PRESSURE MAKES DIAMONDS

Becoming the Woman I Pretended to Be

A Memoir by **Valerie Graves**

OPEN
LENS

Published by Akashic Books
©2016 Valerie Graves

ISBN: 978-1-61775-493-7
Library of Congress Control Number: 2016903687

First printing

Open Lens
c/o Akashic Books
Twitter: @AkashicBooks
Facebook: AkashicBooks
E-mail: info@akashicbooks.com
Website: www.akashicbooks.com

To my husband, who makes me happy so I can work

TABLE OF CONTENTS

**Part Four: Making It Big, Making It Work,
and Making It Matter**

Mining for Gold in Muddy Water . . . Returning the Page

The city of Pontiac, Michigan was celebrating its 150th birthday in March 2011, and my role in the festivities was "hometown girl made good." Being honored as a lifetime achiever by Pontiac is no small thing—my hometown has produced two Olympic gold medalists, renowned jazz musicians Hank, Thad, and Elvin Jones, and the noted playwright Phillip Hayes Dean, a Chicago native whose family moved to Pontiac when he was young. I am flattered and pleased, though the achievements for which the city recognized me could never have happened if I had stayed within its boundaries. I could describe my blessings as unimaginable, except for my belief that they came to me precisely because of my imagination.

My life in New York and improbable career in advertising have taken me into the world of famous people, from President Clinton, Bill Cosby, and Johnnie Cochran to Magic Johnson, Beyoncé, Jay-Z, and Spike Lee. *Advertising Age* magazine once named me one of the best and brightest in a mostly white industry. The leading organization in multicultural advertising has awarded me the standing of "Legend." I have been a senior vice president of Motown Records, home of musicians I idolized during my youth in Pontiac. The work I am lucky enough to do for a living, my hometown watches on TV. That night in Michigan, my fellow honorees would include a retired NBA basketball star, a billionaire real estate developer, a noted author, a legendary union leader, and an award-winning New York journalist. I wondered how many of them, like me, were motivated to succeed by the feeling that their hometowns were too small to hold their dreams. Had they, like me, ever fallen from grace and had to pick themselves up? I thought of the years I had spent longing to leave Pontiac in order to "make good," and of the time I had spent clawing at the imaginary walls that held me there. I even wondered if a bit of prodigal confession should be part of my remarks.

On the way to the program where I was to be honored, I attempted to drive through the former site of the public housing project where I grew up, only to find it impenetrably reclaimed by nature. The sapling trees of my childhood were now tall and strong obstructions to my attempt to revisit the past, and the land was overgrown with thick brush, grasses, and cattail reeds. The location of my childhood home once again belongs to creatures that were there long before me, and nature's reliable cycle of destruction and resurrection was not to be interrupted. Gone was the horseshoe-shaped drive where fresh-off-the-line cars had once cruised in search of fast young girls. A pleasant memory fragment of a passing white convertible, the R&B tune "Knock on Wood" wafting from its radio, drifted through my mind. Trailing behind it was the realization that nostalgia blunts the pain of the past by filtering it through the comfort of now. My adolescent angst was now as ephemeral as a recollection floating on a brain wave. From the condos across the lake, the view is now of a tranquil natural habitat. When economic times are better, and we humans make our presence felt again, the critters will likely be displaced by housing befitting the valuable waterfront setting. An unexpected surge of real affection for my working-class homestead washed over me as I realized that it, too, is destined for change and upward mobility. I drove away from my invisible past, finally understanding what it could tell me about my present: that life is a constant process of becoming and transforming. As I sped away toward the equally hidden future, there was a comforting clarity. I recognized that the weight of my challenges helped shape the successes I hold dear.

Before Michelle Obama forced America's consciousness to accept black female intelligence as more than science fiction, I was a precocious little girl in the Lakeside Housing Project, sensing a larger life beyond it. I developed the strong conviction that I would be somebody in life and achieve things that most people around me only dreamed of. In the midcentury environment into which I was born, I had few light posts en route to my destination. I saw no black people like the person I am today. To be sure, there were smart people, hard-working people, talented people, and accomplished people. Yet, none of them lived in the buttermilk churn of big-league advertising, where, like a pesky and resilient fly, I would survive and become part of the mix.

Pretending, for me, has ever been the ultimate creative act and a form of self-salvation. Early on, I became adept at imagining a life I could not see, and then acting "as if." Like irrationally ambitious little Eddie Murphy, who performed the entirety of *Elvis: As Recorded at Madison Square Garden* in the family basement while his brother stood shaking his head and saying, "You crazy!" Or like young Marguerite Johnson pretending Maya Angelou, *my* hero, into being, I was given the gifts of blindness to obstacles and of making a fool of myself without surrendering to shame. While pretending to be that successful, creative person, I began to become her.

Pressure Makes Diamonds is meant as a beacon to my fellow foolish dreamers. Though every journey is different, and there are parts of mine that I would not wish upon another, I have every confidence that pretending leads to believing and belief creates reality. My journey is about seeing oneself winning the race from wherever the starting line might be, even if that place is a project on the wrong side of a muddy Michigan lake.

These days, Pontiac is being tested as I was in my youth. When I was growing up, the city was a thriving municipality. Tax dollars poured in from factory workers' pockets and corporate coffers. That abundance built a new downtown city hall, library, and police station. The sprawling new Pontiac Mall bustled with optimism as customers purchased everything from kids' clothes to riding mowers and boats. Young people had the option of going to college or taking abundant factory jobs right out of high school. The streets reverberated with the throaty roar of Firebirds, GTOs, and Camaros that were bought on the ninety-first day of employment, when young men completed probation and received the almighty union card. Young people from as far away as affluent Grosse Pointe came to hang out and car hop at a Pontiac drive-in hamburger joint called Ted's.

Then, when the auto plants closed and GM's Tech Center relocated, Pontiac moved steadily to the brink of extinction. The city is now broke, and nearly broken. Almost every municipal building is up for sale, with no takers. The finances of

Pontiac are in the hands of a state-appointed manager. The Silverdome that hosted a Superbowl is a ruin that recently sold for a relative pittance. Plan after plan to revitalize the downtown core has sputtered and stalled. Saginaw Street, the main drag that was home to two banks, multiple department stores, two five-and-dime stores, and five movie theaters, is so deserted that a tumbleweed would hardly look out of place. The last great hope, a parking structure, office building, and train station called the Phoenix Center, seems destined to fail. Pontiac is a city that no longer pretends good things will happen.

Waiting for the ceremony to begin, I looked across from the stage to the audience of hometown faces. Many were people I had all but forgotten. A handful were central to the evolution of my dream.

Right up front was Ruth Ann, my best friend of more than forty years and my doppelgänger in this place where we bonded as teenagers. I left; she stayed. She married early and later divorced; I married in my thirties and remain with the same man. She has been a career social worker; I have changed companies and cities chasing advancement. We have remained close, vicariously living the choices we did not make. Our sons are our mirrors. Her son Burt has forged a stellar career as a Ford Motor Company executive; my son Brian has followed his heart around the country, working his dream job as a sales executive with NBA teams.

Next to her sat my mother, a constant of my life whether near or far. Always too cool and too Christian to brag or lose her composure over the straight-A report cards of my childhood or the recent six-figure salaries, her presence reminds me never to think that mere achievements make me better than anyone else. My eldest brother, Gary, serious and still handsome, was also in the house. Gary taught me a lot about falling and getting back up. As a youth, his classmates called him the Sidney Poitier of Washington Junior High. After college, youthful rebellion and drugs led him to prison, like so many black men. Yet he quickly found redemption through his Islamic faith. After his release he rose to become imam of his mosque.

Hubert Price Jr., the former state legislator who made his way to the stage to officiate the proceedings, was a fellow smart kid who saw something special in me, and the respectful, loving relationship we developed after the birth of my son reminded me who I was and helped bring back my self-esteem. Long after we amicably parted and he married his wife Carolyn, I was grateful for the two years we were together.

Without Pontiac and its people, I might forget that my life today was once the dream of a little black girl trying to see past a polluted lake. I might not remember that their expectations helped create my own. I might lack the resilience to punch out the dings of life like an auto repairman envisioning something shiny and renewed. I might have no useful words for teenage mothers, black women, or people of color wrestling with corporate demons on the road to getting "somewhere."

I searched my grateful heart for something I could say to give hope to the people of Pontiac. I decided to speak about Harlem, my classic New York neighborhood that has risen from disrespected no-go zone to vibrant, desirable enclave. What I really wanted to say is what my straying life has taught me: *Believe you are meant for great things. Dream big, pretend accordingly, and nothing can keep great things from you.* But without knowing my life story, who would believe the answer could be that simple?

"Was It Something I Said?"

I could feel the Thing gaining momentum as it came around the table and headed for me. I felt my anxiety rising and briefly wished I'd had another drink instead of stopping at one. I hadn't thought it wise to get too high, but now that my nemesis was coming my way, a little liquid courage wouldn't have been bad to have. The Thing had the guys in the room in a frenzy, each one trying to best the man who had spoken before him, and avoid the wrath of the Thing. The Thing was the ferocious one-upmanship my white male colleagues called on to cut each other down to size, to carve out the pecking order. The Thing was an unexpected guest at the big ad agency dinner. Like the popular TV series *Mad Men*, the advertising agency was a clubby drama full of anxious, driven white men seeking money and power of every sort. Power in the marketplace. Power with clients. Power over colleagues. Power over the few women who had managed to find their way into the business. The quest to gain and wield influence had long since taken on a life of its own. The Thing was its weapon. Tonight, I was the least powerful entity in the crowd: a black girl trapped with the Thing in a room full of madmen.

I racked my brain for something to say that would show I could hold my own. I felt like a schoolmarm in a frat house.

In the office, I could opt out of this competition and let my work—created with time and thought—speak for itself. In this intense, liquored-up room, the new girl—in 1976, the office's only black—had no choice but to show and prove on the spot. As I scanned the crystal and china–laden room, I could see the tension in the bodies of the white-uniformed, brown-skinned waiters and female attendants who looked like my cousins and great-aunts. All evening I had tried to read their averted eyes as they quietly went about their jobs. Now those eyes were all on me, the only black person in the room not serving canapés or drinks. Would mine be the cringe-worthy words of a happy-to-be-here Uncle Tom, or some militant mess that would make the white folks scared and mean? No one knew, least of all me. I was about to perform live at the Bloomfield Open Hunt Club, direct from the Lakeside projects on the shores of Mud Lake. The Thing picked me up and threatened to throw me back into that polluted pond. "Go for what you know, kid," it snarled. It didn't give a damn whether I could swim or not. In the grip of the Thing, I said the only words I had been sure would come out of my mouth: "Valerie Graves." Then, something else safe: "Copywriter." I looked at my half-drunk colleagues waiting to see if the Thing would drown me, then I listened as the next words tumbled recklessly out of my mouth: "And token." There was an audible intake of air from both white and black folks, for entirely different reasons, followed by gales of laughter from the agency crowd. My black brethren gave me looks that said, *Girl, I hope you know what you're doing.* I didn't, but whatever it was, the Thing would not take me under that night.

The next morning, the CEO paused as he passed my doorway. "Token, huh?" he said with a beaming smile and an *Oh, you're such a kidder* gesture. Two weeks later, I was out of a job.

They had other reasons, but reliable sources told me that my quip had sealed my fate. Fuck 'em if they couldn't take a joke. I had been saying what they wanted to hear my whole damn life.

PART ONE

MUD LAKE MEMORIES, CRYSTAL LAKE DREAMS

CHAPTER 1

Watching the Shimmer from the Shore

I n Michigan, it is impossible to be far from a body of water. That pretty much explains Lakeside Homes, the public housing project where I spent the first fifteen years of my life. Lakeside was built on the shores of Pontiac's Crystal Lake and designed to shelter the great influx of workers who flocked to the auto manufacturing jobs in the Detroit exurb of Pontiac. This public housing project was not the urban nightmare that springs to mind when the term "projects" is used. Instead of the fatherless welfare-dependent families stereotypically associated with public housing, Lakeside was home to many young nuclear families with working fathers and even stay-at-home mothers. Most of these families comprised recently migrated black Southerners, with a smattering of Mexicans and even the odd white family. The renderings in the project offices depicted a cheery tree-filled community of garden apartments with landscaped public lawns, playgrounds, and private, fenced, and gated backyards, all set on a sparkling body of water. It should have been idyllic.

In reality, the lake was polluted, the constant wear and tear of hundreds of young children soon turned the common lawns into patchy, dandelion-dotted turf, and the sapling trees struggled to survive the kids' constant assaults. The playgrounds were the site of much fighting and bullying, and the small lake, though pretty on sunny days, was surrounded by tall reeds and was rumored to be habited by a green man who would carry off any child foolish enough to wander into the weeds. Occasionally, bigger boys and men would venture onto the lake in small boats and catch huge, inedible, scary carp with scales as big as a man's fingernails. The housing commission did its best, routinely maintaining and improving the brightly trimmed housing units and protecting the young trees by coating them with thick, tarry goo. Some of the families maintained neat yards, even planting flower beds and growing morning glories in the chain-link fences. Others had to receive threatening notices from the project office before they would mow their ankle-high growth. The sprightly yellow tulips my mother planted on the sides of our front door quickly had their heads snapped off, presumably by the "bad" kids who roamed the projects casually vandalizing whatever struck their fancy.

Our neighbors included the Reverend Morris, his kind, pretty wife Miss Bertha, their tall son Leo, and the good-looking Pryor family at the end of our row, with names like Kirjathous, Kirlather, Mentre Jean, Lady Mae, and Lorisul. In the row behind us was a family of misbehaving kids who I'm pretty sure stole our clothes off the backyard clotheslines after dark. Two doors away was the Gonzalez family, whose parents seemed to speak no English, but whose numerous children quickly picked up black English and became honorary Negroes. In those early days, there was a white family next door to us. I forget their last name, but their pudgy kids Tony and Mary used to talk to my brother and me over the backyard fence. Some of the families belonged to our church, Trinity Baptist, and socialized with us at the occasional potluck dinner. There was always someone to play with, and most days no one tried to beat me up. Until I was old enough to know what I was missing, I was pretty happy.

For my mother, a pretty young divorcée raising two of her three small children alone, the project apartments were a dream come true. When she married my father, she had left her firstborn, my brother Gary, in the care of our great-grandparents. They doted on Gary and were appalled at the notion of his being subject to the will of a stepfather they did not care for. Their fears might have been unfounded, but their low expectations for the marriage were not. Within three years, my mother had filed for divorce. Her ex-husband, my father, was a known figure in town. We certainly knew ourselves to be his children; my brother even carried what I felt to be the burden of his unusual first name, Spurgeon, but our father provided only the minimal financial support the court required him to pay, and gave us nothing emotionally. He was a union steward, a self-made man, and a bit of a blowhard who wielded a small amount of power with a great deal of brio. I remember telling my fellow neighborhood preschoolers that my father was "the president of the world" and not being challenged. He was the kind of man who would drive by in his latest shiny new car, toot the horn, and wave without stopping to say hello or offer us a ride. When we asked our mother why they had gotten divorced, she gave us one unchanging answer: "Because we couldn't get along."

Our father quickly remarried, to a Southern homemaker who was almost the opposite of our stylish, striving mother. They lived in a small single-family home not far away on the South Side, with a young brood of two girls and two boys who we occasionally saw at my father's sister's house. Having had the audacity to leave him, my mother was pretty much on her own.

Finding a nice new apartment with a fenced-in backyard was quite a coup. With the help of her family, Mama completely furnished our small two-bedroom apartment in 1950s décor. In the living room, there was an overstuffed, navy chenille-upholstered sofa and a matching chair, blond end tables with tall geisha-girl figurine lamps, colorful framed prints of birds on the walls, pull-down shades, and snowy sheer curtains at the windows. There was a sunny yellow faux-leather-and-metal dinette set in the kitchen, twin beds and matching dresser for the kids' room, and a handsome double bed and dresser for her masterless master bedroom. When I recall the first home I knew, I see evidence of the mother who raised me everywhere. Always accentuating the best of her life, she outfitted the place to please herself, not to impress others, and the result was a compilation of items that reflected her idea of what was pretty and her pleasant, unpretentious view of the world.

We weren't the Cleavers—except for his annual half-hour Christmas visit, my father was little more than a name on checks that arrived from the Oakland County Friend of the Court—but we were a family. I idolized my attractive, smart mother, and it was awhile before I realized that our circumstances were less than ideal. Mama lavished affection on us kids; when I was old enough to visit my neighborhood friends, it slowly dawned on me that not everyone was hugged and kissed daily as we were. Their parents might have been too stressed out to indulge them in the little ways our mother did with us. If I bumped my knee on the couch and cried, my mother was likely to give the couch a whack and a stern, "Don't you ever hit my baby like that again!" Even as a small child, I knew this was silly, but I loved it that my mother cared enough to attack inanimate objects on my behalf. We had nice clothes, new shoes, and enough toys and books to junk up the apartment that my mother straightened up after we finally went to bed. Having never lived with my father, I was oblivious to his absence. With the casual acceptance that children enjoy, I assumed a father was optional. In those early days, the charming camouflage of new furniture, a clean house, reliable meals, and a peaceful environment shielded me from a harsher reality. Over time, the realization seeped out of the TV that our family and our neighborhood were somehow lacking, and I began to feel deprived, a sensation that would be with me for many years and later be given names like "underprivileged" and "disadvantaged." When I learned that our side of the lake was called Mud Lake, I felt ashamed and wondered why God hadn't put us on the Crystal Lake side. When I noticed that the people on that side of the lake were white, I wondered why God liked them better than us. I don't remember blaming white people for anything; since they seemed to have so much, I wanted to be like them.

*"I never cut class. I loved getting A's, I liked being smart.
I liked being on time. I thought being smart is cooler than
anything in the world."* —Michelle Obama

The first thing I remember knowing about myself is that I was smart. I got a lot of attention for being articulate and curious. The more grown-ups told me that I was smart, the smarter I wanted to be. One thing I quickly noticed was that being smart was associated with "going places" and "getting somewhere in life." I took these phrases literally and quickly came to the conclusion that everyone knew leaving Mud Lake was a smart thing to do. I felt that desire increasingly validated within me. Where did I think I would go? At age four or five, I was thinking that wherever Wally and Beaver lived, with the neat lawns and cute houses, would be nice, and that Ricky and Lucy Ricardo seemed to have it pretty good in a place called New York. I was also drawn to wherever John Forsythe was living (Malibu?) in his TV series *Bachelor Father,* but at that age, "ocean" was only a word, and for all I knew, the sandy dunes of that show might only exist within the brown box of our tabletop TV. My impressions of "somewhere" and "places" came almost entirely from television and glimpses of the impressive homes of Bloomfield Hills, an affluent neighboring community. When I think of some of the places I have been—the White House, Beverly Hills, the Waldorf Astoria, the Plaza Hotel, the Eiffel Tower, the Apollo Theater, the Amazon rainforest, and too many mansions to count—I realize my quest to get "somewhere" and go "places" had very little to do with tangible physical destinations. It was much more about not staying on the scruffy shore of Mud Lake, a place that was all too real.

One very early experience of "going places" was the monthly family trip to Jackson, Michigan. In those pre-expressway days, the journey to Jackson was a long, drowsy-making excursion through foreign farm country: green, open meadows where languid cows and grazing horses lifted their heads to glance at my great-grandfather's slope-roofed, aging Pontiac, and where weathered roadside Burma-Shave signs seemed to outnumber human beings. When I could manage to capture a window seat, I stared out at the foreign territory that is rural Michigan, feeling disconnected from this world without the cracked pavement, chain-link fencing, and cacophony of voices of my everyday surroundings. I remember a slight fear that we might somehow be stranded in these hamazulas of the Lower Peninsula, and I was anxious that we keep moving toward civilization as I knew it. My future as a city-dweller was probably foreshadowed by my unease with the lonely distances between farmhouses and my relief when the buildings of the University of Michigan and the city of Ann Arbor appeared on the horizon. After we passed these, I knew we were not far from our destination: the long, flat-roofed edifice of the Southern Michigan Correctional Facility, known to us as Jackson Prison.

There, my grandfather, a small, gentle man who held me tightly and kissed my face lovingly when families were allowed to embrace at the beginning of a visit, was imprisoned for all of my childhood, having been sentenced to natural life for the crime of murder.

Until the day I worked up the courage to ask my mother what her father Walter had done, no one in the family ever discussed the crime or his conviction, and as a small child I simply accepted those trips as a normal part of life. There was invariably a wait after we arrived at the prison. Later, I found out that my grandfather always took the time to shower, shave, and change clothes before greeting his family. Before the visitors' grille was replaced by a microwave oven and automated food vending machines, we used to lunch on delicious, greasy hamburgers that were prepared by trustee prisoners in white clothing, aprons, and hairnets.

Eventually, a uniformed officer would call out my grandfather's last name, and our family would proceed through a series of locked gates, with the adult males being patted down by prison personnel. (The ladies' purses had been checked in at the front desk.) Before I was old enough to understand its terrible significance, I loved the sound the barred metal doors made as they clanged shut behind us. We kids were sometimes allowed to play with the numbered metal disk that served as a receipt while the adults conversed in quiet tones, sitting opposite my grandfather with a wooden half-wall between them. Over the years, the visiting room became less restrictive and our family was allowed to sit in a small cluster without barriers, but my childhood memories were of watching my grandfather's face behind a wire mesh screen, with the whole room being surveyed by an armed guard seated on a platform. Even when the procedures were at their most restrictive, they never stopped my great-grandmother from passing the tiny, folded hundred-dollar bill under her tongue to her beloved son, whom she was allowed to kiss on the mouth at the beginning of the visit. My grandfather had nicknames for everyone; I later learned that this was to keep our names from being known by other inmates or by the prison officials whom he assumed read every one of the letters that regularly arrived at our homes. They were written in his ornate cursive, with salutations like *Dearest, Most beautiful, Most loving, Most wonderful, Most devoted, Most intelligent, Most caring,* etc. I was told that these long greetings were meant to frustrate the prison "screws" who had the right to invade his privacy and try to fathom the meaning of his references to *Big Shot* (his sister Dean), *Boss Man* (my infant son), and many others who were never referred to by their given names.

Occasionally, our long ride to Jackson would turn out to be in vain. My grandfather was sometimes in "the hole," usually for fighting. These infractions were sometimes the result of fending off attempted sexual assault. As I grew older, I learned that despite his diminutive size and soft-spoken manner, my grandfather was a "tough guy." Men who knew him spoke of a fearlessness that no one could explain. "He just ain't scared of nobody," my cousin Henry said, with a look that contained both admiration and the knowledge that fearlessness can be a dangerous quality for a black man to possess.

My grandfather's reputation—built on incidents like the time, feeling he had been cheated, that he reclaimed his losses from a local gambling joint at gunpoint—probably contributed to his being convicted twice of a robbery/murder committed at a local pool hall. Those verdicts, based on circumstantial evidence, robbed him of twenty-one years, seven months, and seven days of his life; convictions that were overturned and called "a travesty of justice" when I was a young adult.

On the day he was freed, as we walked away from the Oakland County Jail, we heard a voice yell out, "Mr. Banks! Mr. Banks!" When my granddad turned around, a huge racket of whistles, clapping, and banging of anything that would produce a sound broke out. Exclamations like "God bless you!" and "Good luck!" rained down from the black prisoners he had left in the grip of the penal system. For these men, most of them at the beginning of the journey that had finally ended for Walter, to see him walking free must have buttressed their hopes of returning to life on the outside one day. Strangely, though as a young adult I was overjoyed to see him free, my own childhood fantasies of escape from Mud Lake had never extended to my grandfather being released from prison. Perhaps because he had always been there, Jackson was simply where he lived. Unlike today's reality, where so many black men are incarcerated that a child could hardly be blamed for seeing prison as a fact of African American life, I can't remember knowing anyone else who had an incarcerated relative during my early years.

I don't remember much discussion of my granddad's guilt or innocence among family members; our loyalty and unconditional love were an immutable fact of life. As is the case with so many jailed black men, he was neither as guilty as society found him nor as innocent as his loved ones might have wished. When he was released, my grandfather seamlessly rejoined what remained of the family he left and took up his life without much talk of the time he had lost. Walter's homecoming was not entirely without dramatic undertones, though. Without a word to the family, a day or so after his release, he visited his ex-wife—the only grandmother I ever knew—to come to terms regarding the house he had built and which she now shared with her current husband. This negotiation carried the potential to be a whole lot less civilized than the peaceful resolution that actually went down. Elders in the family told me that as a younger man, Walter might have approached this kind of discussion accompanied by a pistol. They breathed a collective sigh when the parties came to a quick and amicable settlement; my grandfather was not known for his patience. With the money he had, he quickly bought a car and a small house in Pontiac's East Side, planted a garden, and reignited his relationship with a lady named Willie, a former paramour whom he fondly referred to as "Bill." The East Side house was rumored to be a near-gift from a hustler named Roy, a hometown brother whom Walter had taken under his protection in prison. The one comment I ever heard my grandfather make on the subject of incarceration was, "They got enough of my life. I made up my mind they wouldn't get any more of it by my thinking about the joint or talking about it. I never opened my eyes one day thinking I was still inside. The first morning I was out, I woke up knowing I was free."

What seemed like aeons later, from my thirty-eighth-floor office at UniWorld, I would watch families from a Herald Square welfare hotel as they boarded an ironic yellow school bus to visit the missing men of their families on Rikers Island.

It was awhile before I shared the story of my grandfather

and my childhood trips to prison with any of my New York friends. Although I knew it must, I felt as if my experience had almost nothing in common with the children leaving those hellish hotels and getting on those ignominious buses. I thought of my granddad not as a common criminal, but as a hothead who had been falsely imprisoned for a horrible offense he did not commit. Perhaps, like my grandfather, I felt that prison had taken enough of my life. The shameful reality of criminal life just didn't square up with my freed grandfather, my image of myself, or the kind of child I had been when I made those long-ago family visitations.

When I was that child, I couldn't wait for school to teach me how to read. I felt frustrated that there was a code all around me that I couldn't crack. One day, riding down a rural highway in a car, I saw a roadside billboard with a big black panther on it. My inability to read the words on it made me so frustrated I cried. When my mother read books to me, I longed for the words to be as understandable as the pictures. I stared at the pages, willing the words to become comprehensible. Our babysitter's grown son, a lean, ramrod-straight soldier whom we called *Uncle*, was a smart guy who loved to test our young brains. He was always posing riddles and showing us cool stuff—like how magnets would stick to metal but repel each other. One day, he challenged my brother and me—the first one to tell him the word affixed to the corner of the window fan would get a nickel. My brother Spurgeon, who in my five-year-old eyes knew everything, may have been distracted by thoughts of the ice cream he would buy with his nickel. I, on the other hand, slid right back into my usual focus: trying to make sense of this arrangement of the ABCs I had known forever. This time, inexplicably, something clicked.

"Is it Country Aire?" I asked.

Our uncle, astonished, replied that it was. "Did somebody already tell you that?" he asked.

"No, I just know it."

I was just as surprised as he. It was an incredible experience. I had willed myself to comprehend something. I had taught myself to read. I don't remember reading anything else until I went to school, but the feeling that I could, through sheer will, break through a barrier and get into a world I had been locked out of was born that day.

While my mother worked, we were left with Elsie Cooper, a stout, Arkansas-born matron whom we called Mama Cooper, and who was more like a grandmother than a paid caretaker. When my mother dropped us off at her house early on cold winter mornings, she let us go back to sleep snuggled next to her in bed, only to wake up to the aroma of thick slab bacon frying in the kitchen. She would serve it up with scrambled eggs and biscuits dripping with butter. After breakfast, I would sit between her knees as she combed and braided my unruly hair and chatted with her friends about the latest diet, deaths in the community, and the disaster of someone having missed the daily numbers jackpot by one digit, or having had all the digits but failed to "box" them and ensure a win. As she prepared dinners of fresh vegetables from her garden, fried chicken, or pork chops, and beat bowls of cornbread batter, we watched her favorite soap operas, *The Guiding Light* and *Search for Tomorrow*. Occasionally, she would call one of her friends and exclaim, "Did you see what that low-down woman just did?" Or, "That dirty dog! God's gonna get him for that!"

In the early afternoon Spurgeon would come in from school with his usual treasure trove of knowledge garnered in first grade. Mama Cooper, though barely educated herself, believed in learning and loved smart children. She would talk with Spurgeon and me about whatever he had learned that day.

Later in the afternoon, her husband, Mr. Henry, her younger son Arthur, and her pretty green-eyed daughter Alla Mary would come in from their jobs at the Pontiac Motors plant. After they dropped their lunch boxes in the kitchen, they sat around the dining table waiting for dinner to be ready and reading the *Pontiac Press* that they had divided among themselves. All three would bring up items in the paper, and we were always included in the discussion.

"Whatcha think about them Russians and that Sputnik satellite, junior? You gonna go to outer space when you grow up?"

"Val, the Queen of England is coming to the United States. You reckon she's gonna make it all the way to Pontiac?"

I doubt that any kid in today's formal preschool gets more individual attention. The Coopers instilled in us a respect for learning and knowledge that neither of us has ever lost. Their questions, devoid of obstacles and limits, also made me an incorrigible dreamer who could easily imagine myself meeting the Queen of England, perhaps with my brother the astronaut by my side.

One of my creative heroes, Gordon Parks, had a theory that he didn't tend to see barriers because in his childhood on the Great Plains, the vista was clear to the horizon. The Coopers exuded an unspoken optimism about the future because life had delivered them from the cotton fields of Arkansas to the promised land of the factory job, homeownership, and a new car in the driveway. After dinner, bellies full, my brother and I would watch TV until my mother picked us up. I favored Pinky Lee, a Pee Wee Herman–type comedian, but Mama Cooper usually insisted we watch *The Auntie Dee*

Show because every once in a while we would see a "colored" faced like our own. I loved being with the Coopers and remain close to the family to this day. Still, partly because of their encouragement to envision myself as part of a world I could sense but not yet see, I longed to explore what lay beyond the comforting bosom of Mama Cooper's care. I couldn't wait to go to school.

Some children cling to their parents and feel abandoned when they are left in a strange place called school. I barely remember my mother being around on the day I arrived, raring to go, at the entrance to the kindergarten of Bethune Elementary School. Bethune was a midcentury-modern building our booming city had just erected, presumably to handle the influx of black baby boomers from Lakeside Homes. I remember learning how to sit still for story time, how to play rhythm instruments like tambourine and woodblock. We walked, marched, and ran around the classroom to music. To this day, I can hum the tune from the skipping portion of that exercise. I remember that we were shown a movie called *A Desk for Billie*, about a little girl who moved around a lot (with her family of migrant workers?). That was the first time I realized that white people could also have money problems and live in less-than-desirable neighborhoods. I loved school, with the exception of recess, which was a waste of time and a boon to classroom bullies. My first-grade teacher was a lovely black lady whom I knew from Sunday school and church. I'm not sure whether she had already noticed me from my brief performances on Easter Sunday, when we children recited short poems about Jesus and the Resurrection, but she immediately paid attention to me as a student and was the first of many teachers to nurture my academic progress. At Christmastime, I was stunned and pleased to receive a subscription to *Chil-*

dren's Digest as a gift from her. I read every issue cover to cover, partly because those magazines were a reminder that my reading ability made me special to someone important.

The following school year, the same teacher was instrumental in having me skip second grade. I had no idea why I was being taken to the principal's office, but when asked to read for her, I was only too happy to show off in front of adults. My new third-grade teacher was an elegant, artsy woman who read us the poverty-to-glory saga of our school's namesake and opened our minds to the possibility of Negro greatness. Mary McLeod Bethune, daughter of freed slaves, founded Bethune-Cookman College by selling sweet potato pies—a fact I later used in an ad about black colleges—and became an advisor to Franklin and Eleanor Roosevelt.

My teacher was a tall, unconventional beauty. She wore stacks of bangle bracelets on her long arms; her thin waist was often cinched with a wide leather belt that divided the swirling fullness of her skirts from the form-fitting turtleneck sweaters and simple shirts she favored. A mass of loose curls— what we called "good hair"—framed her bronze face with its sharp, birdlike features. She was the first sophisticated woman I knew, and her class was my introduction to culture. She taught us a few French phrases and ignited a lifelong love of that language in me. After school, she taught the basics of ballet to those of us who were willing to stay, which led to years of dancing lessons that my mother somehow managed to pay for. Our teacher spoke of her daughters, Piper and Kyle, and their unusual names were a beacon to an exotic world I wanted to enter. When our school performed an abbreviated version of *The Nutcracker Suite* at Christmas, the teacher provided the costume for my dance as a Chinese doll: a pair of pajamas with black pants and a pink top with black frog closures and a cheongsam-style neck. She gave them to me as a Christmas gift and they became a prized possession.

My mother was an involved parent; our teachers were invited to our home. Lunching on the tuna salad sandwiches and Campbell's French onion soup my mother set out on our cloth-covered kitchen table, the teachers who came to the projects seemed at ease in their surroundings. They also seemed to appreciate my mother's efforts to provide my brother and me with some semblance of the idealized life we were bombarded with by *Father Knows Best* and *Leave It to Beaver.*

It wasn't until years later that I realized our teachers might have come from similar situations themselves, raised by striving parents to lift themselves out of poverty via the well-trod route of higher education. I was proud that my mother was not intimidated by my teachers and conversed with them easily using the Standard English that to my young ear sounded so much more refined than the black Southern dialect that wafted on the air in our neighborhood. When my mother made an appearance at the school, I was always bursting with pride at her neat, well-groomed, and undeniably attractive appearance. Her hair was always pressed and curled, not nappy even at the "kitchen" near the nape of the neck that often announced the need for a visit to the hairdresser in those days. Her stockings were absent of runs; her shoes were polished and not worn out at the heels like those of some of my classmates' mothers. Chatting with the teachers, she looked like one of them.

In fourth grade, there was stern and wonderful Mildred Garling, also a member of our church. Mrs. Garling was a teacher who appreciated my abilities but gave me less special treatment than I had received in first and third grades. When I finished my class work early, rather than let me help out in the school office, collect weekly milk money, or grade other students' spelling tests, Mrs. Garling gave me more work to do. When she noticed that I was not as proficient in math as in language arts, she requested that my mother drill me with flash cards at home. The gifts she gave me, while less enjoyable than a magazine subscription or pretty Chinese pajamas, were more valuable. From Mrs. Garling, I learned discipline and not to expect that the world would let me rest on my laurels.

Elementary school was filled with memorable characters and experiences. My fifth-grade teacher, Mr. Hull, an Ichabod Crane–like Appalachian white man, cautioned us against underestimating hillbillies. His admonition completely baffled us. Before television's *The Beverly Hillbillies,* most children of my Negro community saw no distinction between groups of white people. My personal assumption was that all of them were from *Leave It to Beaver* land, and went home at night to manicured lawns and neat houses where they ate steak and creamed peas for dinner. I would eventually find out how deeply our teacher was affected by the sense that other teachers saw him as being from the Mud Lake side of white America. Red-faced and nearly apoplectic, he sent me to the principal's office after my friend Delores and I circulated a petition protesting his decision to appoint our student council representatives—choosing two bright but shy students—rather than allowing us to elect them. The fact that his fellow teachers agreed with my position greatly exacerbated my crime. I was sent home until my mother could come to the principal's office with me. As far as I was concerned, my petition was democracy in action, a peaceful protest against a dictator. Mr. Hull was violating our student rights to hold an election that, incidentally, I had lobbied all summer to win. My mother supported my actions in principle, but was furious with me for causing her to miss half a day of work. "Why can't you just go to school and act like other kids?"

In time, she came to accept that being "like other kids" was something I would never quite get the hang of. In the end, after hearing my impassioned plea for justice, the principal convicted me on a technicality: I had circulated a document throughout the school that had not been cleared through her office. The previous afternoon of suspension constituted my punishment. This was my first inkling that the system might be rigged against me. I was a little upset with Mama for not being angrier with Mr. Hull. He later felt her wrath, though— not for this, but for referring to a dark-skinned, chubby class-mate of mine as Aunt Jemima. I was proud that my mother stood up for her and demanded an apology from Mr. Hull. Justice delayed felt better than no justice at all.

My sixth-grade teacher, a very proper lady, gave our class a memorable lecture on avoiding "niggerisms"—i.e., loud and unruly behavior and bad table manners—before a field trip to the Detroit Institute of Arts. This clearly did not have the desired effect. A couple of us watched, mortified, as several stu-dents decimated the ketchup, relish, and mustard packets of-fered at the end of the cafeteria line. Today, I realize they might have been hoarding food so they wouldn't go hungry later.

Among my small but cherished memories of elementary school: my pride the day my Aunt Dean's husband chauf-feured a carload of us in their turquoise Cadillac on a class trip to the zoo; and the time my dance performance as Ru-dolph the Red-nosed Reindeer was written about in the *Pon-tiac Press*, though I'm still not sure why.

When I was in fifth grade, my brother Spurgeon and I took part in a school-wide speech contest on the subject "What

Good Sportsmanship Means to Me." I relished the opportunity to show off my ease with public speaking, a blessing that had been nurtured by Easter Sunday pieces and other church programs. Though the specifics of my talk are long forgotten, I know that like so many things in my life, much of the content was gleaned from the lessons of *Father Knows Best, Leave It to Beaver,* and other sources from the TV world, where cheaters never won and kids settled their disputes without the physical throw-downs that happened every day in the projects. I transcribed my carefully wrought words onto the index cards we were encouraged to use onstage and practiced my delivery in front of Mama's vanity mirror. Never one to suffer from stage fright, I made it through the preliminary round of the competition, as did my brother and several other of the more attentive students.

On the night of the finals, after all the contestants had spoken, the judges' deliberations dragged on and on. The contest audience grew restless, and our elementary school band was asked to entertain them with an unrehearsed number. Our band teacher, eyes cast heavenward, prefaced our off-key, squeak-laden rendition of "Clare de Lune" with these words to the audience: "You know not what you ask."

When the judges finally emerged, the decision was first place for my brother, second for me. Although I felt my speech had been the best, in those prefeminist days, losing to my older brother was an acceptable outcome. The judges' decision later led to some very unsportsmanlike reactions from other parents, and culminated in one contestant delivering his speech months later at sixth-grade graduation, a head-scratching non sequitur as far as the audience was concerned. Just a couple of years ago, my mother disclosed that on her next visit to the beauty shop after the contest, our hairdresser remarked, "You must be very proud of your children taking first and second like that. Your son didn't win, though. Your daughter did." Even now, it makes me smile to know that at least one adult shared my opinion of that performance.

At Bethune, I also unofficially began my advertising career by creating the slogan for my brother Gary's winning campaign for student council president: *You'll Rise to the Highest Ranks If You Vote for Gary Banks!* At the time, a decade before innovators like Bill Bernbach ushered in advertising's creative revolution, I'm sure I was influenced by ad slogans from my early childhood, like, *You'll Wonder Where the Yellow Went, When You Brush Your Teeth with Pepsodent.* I was also secretly gratified to have been part of vanquishing Gary's opponent, the undisputed light-skinned diva of Bethune elementary, who, as I prepared for my role as Rudolph in the school Christmas play, had advised me, "Just go outside in the cold until your nose turns red." She said this knowing that my chocolate-brown nose would probably turn blue before it reddened like hers. Her "advice" was a stinging, deliberate reminder of the advantages that her complexion bestowed. My brother's student council victory was my very satisfying rejoinder.

All in all, Bethune Elementary was a positive experience. The school cemented my early identity as a noticeably smart kid, which was more than fine with me. Having not been blessed with the light skin, long hair, or professional parents that conferred status in those days, I was happy to flaunt an attribute that could make me stand out. I loved basking in the spotlight, and cultivated a community of people who expected great things from me. Adults, unlike kids, placed high value on doing well in school, as if they knew we good students would pay the price among our peers for our straight As, and they cheered our accomplishments in the neighborhood's churches, beauty parlors, and barbershops. Being one of those kids was worth the price of being far from the most popular kid on the playground.

Soon, it was time to move onward to Jefferson Junior High. As usual, I was chomping at the bit.

They were calling all the smart kids first. One by one, home-room 202 of Jefferson Junior High's class of 1964 was assembled at the front of the gymnasium on the first day of school. Many of us had heard of each other, though we came from four different elementary schools. In Pontiac, if you were a brainy Negro child, word got around. Bespectacled Veta Smith came from Bagley School, but lived on the other side of the projects. Alvin Bessent's parents were friends of my step-grandmother. His name had stood out when she mentioned him as someone who might be even smarter than me, a speculation I highly doubted. We were gathered into a group of about twenty and ushered to homeroom 202 as other kids in the gym murmured their awareness of who we were—"That's the smart room." They said this without a great deal of envy; other kids had their own, more admired claims to fame. Athletes, cool kids, great dancers, and girls with precociously developed bodies were quite secure in their identities. Being smart was okay, but it had limited appeal. Kids could aspire to become better football and basketball players. They could find ways to become more popular. God willing, they might develop the breasts and booties of the precociously hot girls. But smarts were considered a gift that you either had or you didn't. Whether this was right or wrong, the school seemed to embrace the concept. Once our collection of future lawyers, dentists, journalists, doctors of philosophy and medicine, advertising executives, nurses, and engineers was assembled, we were never separated during the three years of junior high school. Of the group we left in the gym, only one student was ever added to our homeroom.

The kids of homeroom 202 were young, gifted, and black, although in those days we would have called ourselves Negroes. Thanks to the magic of academic tracking, we no longer ran the risk of catching an after-school beatdown for being a teacher's pet. All of homeroom 202 was the teacher's pet, and the beauty of it was, no one else was around to see it.

We became leaders of Jefferson Junior High. Whereas in the past, we might have felt competitive with other bright kids, as a group we took on an expanded identity. For the first time in our school careers, we were not oddities to be put on display like trick ponies: *Watch this, everybody! Valerie, spell antidisestablishmentarianism!* We were part of a group. In the confines of the classes we shared, we were free to fully express our potential, to speak Standard English, voice our unrealistic aspirations, even ask our dorky questions—*Where does the wind come from? Who writes the dictionary?*—without fear of being mocked.

For me, the three years of junior high school were a time full of creativity. A poem I wrote, "Mountains," was even published in a national anthology, *Songs of Youth*.

One night, as I lay on my bed daydreaming, an idea came to me for a Jefferson Junior High personal growth event— "Personality Week" would benefit the girls of Jefferson; it would consist of inspirational talks from prominent local women, beauty and fashion events, and a contest for the title of "Miss Personality." I called my girlfriends Veta and Dorethia to help flesh out the details, and somehow we convinced the school to actually put on Personality Week. Two of the speakers we recruited were the artist wife of one of our English teachers and a nurse who was married to my family doctor. The doctor's wife was especially memorable because she arrived in a powder-blue Lincoln Continental convertible with a white leather interior and elegant suicide doors. That swanky car was as inspiring to me as anything she said during her talk about how to achieve professional success.

As commentator of our Personality Week fashion show, I practiced the sophisticated delivery I admired in television hosts and local TV news anchors. Even though Personality Week was a scaled-down version of my daydream, it was a big enough deal that I didn't even care that I had no shot at being voted Miss Personality. I was too much of a mouthy show-off to win a popularity contest. In fact, the girl who won was a popular hairdresser who had been a stylist to a thriving clientele at her family's salon since she was twelve. Veta, Dorethia, and I were satisfied with the outcome. After all, Veta remarked one winter day as we trudged the icy two-mile trek from Jefferson to Lakeside, "We're too smart to be really popular. Most of the kids we know couldn't even fathom the things we talk about." It was certainly an immodest statement, and probably untrue, but we wrapped ourselves in it like an oversized blanket and huddled in its warmth. We girls of homeroom 202 were at least smart enough to stick together.

The incongruity is that the environment in which we flourished was at least 99 percent black. In high school, where the kids of 202 would later find ourselves among very few other black students in college prep courses, it was easy to see that our de facto segregated junior high was indeed unequal. We had received enrichment assistance; the "white" schools had received more. Just as Michigan had so many lakes that even the projects could be built at the water's edge, there was so much factory money fueling the school district that even "black" schools could get a few extras.

Still, there was a benefit to being in a virtually all-black school—at Jefferson we could compete fairly to do whatever our talents would allow. In high school, the teachers' imaginations could not stretch far enough to envision any of us playing the leads in the school musical or the children's play put on by Pontiac Central High each year. At Jefferson, even as Rosa Parks refused to sit in the back of the bus and Dr. King marched into our awareness, we were thriving in a school where the only white faces belonged to teachers.

I later tapped this experience as the basis of my first ad campaign for the UniWorld Group. The campaign was created to support historically black colleges. Through my research, I learned that most of the towering figures of black America had been educated in all-black environments. Some of them wrote essays for the campaign, detailing the benefits of their undergraduate educations. Jesse Jackson played college quarterback—a position denied to blacks at white schools. Astronaut Ron McNair credited his black college counselor with making him believe he had the intelligence to major in physics and earn a doctorate at MIT. The campaign's first print ad featured a handsome black Cyrano de Bergerac. The campaign was tagged, *America's Black Colleges: Are You Smart Enough to Go?* My years at Jefferson had taught me that in segregation, there could be a surprising benefit: freedom from discrimination.

Decades later, my experience as an advertising creative working in an African American agency would amplify the same contradiction, which persists to this day. In those junior high days, though, the inconsistency flew below my radar. I was too busy enjoying success to negotiate better terms.

CHAPTER 2

Mom Drops the Nuclear Family Bomb

When I was thirteen, my mother married the man next door. Albert Munson was a nice-looking, dark-skinned man who moved into his Lakeside apartment with his children Mack and Sharon when I was ten. Mack and Sharon's mother lived elsewhere in the projects with several younger children from a different marriage. Mack was a fairly good-looking guy, but Sharon was really quite beautiful, with a lovely face and a body that attracted a lot of attention from older guys. One day Sharon, who was two years older than me, was bored enough to cross our shared front lawn and talk to me. We bonded over the revelation that her favorite aunt was married to my cousin and that my little cousins were also hers. From that time on, if her real friends, a couple of tough girls named Ritchie and Mary Jane, were not around, we would watch TV, gossip, and bake cookies or cupcakes together. If Mr. Munson came home while I was at Sharon's, we might exchange a few words. Like most of the fathers I knew, he did not spend a lot of time hanging out and talking to kids. I was very surprised when Sharon angrily told me that her father had decided that my brother Spurgeon and I would be the only kids allowed in the house while he was not there. Sharon largely ignored his directive; Ritchie and Mary

Jane stopped by often to hang out with her, puffing cigarettes and blowing smoke out the windows of Sharon's bedroom.

Once, Sharon and I spent Thanksgiving night and the following day visiting our mutual relatives and babysitting while the parents worked. We got into a long, rambling conversation about how our race was perceived, which turned into a verbal example of the Stockholm Syndrome, and I blush when I recall the conversation. We tongue-lashed our people like a couple of crackers at a Klan meeting, egging each other on as we recalled loud, unruly public behavior, messy restaurant counters left behind, boisterous classroom behavior, fighting instead of studying in school, and all manner of missing decorum when it came to the behavior of Negroes. If we wanted to be treated better—and I can only hope we used the inclusive term "we"—we would have to learn how to conduct ourselves in polite society, instead of showing the ignorant side of ourselves that was so often on display. Something possessed me to write all this down.

When my cousin's wife, Sharon's aunt, came in from work, we proudly shared our dissertation. As proof of the damage racism inflicts on the self, she agreed with us. So did the president of the local youth chapter of the NAACP, who invited us to read our work at the next meeting at the Lakeside Community Center. Sharon was a no-show, but since I had shot off my mouth, my mother made me go. Eleven years old and still wearing lace-trimmed socks with my black patent-leather church pumps, I stepped to the front of the room and proudly read my excoriation of all of us for being the cause of much of the treatment we received from the white world. I sat down to a thunderous ovation that may have been further proof that racism drives people out of their minds.

As the hip organ music of Ray Charles's "One Mint Julep"

signaled the start of the partying that most of the teenage audience had come for, I thought, *Wow, Sharon is so stupid. She missed it.* Savoring the spotlight and the rare privilege of being present at a teenage social gathering, I watched from the edge of the stage as one of the neighborhood's best dancers swung his partner onto the dance floor. Whirling past, he shot me a smile that was icing on the cake of my evening as the Lakeside projects' official social activist smarty-pants. By the time I was twelve, I realized that Sharon, in skipping out on that celebration of self-hatred, had made a wise decision.

My mother's first meeting with Sharon's father was so cute that it became a favorite family story. As she was hurrying to her job as a church secretary one morning, Al Munson appeared at his front door and called out to her: "Miss Deloris, can I speak to you for a moment?"

She wondered what we kids had done now that required a neighbor to talk to her. "Can I stop by when I get off work? I'm running late."

He agreed; she went to work and worried off and on all day about what had happened. She knocked on his door as soon as she came home from work.

He came to the door and quickly started talking: "Thanks for stopping by. Um . . . listen, what I wanted to talk to you about . . . I heard that you broke up with Don."

Don had been my mother's boyfriend for a couple of years. He was a decent guy who turned ugly when he drank alcohol. Don was never mean to us kids, but one night after a few drinks, he made the mistake of hitting my mother. He promptly found himself without a girlfriend. My beautiful mother would not lack for replacement suitors, and Al Munson hoped to be one of them.

"I don't know if you heard, but I broke up with my girlfriend too. I was wondering if maybe we could go out sometime?"

My mother, shivering on the doorstep, said, "Well, maybe you could ask me to step inside. It's cold out here." She walked into his living room and he walked into our lives.

The first time I heard my mother call Mr. Munson "honey," I felt a shock pulse through me. I had answered the phone, so I knew who she was talking to. Mama and Mr. Munson had gone out on a couple of dates by this point. One time, they went to a music club and stopped for Chinese takeout on the way home. This was cool with me; I loved the spicy jumbo shrimp Mama brought home from their date. I was hoping for more dates and exotic leftovers. But "honey"? When did Mr. Munson turn into "honey"?

Before Don, there had certainly been men buzzing around my mother: Emmett, a friend of our Detroit cousins, used to come by. Captain B., an army officer who had been Mama's teenage boyfriend, took her to the movies while visiting Pontiac one summer, provoking no end to my fantasies about life as the captain's daughter. The owner of the local record store, whose name I forget, came by one Christmas Eve to personally deliver the console hi-fi my mother had purchased. He brought Ahmad Jamal's new jazz album as a present and hung around for a holiday eggnog.

Guys hitting on my mother were nothing new. "Honey" was. I was right to think this relationship was different. Mama and Mr. Munson grew closer and their relationship grew more serious. After making dinner and feeding us, Mama would now spend most evenings next door at Mr. Munson's watching his Zenith remote-controlled television, the first I had ever seen. He began to be included in family gatherings and we started meeting other members of the Munson clan. Increasingly, we traveled in his used but freshly painted black-cherry

Oldsmobile Ninety-Eight. If he were around on hot days when the ice cream truck came jingling through the neighborhood, he would give us money for frozen treats, and on cold winter mornings, if we were ready, he would drop us at school on his way to work. Riding in the car, cozy and warm, listening to Jackie Wilson crooning "Lonely Teardrops" or Howlin' Wolf wailing "Smokestack Lightning" from Mr. Munson's state-of-the-art mobile record player, I thought that if only he liked Marvin Gaye, the Supremes, and Smokey, life with Mr. Munson in it would be pretty cool. Later, when he and Mama decided to marry and become a family with four teenagers who had little in common, I changed my mind.

Actually, their wedding was pretty cool. After I had thrown a heroic tantrum, cried myself weak, and made an empty threat to move in with my father—"Go ahead," was my mother's knowing response—I accepted the inevitable and hoped for the best. Mama's maternal grandmother, Allie Williams of West Blocton, Alabama, whom we called Mama Allie, came up for the wedding at my great-grandparents' house on Houston Street. My mother wore a bright fuchsia two-piece silk sheath dress for the occasion, which scandalized her grandmother. "So, they're marrying in red, now?" Nevertheless, Mama looked gorgeous and Mr. Munson was beaming.

After the ceremony there was a big family party of my favorite kind, where nobody paid attention to us teenagers and we hopped in and out of family cars that went on seemingly endless trips to the store for more ice, beer, and ginger ale. The highlight of the evening was when we rode with a couple of older cousins to roust their husbands from a local bar. One cousin's wife, the instigator of the expedition, was a big-boned, outspoken Southern belle from Macon, Georgia. She had a personality as large as the shapely hips that had attracted my cousin in the first place, and was always the source of some manner of outrageous good time. The guy cousins had sought refuge from our too-tame family gathering at the notorious Club 88, steps from the infamous corner of Bagley and Wesson streets where gamblers and bums hung out. We kids didn't get past the bar's blue neon sign, but watching my bad-boy cousins make a hasty, shamefaced exit was worth the trip. Their indignant wives chattered all the way back to Houston Street.

"Did you hear Henry trying to say he wasn't sitting with that cheap floozy?"

"Well, James couldn't even try that. He was sitting there big as life with his arm around some little hussy."

Neither of these women was worried about losing her man; they just weren't about to be disrespected in front of the whole family. For us teenage girls, the incident was a fun sidebar to a memorable evening. No two ways about it, my mother's wedding was fun. While it lasted.

Maybe Mama and Mr. Munson had been watching too much TV. What was their vision? A perfect family where the motherless kids and the fatherless kids lived happily as one united crew? In fact, my fifteen-year-old brother Spurgeon had become too much the man of the house to accept a father figure whose permission was now required to do almost anything. My slightly wild stepsister thought she had been stuck with the silliest goody-two-shoes sister in the projects. My stepbrother, a poor student, had already developed some bad habits like shoplifting, though the adults didn't know it. I, while happy to have a daddy figure, had a bad reaction to my mother's sudden deference to her husband. Every time I heard, "What do you think, Al?" my thirteen-year-old mind interpreted this as a stunning loss of self-confidence. It was a phrase she uttered far too often for my liking. I also thought my stepsister Sharon, with her tough friends, cigarettes, and grown-man suitors, was fast and embarrassing.

For a short time, we all lived in the two-bedroom apartment I grew up in. To my mind, the roll-away bed in the downstairs hall was a booger on our cute, modern living room—by then updated with a sectional sofa and blond corner table—and offended my upwardly mobile sensibilities. Shortly after Mama's wedding, I awoke after sharing that roll-away bed with Mama Allie to the sound of the television, and was greeted by the sight of tens of thousands of marchers in the streets of Washington. The night before, having heard of the intended demonstration, I had said a silent prayer that at least a few hundred people would show up. I did not leave the TV for the duration of the day's activities. I was buoyed by the spectacle of so many of my brethren gathered together to demand participation in a world that was as omnipresent as the propagandizing television screen, and as unattainable as a two-week all-expenses-paid trip to Disneyland. The multitude marched for jobs and equality. I was too young to work, but my snotty idea of economic justice had a lot to do with a single-family home with three bedrooms and a new living room suite, in a neighborhood where the furniture would not be called a living room "suit."

For Mama and Mr. Munson, hereafter known as "Daddy," things were already getting better. Two incomes and one rent afforded them a bit of economic relief, both were taking steps toward better jobs with the federal government, and they were in love. Even for me, those days were not all bad. One bright, indelible spot is the night I persuaded my brother Gary to use his new driver's license to chauffeur Spurgeon, our cousin Dorethia, and me to Berry Gordy's Motown Revue at the Fox

Theatre in Detroit. For about three dollars, we saw thrilling live performances by the Supremes, Smokey Robinson & the Miracles, the Temptations, the Marvelettes, Marvin Gaye, and other acts from this celebrated label where I would one day work. Our senses were nearly overwhelmed by the lights and the tuxedo-clad Earl Van Dyke Orchestra, the glamour of silk suits, mirror-shined shoes, sequined dresses, deftly coiffed wigs, and sophisticated choreography. All the way home, we relived our favorite parts of the show, singing snatches of songs, talking over each other, so excited we hardly noticed that the heat in my mother's old Buick had stopped working. When we got home, our delight was so apparent that even Mama and Daddy were happy we had gone. For at least that night, we were a happy family.

Our move to a larger project apartment eliminated some of my superficial concerns, but I was still dismayed by the changes in my mother's behavior. My stepsister, though never verbally disrespectful to Mama and Daddy, became ever more incorrigible outside the house. Despite my mother's kindness, Sharon wanted an adult life more than she wanted a mother, and was soon placed in a residential facility because of school truancy. My stepbrother remained aimless. My brother Spurgeon was smoldering with resentment, and Daddy's attitude—"This is my house; whatever I say goes"—was a perfect accelerant. It wasn't long before spontaneous combustion between the two of them became a feature of our lives. Once, despite the truth of what Spurgeon was saying, I thought a lightning bolt would strike him when he said to Daddy, "You know, you just keep repeating the same thing over and over. I wish you would just shut up." By today's standards it seems almost innocuous, but in the 1960s, a black child who spoke to a parent like that was likely to be physically assaulted. I wondered why

Mama and Daddy couldn't have been content to just be boy-friend and girlfriend living next door to each other.

I should have been careful what I wished for. In a little less than two years, fearful that his conflict with my increasingly insubordinate brother would lead him to commit violence—something that never happened—Daddy moved to a small apartment on the South Side. My mother was welcome to visit him. Between work, night school classes, a twenty-five-mile commute, and her efforts to save her young marriage, my mother, the most reliable person in my life, had less and less time to spend with me. I developed a rough, persistent facial rash that threatened to make me miss our class trip to Washington, DC; otherwise, there were few outward signs that I was losing my way. A dermatologist declared me not to be contagious, my skin cleared up, and I enjoyed a wonder-ful class trip, prom, and graduation. My grades had faltered slightly, but I managed to get through ninth grade without anyone realizing that I might need help. Coincidentally, I was making new friends, and like most teenagers, I had no idea how much I needed my mother's guidance.

My new friends were already in their first year of high school. Because I had skipped a grade, I was hanging out with girls who were two years older, a big gap when the ages are fourteen and sixteen. My friends were nice girls like Ruth Ann, from good Pontiac families, so my mother didn't seem to worry that I spent so much time with them. Her mind was on bigger and more obvious problems. Marriage, which was supposed to bring our family together, seemed to be pulling it apart.

CHAPTER 3

High School, Low Point

The summer before high school, my desire to learn shifted from school to all things social. My best friend Ruth Ann, almost two years older, had whetted my desire for high school life while I was still at Jefferson. During our frequent sleepovers, she shared everything about how to be part of the "in" crowd and their activities. I even participated where I could.

The year I was in ninth grade, my cousin Melvin DeWalt was the star of the Pontiac Central basketball team. I basked in the status of being related to Melvin and his predecessor, my uncle Willie DeWalt, who in the late fifties had been the Michael Jordan of the squad. With my friends, I went to every game.

Summer gave me an opportunity to get the jump on being asked to join Les Jeunes Filles, an invitation-only club. Les Jeunes Filles was one of two girls groups that guaranteed a certain level of acceptance. The most popular girls were members or alumni of one club or the other. The differences between the clubs were fuzzy. Devonaires, the other group, may have been a bit prettier and more circumspect, Les Jeunes Filles a little spunkier and more irreverent, but all were cute, smart girls, and belonging to one of the clubs was what mattered. I tagged along with Ruth Ann doing grunt work for LJF summer parties: carrying and cleaning folding chairs, setting up tables and spreading paper table cloths, doing whatever I was asked in hopes of becoming a member in the fall.

During summer, the fun moved to the Hayes Jones Community Center—named after a hometown Olympic gold medalist—where the crop of males was not limited to junior high boys. The parking lot was crammed with twenty-something guys in fresh-off-the-line cars. Chuck's fire-engine-red Catalina convertible, James's black Mustang, Clifford's midnight-blue Grand Prix, Bobby G's yellow Chevy Impala: all gleaming with the promise of plentiful joyrides and fodder for fantasies. My friends and I would pile into these chick magnets for raucous trips to the local McDonald's, Motown music blasting. Our newly found sex appeal radiated from us like Martha & the Vandellas's "Heat Wave." Finding safety in numbers, we flirted with these older guys like crazy. For that summer, we girls were young and invincible and life was a feast on shiny chrome wheels.

Academic life in the new school year just wasn't the same without homeroom 202. Even though all of us had selected a college prep curriculum, we might have only one or two previous classmates in any given class. At Pontiac Central High, we college-bound black kids were once again isolated, standing out first because of our skin color, then because of our unexpected intelligence. In advanced biology, I sat next to the sons and daughters of doctors. In civics classes, I defended the "equality now" stance of the civil rights movement against the "steady progress" arguments of the children of attorneys. My years at Jefferson and in homeroom 202 had imbued me with the belief that I could compete with anyone academically, but they could not provide me with the experiences and intellectual arsenal that these kids took for granted. Family trips to Europe, summer camps focused around particular interests, the ability to have complex science questions answered at the dinner table—these were among the privileges that my new classmates took for granted. When Chris Blakeney opined, "Chiang Kai-shek is a fool," I intuitively knew that she was parroting someone, but I was struck by the fact that the struggle between Taiwan and Mainland China would never have come up in any setting of my life beyond the classroom. At Pontiac Central, I began to see what I was up against in life. The enormity of disadvantage was suddenly as real to me as a fifty-foot concrete wall that I would have to climb by finding footholds in the cracks. I admitted to myself that Dr. King's dream might never be achieved in my lifetime. I understood what all those relatives and church people had meant when they exhorted me, "You gonna be somebody. And don't let anyone stop you." But whoever was trying to stop me was big, powerful, and invisible. Who had given me the same IQ and talent as these white kids, but seemingly given them so many more advantages? I directed an ever-increasing amount of my attention to social life. There, I was once again comfortable in a nearly all-black world, one that we considered superior to the white students' world.

In our view, white kids couldn't dance, the guys were not cool, the school-sponsored dances they attended were wack, and the girls were so silly they actually dated boys their own ages. We were convinced of our social superiority—white kids could never out-cool us—it was an incontrovertible fact that was borne out in our style, swagger, music, and dance. Even the names of our beloved Motown groups—the Supremes, the Miracles, the Temptations, Little Stevie Wonder—exuded the conviction that buoyed us and lifted us above the daily discomfort of being surrounded by white peers who enjoyed a favor that no amount of achievement could neutralize. Where once, being smart had seemed the way forward, being cool became the Holy Grail that propelled me.

My shift away from studies was not complete, though. Certain teachers, like my stern but cool biology instructor, pushed me to apply myself. Sporadically, I complied. For some reason, when our class studied the human electron transport chain, I took notes and crammed for the test. A pretty blonde named Lynne got a C on that test. Disappointed in her grade and seeking company for her misery, she stopped by my desk for the first time ever and asked, "So, what did you get?" She couldn't hide her surprise when I answered, "An A." I was happy to disappoint her, but I wondered when people had stopped expecting me to be at the head of the class.

Studying just couldn't compete with Les Jeunes Filles, sporting events, dances, parties, and older guys. I had always liked Hubert Price, a handsome, smart cousin of Ruth Ann's who took me to ninth-grade prom, but he had gone on to Michigan State. I set my sights on Richard, a nice-looking factory worker. We had almost nothing in common; I can't recall a single conversation we had. With too much unsupervised time on my hands, I made out with Richard until my lips were sore and frustrated him to no end by refusing to take things to the ultimate level. Finally, after a dance, as we sat in his car in the parking lot, he told me that if I wasn't going to have sex with him, he wasn't going to drive me home. He wasn't interested in anything I had to say. "I know you're not going to do it, so get the hell out of my car!" I stood next to the car wondering what to do. I wasn't infatuated with him, and he was too unconcerned to pretend I was special to him. No way was he going to be my first.

A soft voice came from the open window of a sharp-looking white Catalina parked nearby. "Are you all right, baby?" I vaguely recognized the driver and the car. One cold day when my girls and I had been walking from Jefferson, I had seen what I thought was Ruth Ann's uncle's white Grand Prix slowly approaching through the heavy snow. I had play-fully stepped into the street and flagged the car down to ask if he would give us a ride home. The car had stopped and I opened the door. When I saw the color of the interior I knew that I had made a mistake. The driver, a nice-looking guy of about twenty, had smiled at me. He didn't seem to think it was so bad to be flagged down by three young girls. As I began to close the door, he had said, "Wait, wait, what's your name?"

"I'm sorry, I thought you were someone else," I replied, firmly closing the door on his entreaty and his smiling face. That same face was now looking at me from inside the same car.

"I'm okay, but I need a ride." I was less afraid of this kind-faced near-stranger than of walking home in the dark at al-most midnight.

"I'll give you a ride. Get in."

As I entered the car, he asked my name.

"Valerie."

"That's a pretty name. I'm Vert." Unromantic as it was, this is how I met my first love. He was six years older and a perfect father figure for a confused girl.

Vert achieved with kindness what Richard could never have bullied me into. He called the day after he drove me home, and the day after that. I had, of course, vetted him with Ruth Ann immediately after our parking lot meeting. He was a well-known guy, popular enough, who was nicknamed "Hat Man" for the jaunty fedora he was seldom seen without.

Given how starved for attention I was, Hat Man did everything right. He took me out to basketball games and movies, bought me shrimp dinners at the L'il Pig barbeque joint, and cheerfully chauffeured me around. He introduced me to his parents, showed me off to his friends, and made me his official girl. I gave myself to the relationship completely. Hat Man took my virginity, but I also gave it. At fifteen, I was madly in love. When my mother found out how old he was, she forbade me from seeing him. I had no intention of breaking up with him; in fact, I intended to marry him.

When Mama came home from work one day and found me sitting in Hat Man's car, she tapped on the window and angrily directed me into the house. He came in with me and declared his love and honorable intentions. "I'm proud of Val," he said, and I melted like ice cream over warm apple pie. I was convinced that our love would last forever. Six months later he had outgrown me and moved on to a young woman of nineteen.

I wondered if anyone had ever died of a broken heart. I thought the pain of losing Hat Man would surely kill me. When our entire circle of couples went en masse to the new James Bond movie, he took Her. My stunning Easter outfit—a white wool cape suit, chic cloche hat, faux-lizard sling-back heels and matching bag—was selected to make him miss me. I attracted plenty of male attention but left my ex unmoved. When our whole crowd picnicked at a state park, he was there with Her. Nearly every day, I endured the humiliation of seeing his car parked near Her apartment in the projects. When I heard that they had become engaged, I removed the white gold and pearl ring he had given me. On their wedding day, I cried my heart out in my room as a caravan of cars passed by, blowing their horns in celebration of the marriage.

Decades later, I saw Hat Man at a family wake, where he greeted me warmly. I didn't recognize him at first, not because he had changed so much, but because I had.

"I know that I know you," I smiled, trying to place him when he approached me.

"Yes, you do," he replied in a tone that almost demanded I recognize him. "I'm Vert."

"Oh my goodness! How are you?" Hat Man had receded to the irrelevance of a sophomore high school romance. Seeing him, I realized that the players in our lives often fade away; it's the lessons we learn from them that leave a mark.

The spring and summer after Hat Man moved on were an achy blur. Looking to replace the intimacy we had shared, I deliberately went after Ronnie, a brooding ex-soldier I had met through my friend Denise, who was dating his best friend. I'm not sure he liked me and I can't remember if I liked him, but getting together was convenient. I needed someone to fill the hole in my heart, and this tall, strong Vietnam vet was right in front of me. He carried the moody vestiges of having been in a war. He didn't talk to me much and probably listened even less. We had sex two or three times, mostly because I knew this was what a grown man expected, and thanks to Hat Man, I was no virgin. I don't remember much about it, except that on one occasion, the condom he used came off. I felt kind of rejected the entire time, as if Ronnie the soldier wondered what he was doing with me. I was too inexperienced to see how this mirrored my relationship with my father, the original unattainable man in my life.

Once school was out, the only thing that broke through my emotional numbness was my excitement over driver's education. Six a.m. was the only time slot available, but learning to drive was worth getting up for. I showed up for class faithfully, walking the quiet streets and enjoying early morning's soft sunlight, damp grass, and chirping birds. My tough instructor's gruff manner was perfect for teaching us the rules of driving and staying alive. A one-way sign doesn't mean some maniac won't come at you from the wrong direction. A red light doesn't mean some fool won't run through it. Expect the unexpected. That last one turned out to be especially good advice.

One evening my Aunt Dean showed up at our house out of the blue. Dean, my grandfather's sister, was normally a lot of fun, a cigarette-smoking, wisecracking, irreverent fixture of my childhood. That evening, though, she strode deliberately into the house, greeted my mother, and then spoke directly to me.

"I want to talk to you. I heard something about you at work and I don't like it a bit." I wondered how she could possibly have heard that I was having sex. Which of her hospital coworkers could have known? "A woman I work with told me that she saw you out on the street about five thirty in the morning, girl! What in the world is going on? You haven't been raised like that." When I told her that I had been on my way to a six o'clock class, she sat back in her chair, let out her usual raucous laugh, and immediately switched gears. "You just wait until I tell that woman you were on your way to school! I'm getting her told as soon as I get to work. Driver's education. How 'bout that!"

I felt like I had dodged a bullet, but I felt guilty too. I hadn't done what I was suspected of, but I was no longer the girl she thought I was, either. Soon enough, that would become clear.

CHAPTER 4

Teenage Motherhood: A Babysitter for the Prom

One sunny morning in July of 1965, I woke up and found myself in a nightmare. My period, which un-failingly arrived every twenty-eight days, had not shown up as expected. For the next few days, I hoped against hope, running to the bathroom so often that my mother asked if I felt ill, but somewhere inside my fifteen-year-old self, I knew that the end of the world had arrived. I was pregnant, and for a girl like me, that was the equivalent of an atomic explosion. The Michelle Obama of the Lakeside Homes proj-ects, the great black hope, that girl was pregnant. Pregnant, and not by my first love, who had deflowered me but also proudly professed his love to my outraged mother. Instead, I might be pregnant from a single encounter with Bobby K., a popular guy who, because of his short stature, seemed to feel more comfortable with younger girls. Bobby was director of a summer recreation program that the kids I was babysitting at-tended. When I picked them up, Bobby would sometimes give us a ride home in his hot little Mustang convertible. He was looking for sex; I was vulnerable to anyone who might make up for Hat Man's betrayal and soldier Ronnie's indifference. On one fateful occasion, Bobby K.'s persistence was greater than my resistance. Now, my disgrace was complete. Not only was my pregnancy a cause of shame—my parents had been married, and their parents before them—it was a looming financial burden to my mother's fragile new re-marriage, and a fall from grace that would require the whole family to explain how such a thing could have happened. That entire summer, I carried my terrible secret and wondered how the world could still look so normal. If Valerie Graves was pregnant, the world as we knew it was over. As it turned out, that assessment wasn't far off.

When my mother learned I was pregnant, she cried for three days. I could feel her crushing disappointment. Her hopes for me were going down the drain. The disapproval of our relatives and church family would be a heavy cross to bear. I did not know it, but she and Daddy had decided to reconcile and buy a house. Just when things might be looking up, I had thrown a giant monkey wrench into the works. As I walked home from school the first day after Mama found out about my condition, I was once again amazed by how normal the world looked. Nothing was normal or would ever be again. The one saving grace was that the burden of keeping my secret was lifted. Daddy came over one day, took me for a drive, and simply asked, "What happened?" My answer: "I messed up." I had forgotten who I had always been. I had violated the standards by which I had been raised. I had even sunk below the monogamous code of my girlfriends. Loneliness and rejection had turned me into someone I did not recognize. Daddy and I talked briefly about Ronnie, but not about Bobby K., whom shame would not allow me to mention. Like a child, I willed the pregnancy to be the result of Ronnie's wayward condom. I acted like a kid, and left what would happen from there largely in the hands of my parents.

We moved to the other side of town at just the right time.

Seward Street, on the East Side, consisted of four nondescript blocks of modest Cape Cod houses on a practically treeless street. Our house was neat, even cute, sitting atop a little rise with a small lawn and shrubs bordering the front windows. The house, though small, was a step up. Mama and Daddy bought a beautiful set of the ornate French provincial furniture that was all the rage, and a marble-topped coffee table. The new cherrywood console hi-fi that Daddy had bought for his apartment now graced our freshly carpeted living room. We even got our first new car, an impressive Buick Electra 225, or "deuce and a quarter" as it was known among black folks. We were the third black family to move to the street. Our neighbors were mostly white factory workers from Kentucky and Tennessee. They were simultaneously cordial and distant. *For Sale* signs soon sprouted on their lawns like dandelions. In those days of real estate block busting, our street turned black overnight—though our new black neighbors were mostly strangers to me. For the first time in memory, I was content to be anonymous.

Once we moved to the house, life was calmer. My stepbrother Mack had decided to live with his mother's relatives rather than leave the West Side. Sharon, after a brief period of compliance, had been truant so many days from school that she was not allowed to complete the school year. Now seventeen, she officially quit and took a job as a live-in nanny. Spurgeon, having briefly resided in our biological father's home, seemed ready to give Daddy's rules another chance

Although I was nauseous from unrelenting morning sickness, I attended school regularly. I hid my condition from teachers under big shirts and loose clothing. I fainted once in the sulfurous chemistry lab, and drowsiness regularly rolled over me in fourth-period French class after lunch. The teacher once instructed me, "Mademoiselle Graves, *dormez bien cette* weekend!" Among my black peers, my pregnancy was common knowledge. I identified Ronnie as the father, and no one other than him doubted me.

At school, my guidance counselor was the only authority who seemed to tumble to the situation. Mr. Ayling was a thirty-something white man who related to students in a cool, nonjudgmental manner that made him easy to talk to. I had come to see him to find out what would happen to my chances of graduating with my class if I dropped out for one semester. It turned out that the extra-credit advanced courses I had taken would be my salvation. If I could complete the fall semester, I could miss the following one, return in September as a senior, and graduate with my class in June. Instead of reporting his suspicions, Mr. Ayling became an invaluable ally. Having studied my entire school record, he was determined that this bump in the road would not run my life into a ditch. Somehow, he talked most of my teachers into letting me take final exams in his office, since by January my pregnancy was apparent. The lone exception was the straitlaced French teacher, who insisted I make my required oral presentation before the class. When I entered the classroom, just shy of seven months pregnant in maternity clothing, her face reflected first shock, then something like sadness. Clearly, she had not been told of the situation. Mr. Ayling had gone out on a limb for me, but to admit knowledge of a student pregnancy could have cost him his job. I walked to the podium and faced the room.

"*Est-ce que les cirques ont eté invade par les anges? C'est possible d'y croisir si on a lu l'article dans cette issue de* Paris Match," I smilingly intoned to my stunned classmates. I still remember those opening lines, which I delivered with all the poise my public speaking experience could afford. My presentation concerned an angel hiding out as a circus clown. I could identify with the situation. I was no angel, but I was determined not to let my situation make me a clown. "*Merci*, Mademoiselle Graves," the teacher said when I had finished. "*Tu t'a fait bien.*" She nodded her respect for my effort to show grace under pressure. Head held high, I walked out of the classroom and went home to await the birth of my baby.

Staying at home with no transportation gave me lots of time to read and watch TV. The nesting phase of pregnancy had taken hold, and television game shows, drugstore novels, and old movies were my daytime companions. I cleaned, dusted, ironed clothes, and peeled the potatoes that Daddy required as a daily side dish no matter what else was on the menu. My pregnant belly bounced and my unborn baby squirmed as I danced around the small living room to the hits on a local TV dance-party show. As usual, my dreams came mostly from books and television. In particular, Darrin Stephens of *Bewitched* piqued my interest. His fun job as an advertising professional seemed right up my alley, and like a surprising number of amateurs, I assumed that I could easily write great commercials. By that time, Bill Cosby's uber-cool character, Scottie, was traveling the world playing tennis and fighting international bad guys on *I Spy*. I resolved to have a job that involved travel. Marlo Thomas's character on *That Girl*, making her way in the big city of New York, where I hoped to live someday, was a female role model. Somewhere along the way, I began to have more positive feelings about the child I would have. I always envisioned my baby as a boy, and I began to talk to him about the life we would make together. I daydreamed the afternoons away, picturing myself and my baby in a cool modern apartment in a metropolis far away. While I still had the occasional self-pitying phone conversation with Ronnie, and sometimes cried myself to sleep at night, the last two months of my pregnancy were mostly a time of calm and reflection.

Nine months pregnant and weighing a whopping 129 pounds, I arrived at Pontiac General Hospital late one Wednesday night, a child about to give birth to a baby. Thirty-seven and a half miserable hours later, I was finally wheeled into delivery. I sucked in the anesthetic as if it were life-giving oxygen. "Take it easy," the anesthesiologist warned. I ignored her; I didn't care if the anesthesia killed me, as long as it stopped the pain. On Friday, April 1, while I was unconscious, my son Brian was born. It was quite an April Fool's Day.

A family friend, the pianist from our church, worked in the hospital nursery. She came out and told my mother, "Deloris, you have a really beautiful grandson." Mama's pride was my first inkling that a cute baby could ease the sting of an illegitimate pregnancy. I think Daddy's plan had been to ignore my infant, but it was an abject failure. The day after I brought the baby home, I began to run a fever as my breasts turned rock-hard and were engorged with milk. Mama took the baby into the living room so that I could get some rest. I was surprised to hear Daddy chuckle as Mama baby-talked to my infant son. By the next day, Daddy was phoning home from work to make sure that the baby was all right. His affection only grew deeper and lasted until the day he died. Daddy's sister Mabel stopped by with shopping bags full of gowns, diapers, and baby undershirts she had bought at a local department store, a kindness I have never forgotten. Baby gifts poured in from other relatives, and even Les Jeunes Filles sent over a bassinet. For the first time in a long while, I didn't feel so isolated and alienated from my previous life.

April was a perfect time to have had the baby. I had spring and summer to adjust to the demands of motherhood and plan my return to school. A baby was a lot of work, but I took pride in being a good mother to my infant. I washed and folded baby clothes and diapers, sterilized bottles, and did household chores whenever Brian slept. My grandfather's eldest sister urged me to breastfeed him, and once I did, I loved the unfamiliar experience. I held my son close and breathed in his sweet baby smell. As he began to respond to the sound of my voice, to look into my eyes and make soft cooing sounds, I fell completely in love with my baby boy. We were alone in the house together all day, and as the touch of my hands and the sound of my voice became the source of his comfort and the answer to his every need, I also clung ferociously to him. He was completely dependent on me and I found in him a love, conditional only on my presence, which filled a need deep in my soul. The closeness of those first intertwined months of Brian's life has resurfaced again and again and helped carry us through trying, potentially estranging times.

My girlfriends made the trip across town to visit and get a look at Brian. Word of my "pretty" baby, with his handsome features and desirable high-yellow complexion got around. I had expected the baby to be medium brown like myself, but I secretly thanked God that Brian shared soldier Ronnie's mother's color.

Then, just as my friend Ruth Ann was preparing for college, she suddenly got married instead. Not surprisingly, the marriage was motivated by an unplanned pregnancy. That situation turned out to be a godsend for me when Ruth Ann volunteered to watch Brian so that I could return to school in the fall. I could hardly believe such a huge problem would be so easily solved, but soon enough I was dropping off the baby at her house and returning to the classroom.

To my surprise, Daddy had expected that I would be going to work, not back to school. I thought he must be crazy if he expected me to be a high school dropout. Predictably, things around the house got tense. One night, after Daddy seemed to want me to simultaneously do the dinner dishes and quiet my squalling baby, things erupted into a screaming argument and I stormed out of the house with Brian and little else. A friend's mother paid for the cab I took to their home, where I remained for weeks, much to my mother's dismay.

I was a big fan of my friend's mother, Shirley B., who had taken me in. Shirley was a tall, fierce black beauty with a big heart, a talent for drama, and a soft spot for slightly dangerous streetwise guys. Shirley, a daddy's girl from an old Pontiac family, took no stuff from her man or anyone else. She had juice; her dad was in local law enforcement and her brother was a pro football player. When Shirley stepped out the door, with an attitude as sharp as her fur-collared walking suit, the world had better watch out. Living at Shirley's was a crash course in the power of female sex appeal and the proper exercise of feminine wiles. Shirley was the sort of woman who left exes wondering what had hit them and how they could get back into her good graces. She schooled us girls—with limited success—in how to command the treatment we deserved. Of the guys who came by to visit us, she pointed out which ones were worth our time and which of them were a waste. Even twenty years later, when she met my handsome journalist husband, she gave an approving nod to his looks and social profile, granting him the Shirley B. seal of approval: "Well, it looks like I raised you right."

While I lived with her, I went on a couple of dates with a guy who, when he came to Shirley's house, immediately picked up Brian and began to play with him. "Hey, little man!

What's goin' on?" After he left, Shirley said, "Now that's a man right there. If you want to know how a man will treat you, watch how he treats kids, and watch how he treats his mama." Since I wasn't seriously interested in the guy, I didn't bother to share that his mother lived with him in a house that he owned.

Life at Shirley's was exciting and cool, but I had absolutely no money. My mother stopped by regularly with milk and baby food for Brian, but it was clear that if I wanted to be provided for, I would have to apologize to Daddy and move back home, something I was too willful to do. I would never wish on anyone the shame of abject poverty, but I think it must strike most deeply the souls of runaway children who have never provided for themselves. I was accustomed to having a roof over my head because someone loved me, to having nice clothes and trips to the movies and being entitled to raid the refrigerator because someone cared if I was fed. Now that the roof was far from assured and groceries not a given, I also felt bereft of love. Like an underage dark-skinned Blanche Du-Bois, my fortunes depended on the kindness of people whose generosity was sure to dwindle. When the family I lived with went out for burgers or ice cream, I was wrenched between the longing for a treat and the indignity of not being able to buy myself a twenty-five cent White Castle hamburger or a meager ice-cream cone.

I sometimes pretended not to want anything when my stomach was doing somersaults and my mouth literally watered. Most of the time, Shirley ignored my protestations and bought me whatever she was getting for her own kids, which made me feel like even more of a loser. What was becoming of my life?

The burden of my situation was plainly taking a toll on my

mother, who was caught in the middle between Daddy's and my battling egos. After Mama, fed up with my being a charity case, came and took Brian to her house, I knew I wouldn't be able to stay with Shirley much longer. It was one thing for my friend's mother to keep an innocent baby out of the street. Adopting a teenage girl was a whole other proposition. Sure enough, when Shirley bought a new house, she advised me to call my mother and work things out. The thought of asking my real father for help never entered my mind. Even now, everything I know of him says that would have been a fool's demeaning errand. Reluctantly, I returned to Seward Street for my feast of crow. After that, I bit my tongue and got along better with Daddy.

During the Christmas holidays, Ruth Ann's cousin Hubert came home from Michigan State and we reconnected. I had always been attracted to his good looks and intelligence, and now that I was a little older, he was equally drawn to me. We talked for hours, in person and on the phone, and he spent every evening during the holidays with me in my parents' living room. Like me, Hubert planned to "be somebody," and everyone in town expected that he would. My family liked him; in many ways he was a lot like my two brothers: smart, cool enough, but basically a good boy. Like everyone else, he gravitated to my darling baby. At last, I had a traveling companion on the trip to "somewhere."

Having a boyfriend who was in college did wonders for my self-esteem. I refocused on school and even managed to participate in some extracurricular activities. People were complimentary of my performance as emcee of the school talent show, and my poem "Middle-Class High" was published in the school poetry journal. I made my first white friend: blond, pint-sized, funny Diane, who had transferred to Central from a Catholic school. Nicknamed "Squeak," she and I shared artistic aspirations and a dislike of physical education class. A few years later Squeak would pass me the first marijuana joint I ever accepted; I trusted her implicitly and she became a lifelong friend. My deepening long-distance romance with Hubert made it easier to stay at home when my friends were out. For the first time since Hat Man, I was in a relationship with someone who valued me. I wasn't looking at anyone else.

As the end of the spring semester approached, my classmates and I focused on writing our first term papers. The black consciousness movement that was inflaming the nation's youth inspired most of our topics. We former Negroes began to refer to ourselves as Afro-Americans. We embraced the descriptor "black," which up to then had been a derogatory term to be hurled at each other when we wanted to be hurtful. Huey P. Newton and the fearless Black Panthers, who had taken to patrolling the streets with their berets and rifles, were a source of pride and wonder. My paper entitled "The Negative Effects of the Ghetto on the Black Child" was a chronicle of the disadvantages of growing up on the Mud Lake side of America. It was an easy A.

I could hardly believe senior year was ending. Hubert was home from Michigan State and escorted me to the senior prom. I wore a fashionable blue gown that was a gift from my proud Aunt Dean. Except for needing a sitter, the night of my prom was just as I had always imagined it would be. I was on the arm of my handsome, educated boyfriend who cared about me as much as I did him. Like almost all of the black students, we swung by the corny official prom only long enough to check out the decorations and have our prom portraits taken. Then it was off to Detroit, over the brightly lit

Ambassador Bridge to Canada for dinner and a glitzy show. Even though I was not a fan of the comedy of Totie Fields, catching her bawdy act over a steak dinner at the Top Hat Supper Club made prom night even more ritzy and special. I drifted into my parents' house at dawn, ending a night that couldn't have gone better.

Now, graduation, the first hurdle between me and the life I wanted, was only a week away. It was customary for graduating seniors to wear mortarboards and gowns for the entire week. I never left the house without at least my cap. Unwed motherhood had not vanquished my dreams, and I wanted the world to know.

I had been so intent on graduating that the ambivalence of commencement took me by surprise. The slightly untethered feeling of no longer being a student was an unforeseen consequence of the end of high school. Even more than having a child, graduation launched me into the world of adulthood at a time when society was changing at warp speed. My generation—the Baby Boomers—was beginning to assert itself in movements that would grow to reflect the size of our cohort. With so many questioning young men in line to be drafted to Vietnam, antiwar unrest was picking up steam. Murmurings of female discontent were evolving into bra-burning demonstrations and a full-throated call for women's liberation. The feel-good exuberance of the Beatles's "I Want to Hold Your Hand" was being nudged leftward by the shaggy discontent of the Rolling Stones's "Satisfaction." As young white Americans surged through the portal of adulthood feeling that satisfaction was their due, my newly minted Afro-American peers were taking their demanding cue.

Dashing young rebels like Stokely Carmichael, Angela Davis, H. Rap Brown, and Huey P. Newton captured our attention as the vanguard of a black movement that dared to challenge the status quo, the Establishment, and the Man. The world I had been so eager to confront was calling my bluff, and a wisp of floating anxiety accompanied my liberation from secondary school. Without the protective, quasi-adult laboratory of college, would I be up to the challenge of everyday life in times that were growing more tumultuous by the day?

"Turn on the TV. The niggers are tearing up Detroit," was how Hubert conveyed the news that the city was going up in flames. His choice of words telegraphed a world of information about which people in our community had set off the rioting in the streets. This was not the organized confrontation of our idolized Black Panthers, militant college professors, or radicalized prisoners. Detroit police had raided an after-hours club on Saturday night, rousted the hustling and hanging-out folk, and set in motion violence that would leave the big city of my youth nearly unrecognizable for two generations.

The whole concept of a race riot was an anachronism to my generation. Just as the killing of John F. Kennedy had raised the phenomenon of presidential assassination from the pages of our history texts, the riot in Detroit brought to life something that had once existed only in two dimensions. Mama, Daddy, and our adult relatives talked about the disruption with unequivocal disapproval, though Daddy was quick to return a Black Power salute thrown his way by a carload of tough-looking brothers.

My own brothers and their friends seemed to sympathize with the anarchistic fervor of their Detroit counterparts, but sat out the riots without taking to the streets. Like my parents, I didn't see the sense of black people running around throwing firebombs in our own neighborhoods. The indignant little girl who had blasted our people at the NAACP meeting was revived within me as I sat glued to the television set. I was half fascinated by the rebellious spectacle, half frightened that the chaos and its clearly dark-skinned origins could place all of us black people in danger. Mostly, I struggled to understand what good the young men skittering past the TV cameras throwing bottles and rocks thought would come of their actions.

The transformative civil rights struggle of my childhood and the March on Washington had been grounded in the nonviolent leadership of Dr. King. Even the black consciousness movement that was taking hold of my peers and me was rooted in the concept of inner growth; we nurtured our connection to the African motherland in an effort to cast off the lingering self-hatred of slavery. My girlfriend's father, incandescent Pontiac attorney Milton Henry, was a local hero who led our young adult revolution by example. Milton was a handsome, charming black man who had explored the traditional American route to success by serving his country during World War II, graduating from Yale Law School, and becoming a catalyst for change in our city government. His military unit was the Tuskegee Airmen—a black fighter pilot group that distinguished itself by never losing a single plane. Home from the war, he had experienced disrespect from a Southern bus driver after fighting for America's freedom, and had been scorned by the Pennsylvania Bar Association after passing its test with a stellar score. He was told that his "black ass" would never practice law in that state, and Pontiac's voting districts were later gerrymandered in a way that made it hard for him to retain his incendiary intellectual presence on the city council.

Milton's discontent with the status quo led him to become a major activist, a confidant and adviser of Malcolm X, and a litigator of black grievances in and outside the courtroom. No cause was too small; when an interracial couple was refused entry to the Pontiac Central High School prom, Milton Henry led protests in the streets. No power structure was too intimidating; in the courts, he challenged the system by objecting to all-white juries in cases with black defendants as not meeting the standard of "trial by peers." In the late sixties, after numerous visits to the African continent, he redefined himself by adopting an African name, becoming a vocal proponent of black nationalism, and wearing the dashiki that would soon be sported by everyone from the brother on the corner to George Jefferson on TV. Ultimately, Milton cofounded the Republic of New Afrika, a truly revolutionary group that urged the creation of a new country made up of five Southern states with majority-black populations. Almost miraculously, he promoted his causes without resorting to violence. Ultimately, he split from his compatriots, including his own brother, over the use of force. Because of Milton, I had seen firsthand how much could be accomplished through aggressive but nonviolent activism. I believed it was the way to achieve our common goals as black people.

Now, apparently in response to violence by raiding police, some of my frustrated brethren were throwing down a blazing gauntlet and being met with armed responses. Looking at the police and military being marshalled against them, I was afraid they were courting self-destruction and risking all of our lives. The fierce lack of give-a-fuck represented by flaming Molotov cocktails, looting, and sniper fire was a new and terrifying feature of a world where it seemed anything could happen. So, too, was the sight of National Guardsmen and the 101st Airborne soldiers patrolling the streets in trucks and tanks, fear in their eyes and guns in their hands. As assault vehicles rolled past ravaged buildings, I felt sympathy for the small-business owners who stood, discouraged and sometimes weeping, in front of stores that might have been built over a lifetime and burned out in an instant. The terror in the faces of mothers whose sons were running wild past gun-toting soldiers was also not lost on me, especially after the alleged murder of at least two black men by police officers at the Algiers Motel.

If the furious looting and burning of stores and businesses had begun as an expression of anger at a system that seemed weighted against the poor, they also provided an opportunity for those same people to take advantage of the "five-finger discount" that broken and breached storefronts put in front of them. During the Detroit unrest, while Ruth Ann and I were visiting a friend in Pontiac, the girl's male cousins came by and used the dining room table to gleefully divide the spoils from a looted Detroit liquor store they had hit that morning. Other people were clearly torn between their disapproval of the riot itself and their desire to grab some free stuff while the getting was good. One black woman, being interviewed by a local TV station, decried the rioters and their violence on camera, saying, "I think it's terrible, just terrible," while diligently searching for the mate to a shoe she had just scavenged from a looted footwear store.

With no past experience to go on, the rumor mill of Pontiac went into high gear. The scenario had the riot "coming this way." My friends spoke as if it were a spreading forest fire. The fact that the riot would have had to leapfrog over predominantly white and affluent communities before it could set Pontiac ablaze was no match for the high drama of a riot watch. Smart proprietors of every race sprayed the label *Soul Brother* on their establishments in an effort to stave off firebombers and looters. A citywide curfew was imposed on Pontiac's citizens. And, like many rumors of war, the prophecy fulfilled itself through a few violent incidents.

A former schoolmate known as "Party Pants" for the red trousers he wore to every neighborhood shindig was shot to death by a South Side store owner during an attempted looting. Unlike the raid on the Detroit after-hours joint, there was little question about who was right or wrong in the matter.

Almost as one, the black citizens of Pontiac seemed to decide that this rioting stuff was big-city business that could do Pontiac no good, and no one was more relieved than me. Although heightened black consciousness and Milton Henry–style Afrocentrism had come to our city to stay, Pontiac largely escaped the physical and economic devastation caused by the conflagration in Detroit. There would still be businesses to hire me, and Pontiac's white residents would soon confine the expectation of violence to an area south of Eight Mile Road where they rarely ventured. Compared to the threat of gunfire and revolution outside my front door, the nonviolent challenges of adulthood began to seem more manageable, even in an era of rampant change. Still, in the aftermath of deadly rioting, a bucolic college campus would have been a welcome reprieve from the unpredictability of life in a black neighborhood.

PART TWO

DREAMS DEFERRED, DETOURS, AND DOWNTURNS

CHAPTER 5

Work Instead of College: Not the End of the World, Just the End of a Dream

Times were booming and businesses were hiring. I registered with an employment service and interviewed for clerical jobs with Oakland County, Consumers Power, and every local department store. Everyone seemed impressed with me, but it was Pontiac General Hospital that gave me a position as a ward clerk. Sitting in the personnel office, I overheard the woman who interviewed me whisper to her boss about my exceptional score on the brief test I had been given. I was hired on the spot. I walked home, thinking about my future all the way. I was thrilled to have landed a "pink-collar" gig, but I would never stop scheming on how to get to college. Being employed would take some of the sting out of watching my homeroom 202 classmates head for Michigan State, University of Michigan, Western Michigan University, Eastern Michigan University, and some of the historically black colleges of the South that had previously been unknown to me. For so long, I had expected to be entering the rarified environs of Harvard or Yale. Instead, with now toddling Brian at my heels, I was bound for the world of hourly wages and thirty-minute lunch breaks. I'm glad I didn't know how long I would be there.

Pontiac General Hospital wasn't a university, but my first job involved a lot of learning. For the first six weeks, we new ward clerks spent half the workday in training. We learned medical notation, how to read and construct patient charts, and how to order medications and treatments. We absorbed the unfamiliar smells, sounds, and routines of hospital life and figured out the all-important hierarchy. The well-dressed attending physicians were gods of the ward who generally visited only twice a day. Without being told, we clerks observed that other than greeting them, they were to be spoken to only if they spoke to us. Residents, most often seen in green surgical scrubs under long white coats, were theoretically more approachable, but they were usually too busy or bleary-eyed from lack of sleep to socialize with the staff. On the ward, registered nurses ran the show. The RN was responsible for the well-being of the patients and supervised a staff of medical technicians, practical nurses, nurse's aides, and one or more clerks. Practical nurses took blood pressure and administered most of the treatments that the doctors ordered. Nurse's aides did the menial and dirty work, like making beds, filling water pitchers, and emptying bedpans. Almost none of the RNs were black; many of the practicals and nurse's aides were.

My hospital training class was like a continuation of high school, and I finished near the top. When I was permanently assigned to the obstetrics unit, I was overjoyed. Aside from the doctors and RNs, I knew many of my coworkers from Lakeside, school, or church. I also knew many of the patients. Though the staff strictly observed the policy of patient confidentiality with outsiders, there was plenty of gossip and speculation about patients among the staff. I was an informed and enthusiastic participant until one of the practical nurses, a former neighbor and a friend of my mother, who had known me since childhood, pulled me aside. "You stop running your mouth and telling everything you know about folks. These people are not your friends."

If I had lighter skin, I would have turned beet red. Her chastisement reminded me that I had no room to talk. It was also the latest in a lifetime of cautionary messages about the folly of trying to ingratiate oneself with white folks, especially if there were even a chance of betraying another black person. As surely as I was in a probationary period as an employee, my mother's friend reminded me, my white coworkers should be "fed with a long-handled spoon" until they proved themselves trustworthy.

There were plenty of more appropriate areas to focus on. Becoming a competent clerk was not the easiest task. Deciphering the doctors' ridiculously bad handwriting was a challenge. All the clerks were convinced that they sometimes wrote poorly in order to disguise the fact that they didn't know how to spell the names of some drugs. Transcribing medication orders correctly was essential; a mistake could cost a life. Pregnant patients sometimes came in waves that made the workload close to overwhelming. Even on a "happy" floor like OB, there were life-and-death emergency cases. Medicine was absolutely fascinating, and doctors even more so. They were the ultimate father figures, and I was always on the lookout for openings to impress them. I paid special attention to my appearance, including wearing a "wiglet" attached to a black velvet headband that gave me the long, straight hair God hadn't. Part of every meager paycheck was spent on cute uniforms for work.

Outside the hospital, my old habit of pretending myself into being was the salvation of my self-image. I envisioned myself as a young career woman and on my days off scoured

the sale racks for fashionable outfits that projected that image. I "lunched" at affordable restaurants like Big Boy with girl
pals who hadn't gone away to college.

Once my training ended, I worked the afternoon shift,
when the hospital slowly quieted from the daytime cacophony of activity and incessant paging to the calm of night, as
most patients were drugged to sleep. The hospital's offices and
shops had shut down, and doctors would make their way to
the nursing station to catch up on the paperwork in their patients' charts.

My first evening on the ward, I heard a baritone voice
that I remembered from the day I had given birth to Brian.
It belonged to Dr. Garfield Johnson Jr., the black senior
OB resident, who had just entered the nursing station with a
booming, "How's everyone doing this evening?" Dr. Johnson's
relative youth, Louisiana warmth, and down-home drawl
made him one of the more accessible physicians. When I had
the chance, I told him that I remembered him as the doctor
who had tried to help me by speeding up my labor.

He looked up at me, rubbing his hand across his beard
with its scattering of bumpy ingrown hairs. "I remember you,
Val. That was a long labor for such a young girl. Did you have
a boy or a girl?" I told him about Brian, and we talked a few
minutes more. After that night, he made a point of chatting
with me when he came to the station. It wasn't long before he
asked me, "What are you planning to do with your life? You
have too much potential to be a hospital clerk forever." Those
words, coming from an authority figure and delivered with
the conviction of the minister he later became, were exactly
the encouragement I needed to hear. It was time to apply to
college.

Like the University of Michigan and Michigan State,

Wayne State is a top state university and was my first choice. Although Wayne maintained high academic standards, its student body was largely made up of commuters from the many nearby suburbs. In a burst of misguided practicality, I had decided to channel my interest in medicine into a career in nursing. I solicited letters of recommendation from my high school biology teacher and from a favorite English teacher, and submitted my application with fingers crossed. When a letter from Wayne arrived, I opened it with trembling hands, only to find the wait was not over. The university insisted that I take the SATs before they would make a decision on my admission.

Arriving to take the test, I wheeled my vintage Oldsmobile—a gift from Mama and Daddy—onto campus and marveled at how the buildings of Wayne State created a real college environment within the city. Throngs of students hustled along crowded Cass Avenue and Wayne's green-and-gold insignia was displayed on jackets, book covers, and bumper stickers. Once accepted, I would feel like any resident student at a big state college.

The next letter I received began with the words, *We are pleased to inform you* . . . In the fall, just one year after my classmates, I would enter a respected four-year university.

By this time, Hubert and I were coming apart. In the aftermath of the previous summer's riots, political activism had become the driving force in his life. As part of a young adult activist group he cofounded, Pontiac Organization of Black Youth (POOBY), he was traveling to places like Chicago and New York to attend meetings and conferences that were raising the political consciousness of young African Americans. His work with POOBY was bringing him into contact with exciting new ideas and people, and his advocacy of fair housing laws was making him a known figure in Michigan. Once, at work, I proudly showed off a *Detroit Free Press* article on fair housing that mentioned him. The next day, I was called into the nursing supervisor's office and gently warned against stirring up trouble. The supervisor was visibly relieved to find out I was only bragging about my boyfriend. Romance was cute; revolution, apparently, could get you fired. In those days, I wouldn't have described myself as militant. Although I shared Hubert's politics, my job and responsibilities made me unavailable to be part of his new world.

It wasn't long before I developed a crush on a young attending physician I'll call Dr. E. He was a very handsome guy in his early thirties with light-brown skin, soft eyes, long lashes, and short, curly hair. He was also married. The female employees often remarked on his looks, but there were no reports of his dallying, as many doctors did, with anyone at the hospital. I secretly resolved to capture his interest. Between my aggressive attraction to father figures and my need to regain some of the status I had lost, I was a seventeen-year-old pitfall waiting for a morally weak man.

Dr. E. didn't exactly play hard to get. Like a lot of young women, I underestimated the appeal of a nubile body and worshipful attitude. The main entrance to the OB ward was a door directly across from my desk. For a couple of weeks, I had greeted Dr. E. with a smile and a sexy greeting every time he entered. At first, he simply nodded and greeted me back, minus the innuendo. One time, he held eye contact for a moment before turning away. Finally, one day he leaned over the counter in front of my desk, glancing around before saying, "Can I speak to you in the hall, please?" I felt a flash of fear. It occurred to me that he might be about to admonish me for my inappropriate tone. He walked toward the elevator at the center of the hall, where our standing together would not attract attention, then turned to me. "Are you serious with what you're doing, or are you just playing?"

Caught off guard, I answered truthfully: "I'm not sure." Attracting his attention had probably been a game, but I hadn't shared that I was playing it with anyone, not even Ruth Ann or my cousin Dorethia. Standing next to Dr. E., being taken seriously by someone I considered so vastly my superior, things felt more serious. Up close, I was even more drawn to his good looks and the possibility of being touched by the same hands that brought babies into the world and performed lifesaving surgery. If he wanted me, could I say no?

He pushed the elevator button. "Well, when you make up your mind, give me a call." He was barely back in his office before he heard from me. Many years later, the whole country would take sides over a sex scandal involving a young female intern and another flawed man with whom I had worked. I was not so quick to judge President Bill Clinton and Monica Lewinsky. I knew that a man who was disciplined in his work and was basically a good guy could also be incredibly reckless and selfish. I also knew too well that needy young women are not always innocent victims. Fortunately for Dr. E. and me, the eyes of a nation were not upon us.

Dr. E. and I didn't just sleep together; we had long conversations about life, family, goals, and even medicine. Protecting both of us, he had immediately put me on the relatively new birth control pill and provided me with an ample supply. He became a vocal supporter of my plan to get a college education and discussed my options at great length. I knew that what we were doing was wrong, but I pushed aside my guilt by determining never to jeopardize his marriage or make our relationship public. In fact, the beginning of the end of our affair was an accidental sighting of him Christmas shopping with his wife. I ran in the other direction before we compounded our sins by trying to hide our relationship in front of her. After that, I began to make excuses for not sleeping with him, and by late spring we were pretty much over.

Endings and change were huge features of the world that spring. On April 4, an event that I, along with millions of others, had feared came to pass. Martin Luther King Jr. was assassinated in Memphis, and black America's heart was ripped open. Back when my mother had been secretary of our church, Dr. King had visited with our pastor, and my mother had met the impressive young minister. The night before the March on Washington, when I was thirteen, I had sent up a prayer that at least a few hundred people would show up to support the cause he led. When I awoke, tens of thousands of marchers were already in the streets of DC. Dr. King's speech had lifted my soul with pride in his eloquence and the scope of his vision. When he died, despite my excitement about the Black Panthers and the black consciousness movement, I was still a product of the civil rights era.

In my concept of black consciousness, there was no contradiction between defiant Afrocentrism and nonviolence; there was evolution. Young rebels like Stokely Carmichael and Huey Newton inspired me, but I revered Dr. King. His death and the loss of Bobby Kennedy that summer were devastating blows that did more to destroy my innocence than any sexual affair could have.

CHAPTER 6

College: That's Not a Work/Study Program, It's My Life

At Wayne State, no one had any expectations of me at all. For most Wayne students, college was serious business. Many had jobs and families; others who didn't mostly did their learning on campus and their socializing elsewhere. Free to reinvent myself, I changed my hairstyle to a short Afro and started to slowly become aware of the rapidly spreading hippie movement.

At the hospital, it became clear that I was not a "lifer"; I was a student clerking my way through college. My daily routine: up at six a.m. to dress myself and Brian and drop him at Mama Cooper's house, catch the bus to Detroit since my ancient Oldsmobile couldn't be trusted to make the trip, attend a full load of classes from eight thirty till twelve thirty, take the bus back to Pontiac, change into my uniform for an eight-hour shift, go home—where Mama had already put Brian to bed—study, and get to bed myself around one thirty a.m. I located every good napping place on campus and learned how to sleep for ten or fifteen minutes at a time.

That first term, partly due to the biology course required to prepare for a nursing major, I only managed a 2.5 GPA. In the spring, as I fulfilled some of the university's liberal arts requirements, my average rose to 3.6. This should have told me something, but my decision to go for a BS in nursing had been motivated by the fact that registered nurses could find employment anywhere, and leaving my hometown was high on my agenda.

My first year of college ended with good grades and the prospect of a summer in which I only had to work a forty-hour week. On days off, I loaded Brian into the backseat of the Oldsmobile and ran around town visiting girlfriends and family members. That summer, I didn't really have a boyfriend and I didn't care. When I got off work, Johnny Carson was all the company I needed, and the sofa was my steady date.

During the summer, I made the decision to move in with Ruth Ann's family, paying a small amount for room and board for Brian and myself. Things weren't particularly bad at home, but after a last small tiff with Daddy, Ruth Ann's mother made me an offer I didn't want to refuse. Life with the Thompson family relieved the day-to-day pressure of Daddy's petty rules, which included a directive not to turn up the heat and a ban on making calls to Detroit—technically long distance, though the fee was about twenty cents and I was willing to pay. At nineteen, with my three-year-old son in tow, I left home for good.

Living with the Thompsons, I envied Ruth Ann's situation. Her parents had decided that the cost of childcare made it more sensible for their only kid to focus on finishing college before finding a full-time job. I couldn't imagine myself with the support my best friend enjoyed. My father had not been a deadbeat dad; he fulfilled his minimal financial obligations to Spurgeon and me, and provided a stable home for the kids he had after remarrying. Still, I felt zero concern from him for my well-being, and no interest in what I would do with my life. It was as if his kids were possessions, and like most possessions, sometimes owning us was a burden. Later, as a mature adult, I came to believe that my father's need to escape grinding poverty had trumped every other concern, and I was able to forgive him, but he did appalling damage with his neglect. The nuclear family my mother had hoped to create by marrying Daddy had had the deck stacked against it, and my pregnancy hadn't helped matters. The love and affection my mother had lavished on us when we were small had formed a bond strong enough to withstand the turbulent early years of her marriage, but the deficit of my father's absence was a hole I would unconsciously try to fill for many years. Living with my friend's family was a blessed relief, but it was also a daily reminder of what I did not have.

The novelty of the hospital had worn off, and as the next school year began, I was questioning my decision to become an RN. Because I had not yet declared a major, I elected to take more courses in English and psychology and only one empirical science course. A female instructor I especially admired was Geneva Smitherman, a pioneering PhD in the English department and a personal friend of counterculture hero Angela Davis. Smitherman's book *Talkin and Testifyin* defined what would later be labeled "Ebonics" as black English, a dialect with set rules that actually tended to regularize the quirks of Standard English. Her book made me proud. Like natural hair, African names, and the Black Power salute, her thesis was tucked into my belief system as affirmation of the majesty of my black people. I joined a student walkout to make her Afro-American lit course available to a larger number of students. During the class, she was highly complimentary of my command of the works of James Baldwin. "Have you ever considered getting a PhD and becoming an academic?"

I thought of how unlikely it was that any science instructor would ever ask me that question. Each day, I realized more how much I enjoyed the liberal arts and psychology—classes that would later stand me in good stead throughout my advertising career—and hated the struggle of most science courses.

Through a psych class, I became aware of a technique called "sensitivity training" and volunteered to be part of a twelve-hour session at the home of a psychology graduate student and his wife. In the session, which began at eight a.m., a group of about ten participated in exercises that ranged from verbal sharing to physical exercises that required increasing amounts of trust. We were all under twenty-five; some of us were outgoing and self-assured, one was a shy stutterer, one a strapping wrestler, another a Vietnam vet missing a leg and part of one arm. There was also a young man a few years out of college who was facing trial for refusing the draft. The group was mostly white, but included two blacks and an Asian. There were several Jews, a few Catholics, a Baptist, and the atheist veteran. As our session leader gently guided us through the day, peeling back layers of defenses and helping us feel safe enough to take off the masks we all wore, a few remarkable things happened. The stutterer, at least for a few hours, gained the ability to express himself without hesitating or stammering. The angry Vietnam veteran was able to communicate his sadness and loss without raging. I could open up about the abandonment I felt. The wrestler confessed his fear of the black men he was forced to deal with in Detroit and shared that the casual racism of his suburban upbringing was the cause.

By the end of the training session, we had built enough trust to perform the now-cliché act of falling backward, confident that one or more of our new friends would catch us. I'm not sure if the effects of the training lasted beyond the eight p.m. cutoff of the session, but for those few hours, caught up in the optimism of inexperience and the zeitgeist of our times, it seemed that with enough understanding, we could solve all the problems of the world.

One question that was answered at the sensitivity group was who my next boyfriend would be. Bill K., a tall white guy with wavy brown hair and beautiful eyes, was the man who had refused induction into the army. Except for his intelligence, Bill, with his longish hair, wire-rimmed glasses, faded jeans, and undeniable whiteness, was unlike any guy I had ever been interested in. In the Vietnam era, before the all-volunteer army turned the service into a working-class jobs program, most of the young men I knew were in peril of being sent to fight a war that they didn't believe in. Many of them were looking for any way to avoid Vietnam. My brother Gary was "lucky" enough to have been diagnosed as a carrier of the sickle cell trait, which would never make him ill, but got him the prized 4F classification. My brother Spurgeon had been hospitalized and even placed in traction with hard-to-disprove back trouble. Pretty much every young man I knew was working some angle to avoid the possibility of losing life or limb in Southeast Asia.

Bill K. had shown up for induction but refused to step forward into the army. Open defiance of the United States government was something I had only seen from Muhammad Ali. Bill, an everyday guy, had shown the courage of a champion, and that drew me to him with magnetic force. Shortly after the group session, Bill and I got together for what felt like a second date. He took me to see *Putney Swope,* a film about race and advertising that would become a cult classic, and whose creator, Robert Downey Sr., would one day become my friend. That date was an epic encounter that was one part interracial exploration, one part antiwar consciousness raising, and—after Bill opened a bottle of wine and introduced me to the Rolling Stones's "Gimme Shelter"—one part mind-blowing sex. Bill the draft resister was my ambassador to white counterculture and that date was the beginning of an on-and-off romance that would go on for years and follow us to three states.

Without a doubt, college broadened my horizons, but working in a hospital also introduced me to people whose worlds informed and enlivened my own. Laverne was a practical nurse who arrived a year or so after I was hired. She was probably in her midthirties, but by the time we met, life had erased softness from her face and demeanor. Her voice was deep and rough, she was not most people's idea of pretty, and her gaze was generally intimidating. Laverne's round, slightly protruding eyes challenged, more than invited, contact.

Twice every shift, Laverne and her coworkers wheeled dozens of bawling babies out of the nursery to their mothers on the OB ward, where I was the evening clerk. Most of the nursery aides brought the babies one at a time, stretching out their easiest chore as long as possible. Unsmiling Laverne hauled the infants out two at a time, dragging the hospital bassinets behind her as she strode the halls with a measured stomp that was silenced by the rubber soles of her white nurse's oxfords. She was a walking dare who scared the hell out of most of us from day one.

A famously inquisitive nurse's aide decided to breach Laverne's space in order to get the 411 on our newcomer. This nosy woman had a habit of following the answer to any question with an elongated, "Oh-h-h," that could have meant, "Oh, right," "Oh, really?" or a lot of things in between. She asked Laverne's name and greeted the response in her customary way. Laverne, frowning, barked, "Oh, *what?* You sound like you know something." As the nurse's aide sputtered, Laverne walked off, dragging her bassinets perilously close to the toes of her inquisitor. I couldn't entirely smother the snicker that came out of my nose at the exchange. Wonder of wonders, as she passed my desk, scary Laverne looked at me and winked.

When Laverne transferred to the ward a short while later, we came to know that the hard shell had a few cracks in it. From time to time, Laverne's dry sense of humor even leaked out. From that first wink, scary Laverne took an inexplicable liking to me, and she and I often had our dinner break together. It turned out that Laverne was one of the wisest and most tolerant people I would ever meet. Her sole exceptions were people she considered fools, like the nurse's aide who had gotten in her face. "She didn't want to know my name. She wanted to be the one who found out my name so she could tell all y'all. I bet she won't ask me nothin' else." Laverne loved the fact that I was a college student and added her voice to the *Don't let anybody stop you* chorus. She praised go-getters in general, like a former welfare mother of ten who had been our coworker until she left to become a teacher via a welfare-related program. "A lot of people don't believe she's gon' make it, but let me tell you something: I been to her house and it's spotless. Anybody who got ten kids and a spotless house can do anything." Nothing I've learned in life since has led me to disagree with her assessment.

Laverne was a never-ending source of what African Americans call mother wit: common sense with a veneer of self-protection. Somehow, Laverne had learned my middle name, Jo, and from that time on, a variation of it became her personal nickname for me. "Let me tell you something,

Jo Jo," she advised me, "when you work with a whole bunch of women, if you try to keep your business private, they will spend all their time trying to find it out. The secret is, tell 'em a whole lot of stuff. Tell 'em so much, anything you don't tell, they don't think you got sense enough to do." Laverne was a master of figuring out the system and making it work for herself. She was the mother of six children who was married to a man she called a "born-to-die" heroin addict. She had never abandoned him, reasoning that without her, he would become a homeless junkie whose children might encounter him in the streets. "He knows he can't do drugs or have no junkies in my house. He don't really eat anyway, and it don't cost nothing for him to soak up a little heat."

A former welfare recipient, Laverne had snapped up the opportunity to become a practical nurse when it was offered through a state program. She had taken advantage of city grants to move her family from the projects to a house she could own and renovate. "I woulda got more if I would've had sex with all those white men that ran the programs," she half joked. In one of the crafting crazes that regularly swept the hospital wards, Laverne learned to crochet and earned extra money making afghans, vests, and adorable caps during breaks and slow times on the ward.

Our coworkers were astounded that the tough, streetwise practical nurse and the clerk with big ideas and hippie tendencies became fast friends. Laverne would sometimes give me the skinny on what the rest of the crew was saying about me, but only if she had some positive advice to attach to it. "Listen, Jo Jo, they got a lot to say about you liking that white boy, but let me tell you something: get what you want. Don't let nobody tell you who you supposed to love. Some of 'em just jealous 'cause you doing something different." One of my favorite admonitions was her nonjudgmental, "Everything don't bother everybody. Don't ever tell nobody what they should or shouldn't put up with. A lot of people couldn't stand a junkie, but I can take that, because my husband is a good man, he's just addicted to that stuff. Now me, I couldn't stand no cheating man. Fortunately, I got one of those motherfuckers don't nobody else want."

Laverne was as Mud Lake as could be, but beneath the ghetto patina was a shaman of human nature and a ride-or-die buddy. She boasted at the hospital about my career after I was gone. Long after I left Pontiac, she would send greetings through my mother, and when I was in town, I would call or swing by for a short visit. Once I was in a position to really bring all that I knew about black people to my advertising job, it was my friendship with Laverne that gave me insight into a culture I had not bothered to delve into because I was too busy running from it. Even now, as I think of her, I reflect on how she and millions like her—the black working poor—remain invisible as far as American advertising is concerned. Having become a nurse and a homeowner, she could have held herself above the Kool-Aid and Kmart culture of the now-decaying projects, but Laverne was better than that. Talking with her for five minutes restored my empathy with a whole segment of my fellow African Americans. Like me, they were just trying to find a way to be black without selling out or being taken advantage of.

Twenty years after I left the hospital, if I asked Laverne how she was doing, she would answer, "You know me, Jo Jo. No sick days; twenty vacation days." And I would understand that she was still working, and still working the system. You got paid nothing for unused sick time, but vacation days were money in the bank. When she died, I learned of her passing too late to send the showy display of flowers that I think would have made her smile. "They can't stand it that the two of us are friends," she used to say. "They sittin' up on the edge of the bed at night trying to figure that shit out."

CHAPTER 7

Rock and Roll, Sex, and Battle Fatigue

I f a song can change a person's life, "Gimme Shelter" revo-
lutionized mine. At the time I first heard it, everything my
generation had been raised to believe was being called into
question: the role of women, the trustworthiness of government and the justness of war, the value of material success,
the sanctity of marriage, the meaning of race, monogamy, and
fidelity, the Christian work ethic, the corporate power structure. From its opening guitar riff and haunting background
vocals, "Gimme Shelter" struck me as a tapestry woven from
those revolutionary strands. Whatever had given rise to this
music, I wanted to be part of, especially the rebellious creativity it embodied. It took awhile before all this inner foment
found an outlet, but as the song says, it was just a shot away.

There is no revolution without destruction, and my personal revolt was no exception. Mama Cooper, my childhood
babysitter, had been caring for Brian since I started college.
After I moved from Mama and Daddy's house, she had never
liked the disruption of my waking him and the rest of her
household at midnight, and suggested that I let him sleep,
spend my hours between school and work at her house, and
take him home with me on days off. Because the Coopers were
like family, and because I welcomed the relief from having

to care for my toddler, I accepted the offer. There probably couldn't have been a worse time for me to be set free. The discipline that Brian's needs had demanded evaporated in the heat of my desire to spend every possible moment with Bill. Predictably, that suffocating preoccupation did not make my relationship with him stronger. Unexpectedly, my frequent overnight absences also provoked disapproval at the house where I lived. I thought of myself as a liberated adult who could not be bound by the narrow conventions of society. After a little more than a year with the Thompsons, I moved to another room-and-board situation with my brother Gary and the widow my great-grandfather had left after remarrying at eighty years old. That kind lady would probably have objected to my behavior too, but the point was moot. By then, Bill had demanded a break, the school year had ended, and I was spending more time with Brian again.

I made a new friend at work who would become my running buddy as I found new boundaries by crashing through old ones. S.K. was an RN who was technically my boss, but quickly became a friend. She was an attractive brunette with blue eyes that made her resemble fashion model Cheryl Tiegs. S.K. had busted out of a boring seven-year suburban marriage and became a nurse in order to support her three kids. Over late-night burgers at a local grill, we discovered that we shared an attraction to counterculture. When not in a nurse's uniform, S.K. was fond of faded jeans, tie-dyed T-shirts, and sandals. Free of her early marriage, she was enjoying her liberation with a nonjudgmental circle of friends: hippies and aspiring hippies who happened to be working stiffs for eight hours a day. I admired her free-spirited outlook, and her new Volkswagen Beetle became such a symbol of light-hearted unconventionality that I was determined to acquire my own. In those early days of our friendship, Woodstock nation held undeniable appeal, but it was a foreign country. I still lived in a mostly black world and meditated on how to revive my dream of being a black That Girl in the big city.

In the late sixties and early seventies, the wave of cultural revolution that was sweeping the country hit my family like a tsunami. The inhibitions and prohibitions that had guided Gary, Spurgeon, and me seemed obsolete and created to justify control of our minds by "the establishment" and "the power structure." All of us became social users of marijuana, and Gary even had the audacity to plant a few seeds in a clay pot on the sunny back porch of the house we shared with Granddaddy's widow, whom we called Mama Al. I began to see the moral code under which I had been raised as a tool in the conspiracy to limit and objectify women. In my version of rebellion, Madonna was knocked off her pedestal and "whore" came out of rehab as "sexually liberated woman." For my brother Spurgeon, change took the form of militant political leanings. Once, looking at an American flag proudly fluttering in the breeze, he was struck by the hypocrisy of all that had been done under its red, white, and blue imprimatur. He risked a year's jail sentence for trespassing by shimmying up the flagpole and setting the nation's banner on fire. The biggest change by far, though, was in my eldest brother Gary, who seemed to go through a postcollege identity crisis and began dabbling in hard drugs and bad companions, with the most disastrous consequences imaginable.

Watching Gary get into trouble was like seeing an airplane explode in midair. One minute he was flying into a clear blue sky with every expectation of a successful journey. The next, all that seemed to be left was a mass of flames. Up to that point, my brother had been the guy parents wanted their sons to be and their daughters to marry—an obedient son, respectful kid, reliable paper boy; before the revolution, my brother had had a corner on the good guy market. In the time of defiance, the boy he had been must have seemed to him to be the creation of other people's expectations. Our great-grandfather, Jason Banks, the man who had raised him, passed away shortly after Gary's college graduation, leaving a vacuum where his rock-solid belief system had once proscribed Gary's behavior. For Granddaddy Jason, work had been like a religion. Granddaddy had faithfully toiled at the auto factory until his real age was discovered and he was forced into retirement. Once his factory job ended, he drove carless shoppers home from the grocery store for money. He was a lifelong Republican and thought every black person should be, because Abraham Lincoln was a Republican and he freed the slaves. Granddaddy Jason had lived his life as he had been taught he was supposed to. When he died, America's young people were in open rebellion against "supposed to," and it seemed my brother was no exception. Like his siblings, Gary was ready to bust out. Unlike us, he didn't do it in baby steps. Gary had no idea how to be a bad boy. Unfortunately, he was a quick study, with some new friends who were experts.

Early one Sunday morning, one of Gary and Spurgeon's childhood friends called the house we shared and incredulously asked, "Val, is it true that Gary shot Walter J. last night? I can't believe it!" I also could not believe it. Gary had a gift for getting along with everyone. He was the only young man I knew who had never been involved in a fight and yet was not considered a punk. Although the recent darkening of his easygoing personality had not escaped me, and I had certainly noticed that he was calling in sick to work a lot, I hadn't thought any of it was serious. Turning on and dropping out of the humdrum world of work was the order of the day; I would have quit my own job if I could. The one or two times I had visited Gary's office at city hall, I had been grateful that the hospital at least offered the potential for excitement—something utterly lacking in the city's stultifying accounting department. I told the Sunday caller, "Well, no police have come to the house, so I don't think so," but I was hardly off the phone before Mama Al informed me that my brother had come in very early, packed some clothes, and gone out again. In the end, police or no police, the news came from all over town that my brother, in the first physically violent encounter of his life, was reported to have shot to death a local drug dealer on Saturday night. When Mama Al rang my mother, she began with the phrase that usually accompanies a death in the family: "Deloris, I'm calling you with bad news." The language was appropriate. A cherished image of my brother had died right along with the man who had been gunned down.

As details of the crime emerged, Gary's trial sparked an explosion of puzzling and sometimes contradictory emotions in me—some of which remain unresolved to this day. The biggest of these was that, guilty or innocent, I wanted my brother to be acquitted. The victim had attacked him—pistol-whipped him in a sneak attack that could not go without retaliation by the code of black males. Up to then, it was all well and good for Gary to have been that rare person who could get along with everyone. Now, if he didn't retaliate, his kindness would be rebranded as weakness. I have no idea if this went through his head, or if some alpha male instinct sent him off in search of a gun. He had, after all, grown up in a house where Granddaddy kept a rifle (out of reach of children). Presumably, it was there to be used in the face of some appropriate assault. Could Gary take a beating from some lowlife and still hold his head up? It's possible he wasn't thinking at all, just feeling the outrage of being someone who never did anything to anybody and yet had been handed this kind of humiliation. In the community where we had grown up, if you took shit, you would be given shit, and whatever his thought process, that night my brother wasn't having any. If I am honest, I have to admit some deep part of me was impressed that my brother had shot the first son of a bitch to physically disrespect him. No matter how much I grieved the loss of his freedom and the future I had thought he would have, I could not bring myself to blame him.

I have spent half a career telling my clients that it is hardly possible to overestimate the value that African Americans place on respect. Four hundred years of contempt has left a powerful thirst for acknowledgment of the folly of fooling around with us. Scholarly studies from prestigious universities have listed respect as the number one value of the black street code. The drug dealer who brutally went upside my brother's head with a pistol over a misinterpreted transaction was breaking him off some major disrespect. Then, he allowed Gary to drive away as if he were nothing to worry about. Walter J. was a streetwise criminal who surely knew better than to leave a dangerous enemy in a position to retaliate. He clearly didn't see Gary as a threat, and not knowing who he was messing with was a fatal code violation. In the end, if he lived long enough to recognize the shooter behind the rain of lead that capped his brief existence, his last thought was probably what the rest of our city's black men were thinking: *Damn, Gary Banks ain't no joke.*

As the story of the night's events oozed out, the mothers and teachers and ministers of our town mourned the demise of a promising youth, but most saw falling in with drugs and dealers as Gary's undoing. Shooting the fool who had taken him for a punk? Like Chris Rock, they weren't saying it was right, but they understood.

Despite remembering a younger, less criminal Walter J., I wanted Gary to be given amnesty based on the exemplary life he had led before. The prosecutor, using psychology on the all-white jury, portrayed Gary as a near-genius who was counting on the contrast between him and his criminal, drug-dealing victim, as well as between our saddened, mostly circumspect family and the victim's boisterous kin, to sway the jury in his favor.

"This case is not about a good boy versus a drug dealer. This is not about one kind of family versus another. This is about a guy with an IQ that's higher than yours and mine, trying to get away with murder."

Sitting across from the rowdy family members of the victim—a guy with whom I had even danced in more innocent days—I truly felt their pain that their loved one was lost to them forever and being defamed even in death. I was firmly on my brother's side, but the trial demeaned us all. The white jury's disdain for a black drug dealer was a given; to make them fear and convict my brother, the prosecutor had to use his most powerful message: "He is smarter than you. Don't let him get away with that." I watched the faces of the jurors tighten ever so slightly at his words. I listened to the obviously embellished and even fabricated testimony of police who claimed to have identified three black men in a black car with a black interior—during a brief nighttime pause at a stop sign—even though they were not look looking for the vehicle or its occupants at the time. I knew they were lying, except for their admission that the driver, my brother, was unknown to them. I wondered if the white jury believed them and if the presence of even a single black jury member would have reminded them, *They all look alike to me.* The lying cops and manipulative prosecutor inspired in me a lingering disgust for the justice system. The simple truth was bad enough; in retaliation for a degrading assault, having had time to reflect, my brother had shot his assailant multiple times. Like our grandfather Walter Banks, Gary was convicted of first-degree murder and sentenced to natural life in prison.

My heart was in pain for my mother, whose pride and joy would now be lumped in with every black killer that white society stereotyped and feared. Mama cried all night when he was sentenced. Gary's crime wreaked havoc on expectations that had been built on years of merit. Unlike my pregnancy, there was no beautiful baby bonus to mitigate the painful offense; just the prospect of prison visits, clanging doors, and futile regrets. "I just keep thinking, if only the jury could know who he was before," Mama wept. Through the fog of our common sorrow, I wished the same for my brother. As his shiny plane fell to earth in a ball of fire, I hoped against the odds there would be a survivor.

It took awhile to realize that one survivor of Gary's disaster was me. And like most survivors, I had to learn how to exist in a reality that was forever altered. Although the reality I continued was not the same, it was different in ways that would not be apparent to the naked eye. Like so many survivors, I lived with an inexplicable guilt at being able to carry on as if nothing had happened. Yet I had my own life to live, my own mistakes to make. I longed to break out of the suspended animation of Gary's trial and sentence.

The summer after my twenty-first birthday, I spent my income tax refund on a trip to visit my uncle Willie DeWalt, the former Pontiac Central basketball star. "D," as my uncle liked to be called, had moved to New York after graduating from college and was a denizen of the city's jazz clubs and hip bars. One indelible childhood memory of my uncle as a teenager was the afternoon I overheard him singing "That Old Black Magic" and looked into his room to see him lying across his bed, arms folded behind his head, looking up at the ceiling, seemingly daydreaming. That moment was an avatar of his Sinatra-inspired, jazzy New York life. Dressed to the nines in an elegant suit and spit-shined shoes with gleaming watch and coordinated cigarette lighter, my larger-than-life Uncle D was seldom seen in these haunts without a cigarette and his signature Tanqueray martini "with a psychological touch of vermouth."

Hours after I arrived in New York, and after introducing me to his pretty, white, live-in girlfriend, D whisked us off to a West Side jazz bar called the Guitar, owned by Pontiac native Freddie Hayes. One of the only other times I had been in a bar, an underage excursion to Detroit's famous Baker's Keyboard Lounge, a friend had advised me to have a Tom Collins, an alcoholic drink that tasted like lemonade. When I ordered the same drink here, D immediately rebuffed my request: "She will have no such thing. She will have a gin and tonic, a proper lady's drink." Before I could react, he was off talking to one of the musicians who had just taken a break. By the time D returned, with a tall, serious, pipe-smoking black man in tow, I had discovered that I liked gin and tonic just fine.

"Valerie, say hello to Ron Carter. Ron, this is my little niece. She's visiting from Detroit." I would later find out that Ron Carter was a legendary bassist who had played with Miles Davis, Herbie Hancock, and other giants of jazz. If anyone had told me that I would one day work with Ron and be introduced to Miles Davis by Herbie Hancock, I would not have been able to fathom such a thing. Sitting in that bar, on vacation from my hospital clerk's chair, just to live and work in New York City someday was enough of a dream. I found Manhattan completely thrilling and utterly intimidating.

I can only remember being out alone once, when my uncle's girlfriend unexpectedly left me in Bloomingdale's with instructions on which bus to take back to their West End Avenue apartment. I did some careful shopping in the famous department store, picking a stylish long skirt and matching top from the clearance racks and splurging on a suede belt for Brian. I had an herb omelet at nearby Yellow Fingers restaurant, where I was convinced I saw the lead actor from the movie *Putney Swope*. Hindsight tells me that my clingy weeklong visit must have been a bit of a nuisance for a busy New York couple, but as far as I was concerned, my trip to my idealized home had been an urbane adventure.

One week in New York left me impatient to change my life, but one night in Keego Harbor, Michigan actually did the trick. In New York, D had taken me to Greenwich Village, which was in full bohemian effect. The long-haired, army-fatigue-and-jean-clad men and flower-child women in long dresses reignited my attraction to hippie culture. Back home, S.K. had suggested that we shift our late-night hang to a local hippie bar, and now that I was of legal age, I was all for it. The Back Seat Saloon was a hole in the wall with rustic wood interior, peanut shells on the floor, and a bell-bottoms-and-patchouli vibe. When we walked in, an acoustic guitar band was performing a Crosby, Stills, Nash & Young song. They were my idea of a real hippie group: all fringe, denim, and tie-dye, the guys' hair as long as the mane on the pretty blond girl singer. The audience—seated at small wooden tables that held pitchers of warming beer, half-empty foam-ringed glasses, and baskets of peanuts—mirrored the performers on the tiny stage. This was S.K.'s scene; these were her people, and I was welcomed with open arms and thumb-lock hippie handshakes. My color wasn't a problem; as the only black and a woman, I wasn't a threat, I was a mascot. That night at the Back Seat Saloon was the first of many forays into a white generation that claimed to have rejected the conventions of its parents. Like materialism, sexism, and monogamy, racism was another box to be checked off, and hanging out with me was proof of their liberation. It was my first experience of a phenomenon I would encounter time and time again.

I threw myself into music and nightlife with a fervor I hadn't felt since junior high school days. I fell in love with live music, the groups who played it, and the culture that surrounded it. I devoured every issue of *Rolling Stone*, which in those days was a broadsheet with long, incisive pieces by Lester Bangs and Ben Fong-Torres. I immersed myself in the music of the Rolling Stones, Crosby, Stills, Nash & Young, Stevie Winwood, Joni Mitchell, Janis Joplin, James Taylor, Jimi Hendrix, Santana, Eric Clapton, the Doors, the Beatles, Led Zeppelin, and many other popular bands of the time.

When my hospital shift ended, my car headed to the saloon as if on autopilot. I made friends with the bands, the bartenders, and my fellow regulars. Ironically, like a fly in buttermilk, I had never been blacker. I cultivated a certain Afrocentric mystique, accentuated by exotic dress and my trademark headscarf and hoop earrings, a costume I only abandoned after the poster for Ntozake Shange's *for colored girls who have considered suicide/when the rainbow is enuf* made me look like a copycat. I was invited to every after-party and late-night jam session. My enthusiasm for music led me to rediscover my love of singing. Before long, I was sitting in with the musicians who played at the Back Seat, although I never seriously tried to join a band.

My passion for nightlife soon made it necessary for me to move to my own apartment. None of the older black people in my life, and few of the younger ones, could tolerate a culture that had *Sex, drugs, and rock and roll!* as its rallying cry. I, on the other hand, was a card-carrying member. I had rushed in through the rock-and-roll door, alcohol was my drug of choice, and sex tended to take care of itself. Once I moved into my own cute little apartment, I was frequently the hostess of late-night gatherings where guests shared cheap wine and candlelit conversation until the break of dawn.

Not surprisingly, my lifestyle was also incompatible with college, work, and motherhood. Looking back, I can see that I had pushed myself to the limit. Years of trying to make up for my teenage pregnancy had taken their toll. At a time when my peers were working temporary summer jobs, I carried a union card, made payments on my beloved VW Beetle, and struggled to afford a college education. One semester, I even added a tutoring job to my already exhausting schedule. Something had to give, and what gave was discipline. I made sure that my son was taken care of, but increasingly that meant leaving my adorable little boy in the loving care of the Coopers or my parents. I missed classes and work with increasing frequency, but rarely missed a night out. I shrugged off S.K.'s warning that I risked getting a rep for hanging out too much, chalked it up to our age difference, and found other companions on the nights she declined to go out.

I didn't register for college senior year, telling myself I needed a break. My steadfast friend Ruth Ann warned me that I might never go back, but I felt she didn't completely understand my exhausting struggle. Bill the draft-resister was going through a similar phase and was in and out of my life until he quit his job and took off on a road trip to California.

Somehow, in the midst of this most laissez-faire period of my life, I made progress toward the creative career I had always thought I would have. My high school boyfriend Hubert was running for county commissioner and put me in charge of writing all his materials.

Walking into campaign headquarters one night, I spotted a homeroom 202 classmate, Alvin Bessent, who in the intervening years had matured into a really handsome guy. I was happy to have him as a collaborator on the campaign, and after I made it clear that I no longer regarded him as the kid I had known in homeroom 202, we took the relationship beyond campaign headquarters. Our first date was a campaign fundraiser, but a lifetime of growing up in "the Yac" together gave us plenty of fodder for dinner conversations and cozy evenings catching up on the years we hadn't been in touch. The time that I had spent as a hunkered-down student mom, struggling to recapture the promise of my adolescence, Alvin had spent in a carefree college career at Michigan State, becoming a leader of his fraternity, Kappa Alpha Psi, and surviving the typical beer-soaked undergraduate bacchanal. As I was faltering under the weight of so much responsibility so young, Alvin shrugged off the callow concerns of college life, married his undergrad sweetheart, and took a job in social services.

When our paths crossed at campaign headquarters, I was only months away from the advertising job of my dreams, and he was back in the hunt for dreams that had been put on hold during his brief, ill-thought-out marriage. Somehow, we sensed that it might be the wrong time for the two of us to get serious and—something very unusual for me—kept the relationship light. We had a wonderful time before our candidate won and Alvin moved to Lansing and later Washington, DC. We parted without drama, a rare occurrence in my life for which I would later thank a benevolent universe.

In addition to working on the campaign, I was delighted to make it through the first round of the *Mademoiselle* Magazine College Board competition, which made me a sort of campus stringer for the New York magazine. Famous writers like Sylvia Plath were alumni. Entering the competition was the sort of thing I hadn't done since high school. When I shared with one of my white friends from Wayne State that I probably wouldn't enter because I'd never be chosen, she said, "Why not you? Why would you think someone else is better than you?" I was reminded of James Baldwin's warning that it is not what others think of us that limits us; it is our belief that their opinions define us.

I was embarrassed that it took a white girl's uninhibited perspective to reawaken my belief in my ability to compete. Although I continued to vacillate and barely made the deadline, I developed and wrote a sample magazine section, "The Now Woman," and dropped it into the mail just under the wire. Along with political and fashion-related material, my entry contained a profile of Graham Nash, whose music often revolved around love and relationships. To score a face-to-face interview with Nash when he was in town, I had called every local hotel and pretended to be his assistant making sure he would not be given a room on the thirteenth floor. When the clerk at Detroit's St. Regis informed me that he would be safely ensconced in their low-rise hotel, I sent him three red roses with a card that simply read, *Hello,* and was signed, *Valerie.* I followed up with a phone call and he invited me to stop by the next afternoon. Seeing Graham Nash and David Crosby—who was probably there to ensure that the meeting would be brief—striding across the hotel lobby to meet me, I felt as if I could make anything happen. I came away with enough material for a cute article, and a conviction that hanging out with superstars was my destiny.

Only metaphysics, a belief system I wouldn't discover until many years later, can explain the way music stars began to appear in my orbit. Once, after making a solo trip to Detroit to catch a Who concert and finding it sold out, I stopped at the posh Pontchartrain Hotel bar (now a Crowne Plaza) for a solitary drink. A hip-looking group of men and women sent over a margarita. They'd been taking bets on why I was alone. Apparently, my African-inspired headscarf, long skirt, and spurning of a barstool in favor of a table made me seem more like an artist than a hooker. Out of curiosity, they invited me to join them. They turned out to be concert promoters, and I ended the evening hanging out with them in Pete Townshend's suite. My external affect was cool, even slightly jaded, as if I were invited to parties with rock legends every day. On the inside, though, a self-invented hippie chick was jumping up and down, mentally calling S.K. and screaming, *You will never guess where I am!* When I jokingly remarked that all the Americans suddenly sounded British, Pete Townshend shot me a look I didn't understand until I read the classic *Rolling Stone* interview where he mentioned that that affectation annoyed the hell out of him.

The ultimate magical hook-up was an assignment to write the program magazine for a local concert venue. Pine Knob Music Theatre was a woodsy upscale amphitheater and a summer stop on the biggest national music tours. I don't even remember the introduction that got me the gig, but I will never forget the elation I felt driving away with my first paid creative assignment under my belt. I had never known anyone who wrote for a living; all at once, my daydreams of doing something so farfetched seemed as achievable as the time in junior high when Personality Week transformed from silly Valerie fantasy into a real achievement.

Suddenly I had backstage access to the biggest rock bands in the world. Every rock star needs an entourage, and attractive girls get picked up in every town like backup musicians from the union hall. My writing gig insulated me from being labeled a groupie; musicians accepted me as a cute freelancer who liked to hang out. My life became a schizophrenic boomerang from limos, VIP suites, and the occasional chartered flight, to the Back Seat Saloon and the nurse's station of the hospital ward.

While I wrote for the music theater, I had sequential romantic flings with a bad-boy guitarist and a lovely drummer/songwriter, both members of very famous bands. One of my good friends still laughingly refers to this time as my "groupie days," but in truth, I didn't even know who the famous drummer was when he sought me out in the backstage area of a Cleveland stadium concert. Having noticed me digging elbow deep in an ice chest, he offered to go find me the beer I was searching for, and returned after he located one. Later, over a more ladylike glass of wine and backstage appetizers, I lit a cigarette with my usual cool-chick flourish, turned to him, and inquired in my best rock-writer voice, "So, Lee, what is it that you do?" When he responded, in the Arkansas drawl that I had initially found enormously disconcerting, "Oh, I'm a musician," I hid my mortification but knew that, despite my voracious consumption of rock-and-roll journalism, I had made a very big faux pas. There were only three bands on the bill that day—all of them rock royalty—and not recognizing him was a major chink in my rockologist armor. I loved the way he brushed it off, saying, "Hell, it still surprises me when people *do* know who I am," and continued acting like any other guy who was a bit smitten. I allowed his raw-boned good looks and Southern charm to permeate the self-protective membrane that reflexively grew between me and any white person with a Southern accent. That day, and in our ensuing meetings, he was a courtly gentleman who introduced me to the band but kept me to himself. Distance and impracticality doomed that and the other liaison to the lifespan of a housefly, but those encounters changed how I saw myself. Having captured the attention of superstars, there would be no keeping me down on the farm.

Meanwhile, my job at the hospital was becoming intolerable. My erratic attendance at work was a constant vexation to my supervisors. Finally, pleading burnout from the pressures of college combined with work, I negotiated a layoff one step ahead of being fired.

CHAPTER 8

The Big Break and How I Almost Blew It

I got my first job in advertising courtesy of a person with zero industry connections. My mother, a faithful reader of the hometown paper, saw the coverage of a speech that had been given to the local NAACP by the president of D'Arcy-MacManus & Masius, a huge ad agency headquartered in nearby Bloomfield Hills. In that 1974 speech—the essence of which is still being delivered today—the president lamented the dearth of "Afro-Americans" in the ad industry, and claimed to be on the lookout for all appropriate candidates. Mama remembered my having spoken of sending them a résumé, which I had, assuming in my naïveté that it would get me an interview. No one had ever followed up to find out if I might be that elusive, appropriate Afro-American. On paper I was, since having left college without a degree was something I thought should remain between Wayne State University and me. Fudging my résumé was not a decision I made lightly; at the time, it was a desperate measure that I resorted to as I was teetering on the edge of an abyss called failure. I rationalized my actions because I felt a degree would not have made one whit of difference in my ability to do the job. I had been a writer for most of my life.

D'Arcy was quick to give me an interview after I called

and pointed out that no one had ever made any attempt to find out—perhaps by offering me an interview—whether I might be Afro-American. I gathered the best samples of my writing for *Pine Knob* magazine and my *Mademoiselle* magazine entry, and walked into the impressive midcentury-modern headquarters of the multinational advertising giant. Just as I had expected, no one questioned my claim to have a college degree. The gray-at-the temples vice president who interviewed me seemed like a genuine guy, and that initial meeting ended with an invitation to take home a few ads, rewrite the headlines and copy, and schedule a second interview. Apparently, he liked my lighter approach to diesel engines and industrial pesticides, because I walked out of the second meeting as a junior copywriter.

My first day on the job seemed like a classic bait-and-switch. The VP who had hired me informed me that rather than being given writing assignments, I would spend the next two weeks shadowing a "traffic" coordinator. Since the job of the traffic department was to smoothly move every job through the various stages of development, he thought this would be an excellent way for me to get a sense of the business. On the way downstairs to traffic, he stopped by a large office, decorated with iconic modern furniture, introduced me to the agency's creative director—a slender, dark-haired, real-life Don Draper—and explained his plan. The big guy's unsmiling response was a dry, "You're very lucky. It took me two years to get out of traffic."

It still pleases me to say that I wrote my way out of the traffic department in four days. The leisurely pace of traffic didn't compare with the urgency of the hospital, and the simple tasks I was given by the traffic coordinator would have been child's play for any experienced clerk. Determined to wipe the smirk off that creative director's face, I ran up to the creative floor during every break and asked if I could help on any writing assignment. When the DOW Chemical Company bought my headline for industrial glue, *Why Not Stick with the People Who Know,* I was brought upstairs, ensconced in a small windowless office—still a step up from the cubicles occupied by the secretaries and other support staff—and introduced to the creative professionals.

It's a good thing I wasn't looking to meet up with an actual version of TV's Darrin Stephens when I got to that advertising job, because no such creature existed. Since my impressions of life in the unfamiliar world of advertising were based on the TV show *Bewitched,* I shouldn't have been surprised that Darrin was mostly fiction. There wasn't enough truth in *Bewitched* to prepare me for the real thing, and even my reliable kit of dreams couldn't provide me with a picture to place myself within. Looking back on the midseventies from a world that now includes marketing powerhouses like Jay Z, P. Diddy, and their predecessor, Russell Simmons, it is hard to fathom how little contact young blacks had with the corporate empire that influenced our choices of what to buy, wear, and eat. In the world I had grown up in, even the successful professionals— black doctors and lawyers—had nothing to teach me about the workings of this alien environment. On the other hand, my affable traffic manager steward, who was flattered to have been entrusted with showing me the ropes, was a fountain of information that washed away some major misconceptions I never even let her know I had.

For one thing, the cool "account executive" job I had been watching on *Bewitched* didn't exactly exist. On the show, dashing Darrin won new accounts, wined and dined clients, and often came up with just the clever creative idea to save the business. In the real ad world of 1974, Darrin would have been doing the jobs of at least two or three people. Today, that number would be much higher.

My traffic guide taught me that accounts could actually be acquired in many ways. Some pieces of business are "walked in," via high-level business or personal relationships. A large agency I later worked for actually acquired a "Big Three" auto account this way. The executive assistant to the agency's CEO was relieved to find out that the hotel rooms she had been booking this man were actually used for top-secret business meetings. She had been convinced her boss was having an affair. In a way, he was, since the auto client was "cheating" on the agency he left.

Other times, accounts are won via "pitches," another word for highly competitive presentations where multiple agencies create campaigns and compete for the business. Major pitches can involve nearly every department in the ad agency, from the high-ranking executive level that gets the agency the opportunity, to the senior account director who supervises the pitch, and the researchers and planners who search for insights into how consumers think about the product. Media experts determine the right vehicles, be they Internet, TV, radio, magazines and newspaper, billboards, or other promotional endeavors.

Finally, "creative professionals" turn all this "ad science" into dramatic, compelling, sometimes funny, and—fingers crossed—motivating commercial messages they present to prospective clients. If the stakes are high enough, agencies sometimes even produce sample commercials, which bring in agency producers, outside photographers and directors, and even the accounting department that keeps track of the money being spent. When I came into the business, these pull-out-all-the-stops pitches were called "dog-and-pony shows." The modern-day cable television series *The Pitch* is a pretty good depiction of today's process.

What was, and is, almost never seen is a jack-of-all-trades account executive/media planner/researcher/creative director like Darrin Stephens. In a real ad agency, there is almost always a healthy tension between account management and the creative department (creative directors, copywriters, and art directors). Even the brightest members of the account team, which handles the "business" side of advertising, were often called "the suits," right to their faces. For the most part, this was good-natured kidding, but the creative input of account management was distinctly unwelcome in the creative department. In turn, many of those "suits" seemed to regard the creative staff as a group of rambunctious children, but a necessary evil. The "creatives," with our jeans and other casual, expressive attire and quick tongues, thought ourselves to be original and, above all, indispensable. One creative director even told me, "Any intelligent person can be taught to be an account executive. Only God can make a copywriter."

To be honest, at the time, "Darrin Stephens doesn't exist" was the information that stuck most in my mind. Shadowing the traffic manager for a couple of days as she moved several ads through various stages from assignment to release to a publication or printer, I quickly picked up the sequence: advertising assignment to media plan to creative idea to client presentation to production. Still, I had no more real understanding of how ads were made than the orderly who wheels a patient into the operating suite knows about performing surgery. I'm not sure the traffic manager did either. Her job was simply to make sure everyone else's job was done on schedule. Her job in advertising was the rough equivalent of my clerk position at the hospital. That alone was enough to motivate me not to get stuck in traffic.

In those early days of agency life, I could have gotten whiplash from the back-and-forth. One minute I felt like a fish out of water; the next I might be positively slaphappy at my good fortune. To me, the work of a professional copywriter was a joy almost beyond imagining. I got paid to sit around with very quick and funny people and come up with clever ideas. Even with the constant pressure to keep up the zingy repartee, the freedom and spontaneity of creating advertising concepts was my idea of a dream occupation. I spent a few moments every day mentally pinching myself to make sure that I was really where I seemed to be. In some situations, my avid consumption of novels and television shows stood me in good stead. Modeling myself as some combination of That Girl and Cinderella, I pretended to be at ease in the design meetings at General Motors to which agency staff were invited. Ditto the fancy lunches in fine restaurants that often followed these out-of-office sessions. *Act like you've been somewhere before,* is a page out of the African American home-training manual, and I used that lesson liberally. Besides, I had not read all those *Cosmopolitan* magazine articles on dining out for nothing. In the movie *Pretty Woman,* dressed-up but unsophisticated Vivian catapults her first escargot into the hand of a discreet waiter. I am relieved to recall that I handled my first snail with a decent amount of aplomb, and only sopped the saucer with a toast round after seeing the creative director swab his saucer first.

In contrast to my hospital job, where one minute late was late and falsifying a time sheet would have been grounds for dismissal, the casual, "just get here before nine thirty or so" standard at D'Arcy was a welcome relief. On the other hand, the informal agency culture, where bosses were called by first names and only top executives were treated with obvious deference, was a sometimes pleasant, sometimes disconcerting change from the clear hierarchy of the hospital. When bosses could be the target of flip remarks, it seemed to me it would be easy to go too far, so I avoided engaging in that kind of camaraderie, and confined my joking remarks to others roughly in my pay grade. Socially, at first, I gravitated toward the assistants—still called secretaries in those days— who inhabited my natural comfort zone. But gradually, the subtle gradations of agency status dictated that time around the water cooler was better spent networking with fellow creatives and chatting about assignments.

Although the creative department was awash in testosterone, there were a few women whose offices I could drop by for an occasional round of girl talk. I knew that some of their friendliness was motivated by curiosity about how I came to be among them, but their gentle, womanly probing was a welcome respite from the rat-a-tat verbal gamesmanship that generally accompanied any gathering of the male writers and art directors. Besides, compared to the skillful snooping of the female-dominated hospital staff, it was the amateur hour of getting all up in someone else's business. I simply followed the Laverne rule and told them so much their eyes probably glazed over.

Meanwhile, I was busily surveying these ladies and their responses to the male-dominated department. There was the mature, capable art director down the hall, whose classic Corvette was the envy of every guy in the agency; my coquettish, miniskirted writer neighbor in the next office; and my Japanese partner, who buttressed the precision of her training as an engineer with the womanly wiles of an urban geisha. Each seemed to have decided on an identity, a perceivable persona to augment her talent and tell the male majority how to think of her. Incongruous-black-rocker-chick-with-a-lot-of-writing-game was the image I chose. Usually attired in colorful heads-carf, hoop earrings, wide-legged trousers, and high platform shoes, my strategy was to stand out while fitting in, a practice I have often observed in successful minorities in similar situations.

To this day, whenever anyone says that advertising is a meritocracy, I have to laugh. Most of the creative staff were talented and professional, but there was plenty of dead weight. The account management team ran the gamut from smart and savvy to clueless but connected. The creatives were given a lot of leeway when it came to quirkiness and unorthodox backgrounds. Knowing this made me feel better about not having a degree. The cute copywriter in the office next to mine had no problem telling me that she got her job because a higher-up thought she had nice legs. She reinforced this every day by wearing super-short skirts even though they had long since gone out of style.

Two of the male art directors in the department were alcoholics who were all but useless after lunch. There were many workplace parties, where I generally had the presence of mind to stay sober. In this milieu, cultural insensitivity might rear its head in drunken conversation at any time. "So, I guess we get two affirmative action points for you: black *and* female," an account manager once slurred, ignoring the fact that the agency did not participate in any affirmative action program. A tipsy executive assistant asked to touch my short natural hair. Even my immediate supervisor, a great teacher whom I genuinely liked, could not resist sharing with me, after a couple of drinks, that he did a killer rendition of "Ubangi Stomp." He was astonished that I had never heard of that tune, a rude homage to an African tribe best known for their custom of inserting huge discs into their lips. At times like these, I could ill afford to have my inhibitions lowered to the level of an in-kind retort. With my lips restrained by relative sobriety, I could assess these remarks with calm reflection. I could consider the source, or even wait to solicit a second opinion from a black friend. The morning after, I would once again remember that the man who made the "Ubangi Stomp" misstep was an ally who was not only thoughtfully teaching me a craft, but cutting me some slack on the tardiness and sick-day front. In all likelihood, he had joked with me about the Ubangi song because he thought it was safe to do so. Safe in the sense that I would not assume he was likening me to an Ubangi, but would acknowledge a connection with Africa that was as plain as the lip on an Ubangi's face.

This is the kind of incident that leads white people to say to blacks, *Where's your sense of humor? Irish people don't get offended at jokes about drunken Irishmen.* For the record, until informed differently, white people in the business world are wise to assume that a black person has no sense of humor when it comes to Africans, slavery, jive talk, blackface, complexion, hair texture, natural rhythm, gorillas, monkeys, and a wide range of topics too extensive to be covered here. Actually, the account man's calculation of my value in affirmative action points was far more offensive than the Ubangi incident. In the absence of the daily interactions my supervisor had with me, the account manager was responded to with a shrug, but placed on my low-priority "watch" list.

Thankfully, I was spared any unwelcome physical advances, though our group creative director thoughtfully gave my partner and me a warning about the roving hands of one very senior executive. Although talent, or lack thereof, is often cited as the reason advertising lacks diversity, the ability to fit into an alcohol-friendly office environment could also have been a job requirement. In those last, gasping days of *Mad Men* culture, it was not unheard of for a red-faced fifty-something guy to drop dead after thirty years of office parties and three-martini lunches.

Luckily for me, my first bosses were smart younger guys. The creative director on Pontiac had the radical idea that it might be good to have a female perspective on a car account. Since our combined salaries would amount to a rounding error in the budget, a talented Japanese American woman art director and I were added to the account. Although it took me a few tries to get the hang of writing headlines and copy rather than prose, my ad for the bicentennial Pontiac Grand Prix, *Your Personal Declaration of Independence*, hit the snarky tone that Pontiac liked. Happy just to be there, we "girls" made lemonade out of lemon assignments like the owner loyalty program, contest ads, and scripts for the pretty girls who delivered a spiel at the auto show.

One memorable mistake, though, was the magazine contest ad we designed for the Pontiac Sunbird. Set against an elegant black background, the car looked like the perfect "hot girl" vehicle and practically begged the reader to fill out the entry form on the bottom of the page. *Win Yourself a Classy New Chassis*, the headline invited. "Are you girls planning to send out white pencils along with your ad?" the production manager demanded, pointing out that our white-type-on-black-page entry form would be impossible to fill out otherwise. It was a humbling lesson in thinking through every aspect of how an ad will be used by the consumer, and a reminder that I still had a lot to learn. Between my partner's degree in engineering and my lifelong immersion in car culture, however,

our contributions on Pontiac mostly made our creative director look pretty smart, and I guess he was. Both of us women
went on to New York agencies like J. Walter Thompson and
Saatchi & Saatchi, and our boss ultimately became worldwide
CEO of the agency.

I might have been a bright light at work, but at my nighttime spot, I was a barfly supernova. The head bartender at the
Back Seat had opened a new bar with live music, and I soon
followed to his more sophisticated venue as a regular, decora-
tion, and friend of the bands. Smiling and murmuring, "Ex-
cuse me," to the long line of patrons waiting to get in, I glided
to the front and was granted immediate entry to the dimly lit
blue interior of the nightclub like the VIP the doorman and I
pretended I was. There was something in this charade for the
bar as well as for me. No matter how crowded the room, there
was space for Val, whose exotic presence seemed to endow the
spot with that soupçon of hipness that a little blackness in the
midst of whiteness paradoxically confers. The entertainment
at the club was stellar. Legendary music-business executive
Clive Davis once flew in to scout an especially gifted pianist/
singer, and Carole King recruited a group that regularly appeared there, Navarro, to give her new album a refreshed
sound. Rock and roll still had a powerful hold on me, and my
semi-glamorous day job simply couldn't compete.

Even with a relatively flexible starting time, getting to
work in the morning was a struggle. The Pontiac group worked
late hours through the summer. I often finished just in time to
shoot over to the bar, catch the last set, and close down the
joint. I felt torn between two white worlds: one aggressive and
competitive, the other carefree and pleasure-driven. In the
nightlife world, I found total acceptance, because there was
nothing at risk. Like the lyrics of the Randy Crawford song

"Street Life," bar culture was a "ten-cent masquerade" where I let the people see just who I wanted to be, and every night I'd shine like a superstar. In advertising, the possibility of rejection was table stakes in a game where the deck by nature was stacked in favor of bosses and clients.

Our night sessions were often held in a conference room. Seated around an imposing table, we wrote headlines on the spot and passed them to our creative director, who either set them aside or push-pinned them to the wall. Once, I tentatively slid over a line that he read, balled up, threw on the floor, and stomped.

"So, I guess you didn't like that one," I attempted to joke.

"No, it was all right," he smilingly one-upped me. "Wait till you see what I do to the ones I think are bad."

Later in my first year in the business, the copywriter/art director team became the prevailing creative format, but those early group sessions among the overflowing ashtrays, half-eaten pizzas, and anxious creatives were a trial-by-fire boot camp that sent me running for the nightly solace of a cold margarita and a warm group of nonjudgmental friends.

My boss eventually decided to throw money at my attendance problem. Nine months into my new job, I was given a two-thousand-dollar raise—no small thing in 1975—and received a five-hundred-dollar Christmas bonus. Despite quick raises and bonuses, the battle for my time and attention raged on at D'Arcy. After they gave up and let me go, I was hired by BBDO Detroit, where, in 1976, I was the only black employee in the entire office. Not a mail boy or data processor interrupted the homogeneity of the BBDO Detroit shop. I probably should have quit when my creative director asked me to come pick up an envelope from him at the hotel room where he was temporarily being housed, then handed it to me as he stood stark naked in the doorway saying, "Oh, hi, kid, you caught me in the shower." The voice of scary Laverne that lives in a corner of my mind tells me that I might have gotten more than an unemployment check when they justifiably let me go after I missed twenty-two days in six months and had the nerve to call myself a token at a fancy company soiree.

By 1977, only three years into my career, I had pretty much found the bottom. I was unemployed, addicted to a melodramatic relationship with a local piano player, hanging out nonstop, and feeling as if I had blown my big chance. As the song says, when you play the street life, "you'd better not get old," and after several years, the hometown crowd had caught my act. My parents and the Coopers were largely raising cute, friendly little Brian, who by now was showing a distinct resemblance to Bob in his small stature and exceptional athletic abilities. Like a lot of neurotic people, I was acutely conflicted about my relationship with my child. On a rare mother/son outing to the BBDO company picnic, I thought my heart would burst when ten-year-old Brian, whom the men had thought was too small for their softball game, smacked a home run and rounded the bases with his shining eyes searching for my approval. He found it; I had never stopped adoring my only child—but at the same time, I was also running: from life as a single parent trapped in a small town. There is a black expression, *Going out of the world backward,* and in 1977, I embodied it.

My high school friend Squeak had a sister who threw me a lifeline. Shelagh was a warm, funny woman who had overcome a struggle with alcohol and had tremendous empathy for my feelings of being stuck in a small town but destined for greater things. I was in awe of her audacious decision, at a young age, to flee her Michigan college, move to San Francisco, and join a comedy troupe before marrying a member of the US foreign service and traveling the world. In the years since I graduated high school, I had gotten to know Shelagh as she visited the States while living in Australia, Zaire, and Haiti. Now she had returned home to finish her degree after a divorce from her diplomat husband.

Shelagh shared my taste in music and added Bob Marley to the list of musicians I put on a pedestal. When she completed her degree in anthropology and was accepted to Harvard for graduate study, she invited me to live with her family and make a fresh start in Boston. Mama and Daddy pleaded with me not to uproot Brian from the stability that they and the Coopers provided. Brian was old enough to express an opinion and did not want to move. I made the decision to head east while lying on my living room sofa, tears rolling into my ears at the thought of leaving my son behind.

I thought back to my impoverished teenage sojourn with Shirley B. and knew that another move like that—with almost no financial resources—would only change the geography of my dilemma. The tears I shed that day were also for the prospect of abandoning the dreams I had held for so long. *No one cares anymore if I ever become anything in life,* I lay there thinking, but something defiant in the deepest reaches of my being would not let that fear take root. *I care!* an inner voice shouted back at me. Inside that compelling message I could sense another: my people still loved me, but only I could save me. Mama, Daddy, the Coopers, and even little Brian were all telling me in their own ways that until I could nurture and make the most of myself, I would not be fit to raise anyone else. Knowing they were right, I left my beautiful boy in their care and went off to seek the life that had eluded me.

PART THREE
THE BIG BOUNCE-BACK

CHAPTER 9

Finding Myself in Boston

There was not a single other black creative professional in the city of Boston. My new boss at Kenyon & Eckhardt, a cool thirty-something white guy, shared this bit of information over drinks at the end of my first week on the job.

"What the hell made you choose Boston? There's almost no place you'd be less likely to find a job."

I didn't bother to remind him that no matter what city I had chosen, there was little likelihood of finding fellow black creatives. I told him the truth he could relate to: I had chosen Boston because a friend offered me a place to live until I found a job. I left out the dynamic that I had learned in my brief career—the secret of success in advertising was to make people feel that I was just like them, only wrapped in black.

Caught up in the hippie aesthetic, I almost believed it myself. After several years as a "magical Negress"—a reassuring black mascot—on the outskirts of rock-and-roll heaven, I was invested in its peace-and-love mantra and its "Come on people now, smile on your brother, everybody get together, try to love one another right now" ethos. Back in Michigan, a rock-and-roll chick had had little in common with the black vibe of the day, and my advertising jobs had made me accustomed to life in a white environment. Over time I had drifted into a reality where other than Ruth Ann, my closest friends were white, and other than Ruth Ann and my family, I spent most of my time as the only black face in whatever room I was in. In that context, the overwhelming whiteness of Boston didn't seem unfamiliar. And, living and working among white people, the most blatant effects of racism became largely invisible to me. My new boss's "What the hell were you thinking?" query might have been a cautionary note, but as I basked in my new freedom and optimism, its pitch vibrated—like a dog whistle—at a frequency outside my hearing.

For the most part, though, my senses were operating with bliss-inducing efficiency. The brick-and-cobblestone charms of my adopted colonial city were a daily treat to my Midwestern eyes. Within the provincial confines of "Bah-ston," where it seemed almost everything was called something different than the name I had for it, my ears perked to learn that a carbonated beverage was not the "pop" I knew or the "soda" I had learned, but "tonic," a term I had previously associated only with a mixer for gin. Likewise, my taste buds were in for a surprise when the chocolate milkshake I ordered turned out to be my idea of plain old chocolate milk. The ice cream concoction I was seeking was called a "frappe." Even trash was discarded in a barrel, not a can, and the subway was known as the T. When the tollbooth agent on Route 128 barked at me, "Fotty cents! I said, fotty cents!" the time it took to understand him was a pleasant reminder that I had left Pontiac for a place where unfamiliar scenes, characters, and dialogue could at last change me and my life. Though the New England accent that filled the air around me sometimes sounded harsh, if I could have adopted the local custom of pronouncing can't as cahn't without feeling like a total phony, I would have. Despite the urgings of my inner eight-year-old, though, I had to draw the line at adopting an affectation that would have set my black "siddity" alarm clanging.

My three years in Boston were the beginning of the life I had always incongruously expected to have. As soon as I found a job, I moved from Shelagh's house in the affluent suburb of Belmont—an address that had visibly impressed prospective employers—to a very nice apartment in Boston's stately Back Bay. Settled in my new place, I could hardly believe I had found, for four hundred dollars a month, a huge living room with twelve-foot beamed ceiling, two eight-foot-high windows, wainscoted walls, and an imposing marble fireplace. Aside from a good-sized foyer, the rest of the place was nothing to write home about; the bedroom was long and narrow and the kitchen was probably a former closet. Still, my grand apartment would have made That Girl jealous. Shelagh was a pro at garage and estate sale shopping, a friend contributed a shabby chic Oriental rug from the basement of his building, and in short order, my place was an elegant mix of castoff antiques and canvas-upholstered furniture from stores that catered to urbanites who might have more taste than money. Mama was so pleased with my success in finding a job and apartment that she sent me money to buy a new stereo system. That (Black) Girl was finally getting her shot.

This time around, I was determined not to blow it, and American culture was on my side. "Yuppie" was a term that hadn't yet been coined, but it was the lifestyle I saw all around me. Young Bostonians worked hard, dressed well, and partied in style. Though I wasn't making a lot of money, I became adept at vintage shopping, and the glamorized bag lady, *Annie Hall* style of the day suited my fashion sense and my pocketbook. I periodically used a mild relaxer on my hair, not so much to straighten it as to loosen my tight kinks into a more

manageable natural-looking state. Sporting a fedora I had inherited from my grandfather, it was all I could do not to toss it
into the air, Mary Tyler Moore–style, in celebration of the new
possibilities of my life.

I didn't know a soul in the city, so at first, everyone I
met—like my super-smart, music-loving office pal Karen—
was a young person connected to advertising. Even when I
took an acting class, something I had wanted to do for a long
time, I made friends with Julie, a beautiful aspiring model who
was an assistant at an ad agency, and a gay male graphic designer from yet another shop. We often hung out over drinks
after class, but everyone was usually home in bed by midnight.
When we could afford it, Julie and I would go out to nice restaurants with a couple of female friends. Our endless conversations about men, careers, and fashion were an avatar of the
Sex and the City phenomenon that would blossom twenty years
later. Julie's boyfriend was a VP art director at the hot agency
where she worked, and through them I was invited to trendy
parties and weekends at summer homes in New Hampshire
and Marblehead where I was always the only black guest. Sip-
ping champagne on the shores of Little Squam Lake in New
Hampshire, Mud Lake—and even Crystal Lake—seemed a
million miles away. That was almost far enough.

During this time in Boston, I started having nightmares about
my little boy. In the one I still remember, I arrived just too
late to save Brian from drowning. I began to see a therapist
who helped me realize that I had not abandoned my child;
I had left him where he wanted to be, in the care of responsible people who loved him. My doctor helped me understand
that having a child at sixteen creates real challenges to any
woman's growth and that the choice I had made was rea-

sonable given the circumstances. She also nudged me to a breakthrough—realizing that I was still dealing with feelings of abandonment by my own father, whom I had long since dismissed as being irrelevant to my life. I called Brian often, but just as I had had trouble making space for him in my own life, I was largely irrelevant to his daily reality with my parents and the Coopers. Yet the universe has more ways of bringing us what we need than our puny minds can conceive. In a spectacular coincidence that I didn't find out about until years later, Brian's father entered his life at just about the same time I moved to the East Coast.

For eleven years, I had kept silent about my son's real father. Mama and Daddy had so filled the parental space in Brian's life that a phantom father named Ronnie, whom he never saw, seemed to somewhat satisfy my son's need to know about his other parent. Trying not to elaborate on what I had come to admit to myself was an untruth, I never talked to Brian about Ronnie unless he asked me a direct question, which didn't happen often. The situation was further complicated by the fact that Bobby K. was now married to a girlhood friend of mine and they had several children. As Brian grew older and sought outlets for his natural athleticism, fate brought Bob into his life as a director of city athletic programs and a mentor.

When Bob and I finally spoke about Brian four years later, he told me that he had quickly recognized something familiar in his son. "I had been watching that little boy. There was something about his eyes. When I found out his name, a bell went off in my head, but I couldn't believe you wouldn't have said something. I never tried to talk to you about it, but I couldn't shake that feeling that he might be mine. I just took him under my wing and tried to look out for him a little." It has taken a lot of years for me to begin to forgive myself for the damage that I caused Ronnie, Bob, and most of all Brian. I can only justify clemency for myself by remembering the brokenhearted girl who clung to her self-image by holding onto what started as a hopeful delusion and grew into a lie. By the time I knew the truth for certain, I was ensnared in a web of mendacity and assumed I would take my secret to the grave. I hadn't yet learned that secrets tend to have their own expiration dates, and the clock was running out on this one.

By the time my son and Bob's other kids were young teenagers, the resemblance between them was so pronounced that they asked him about it, and I was forced to have the conversation with my son that I had dreaded. People say that what's done in the dark will come to light. They also say that the truth is the light and will set you free. Life has made me a believer in both of these adages. I don't know if Bob would have been so accepting of paternity back when I was fifteen, but now he embraced it, as did his children and his wife, my friend.

"Well, well, well, look what we've done," were Bob's words to me when we spoke for the first time in fifteen years. As it turned out, Brian was happy and relieved that the man who had taken an interest in him—not the absent, shadowy Ronnie—was his father. Brian was overjoyed to have brothers and sisters, especially since they all looked so much alike. Bob's wife, my friend, was satisfied to know that the encounter between Bob and me happened before they met. The most painful part of my past ultimately came to a happy ending, but it was a long time coming. During the years I was in Boston, Bob kept his suspicions to himself and a watchful eye on his son.

For the most part, my life in Boston was a dream realized. I lived within walking distance of my office in the bosom of the city, and every time I passed the verdant Public Garden with its serene swan boats and wrought-iron fences, I could hardly believe that I lived just up the cobblestone block. My Beacon Street apartment was only a block away from the Charles River, and watching the Harvard crew team rowing their daily practice on that glittering ribbon, I gloried in the unfamiliar sight. In those days, anyone who accidentally fell into "the Chuck" was advised to immediately have a tetanus shot due to its polluted state, but never once did I allow that warning to lower my esteem for the storied river. Nor did it occur to me to elevate my estimation of ignominious Mud Lake. I wished that my family and friends could see the beauty of my new surroundings, but the recent and raw wounds of Boston's fight against school busing and a few despicable racial attacks kept most hometown visitors away. While I lived in Boston, a terrified black couple was chased through Boston Common, a young black football player was shot near the Bunker Hill Monument, and another black man was killed waiting for a late-night bus transfer in South Boston. Although the racial ugliness of Charlestown and South Boston would eventually seep into my awareness, the affluent Back Bay and Beacon Hill, where everyone I knew seemed to live, were generally like a DMZ where you could live in peace if you could pay the freight.

Boston was home to a proud and somewhat insular advertising community of notable local shops and a couple of regional branches of big agencies like Kenyon & Eckhardt. I was given a mixture of accounts to work on, from the quirky Pewter Pot restaurant chain to B&M Baked Beans to a staid savings bank and Timex alarm clocks. My Neil Sedaka–inspired radio campaign for Timex, *Waking Up Is Hard to Do* . . . went over

well. And while I was upset when the creative director who
had hired me left to take a job in New York, it was during
this fairly long leaderless stretch that my first TV commercial
went into production.

The spot, for Bell's Seasoning and Bell's Stuffing, featured
a modern grandmother and a traditional young mom, each
making Thanksgiving stuffing. Our challenge had been to promote a venerable "from scratch" recipe and a premixed convenience product in the same commercial. The young mom
was excited to be cooking from scratch; the grandma loved
the convenience of the premixed stuffing in a box. Over the
tag line, *For Stuffing Just Like Grandma Used to Make*, the feisty
grandmother yelled, "What do you mean, *used* to make?" The
commercial had been easy to sell, and the art director and I
had to chuckle that the client saw this concept as a daring
departure for a traditional brand. Mostly, we were overjoyed
that our spot was about to be made. One night, lying in bed
watching TV, I saw the spot that had once existed only inside
my head, and I knew that millions of others were seeing it too.
Not bad for a girl from the projects, I thought. From somewhere
deeper inside, I heard, *Not bad for a girl from anywhere.*

Bill the draft-resister was living in Maine, and soon we were
back in contact. Maturity and the move to Boston had cured
me of the need to smother him with my presence. Now that
I no longer clung to him out of fear of being stuck in a small-
town rut, we quickly rediscovered the mutual interests that
had attracted us in the first place. His curious, artistic nature
and my desire to live a creative life had landed us both in
advertising, something Bill had never planned. Through his
interest in photography, he had ended up working for a small
Maine ad agency. When I visited one weekend, he showed

me around their country-cool offices and played a TV spot that they had shot for a local supermarket chain. I kept my mouth shut about the amateurish lighting, lack of extras or a compelling tag line, but I felt very grateful for the exposure and training big-name agencies had given me.

Not voicing any criticism turned out to be the right choice. Through absolute coincidence, when Bill's agency lost the Shop 'n Save supermarket account, my agency picked it up. The campaign they chose, *Check Out the Values!,* was one that I created, and our television commercial later won an award from the Maine Advertising Club. Thankfully, Bill was a good sport, musing, "Yeah, we would have done something that nice if we'd had that kind of money." Rather than attribute our superior production values to just a larger budget, I would have given the credit to my talented art director partner and our producer, but I was glad Bill wasn't mad about the shift in our roles. Having my old friend living in Maine was like having a favorite old sweater in a dresser drawer: handy and warm.

In Boston, I finally got into Harvard. It was a far cry from the officially admitted, legitimate student experience I dreamed of as a child, but I became a member of Harvard's Black Community and Student Theater Group. I was cast in an experimental piece, appropriately titled *Mars.* Alongside Courtney B. Vance, who would later appear on Broadway with James Earl Jones, I played a bus passenger, a revolving door, and a cockroach. As a member of the cast who looked as young as my fellow performers, I hung out on campus, was invited to student gatherings where twenty people partied in dorm rooms the size of walk-in closets, and was asked out by guys less than ten years older than my son. I also witnessed the stress my new friends went through in preparation for grueling end-of-term exams. By then, in my late twenties, I was more than content to have my Harvard without the gruel. I saw myself, circa junior high, in almost every one of the young people I met doing the show. They were Dr. W.E.B. DuBois's "Talented Tenth," bright, self-motivated, confident, and as optimistic as I had been before life went left. Like me, they had spent too much of their lives being told that they were different from other black kids. At Harvard, brilliant and talented Suzanne, perfect gentleman and Philadelphia Central High scholar Kevin, future filmmaker Rhonda, and Yale School of Drama graduate and movie-star-to-be Courtney found their tribe. Despite the gulf of age that even their intelligence could not entirely bridge, among them I also found my own tribe.

After our play's first run at Harvard, we received requests to perform the show at venues as varied as Yale University and Walpole Prison, where our trip brought back clanging metallic memories of childhood visits to my grandfather. Even after our wrap party, held at my undeniably grown-up apartment in the Back Bay, it was not easy to break up the group. I was invited to join Kuumba, a theater and music group that several of the cast belonged to. Later, I learned that even one of the young women whom I thought didn't particularly care for me had unsuccessfully looked for me to direct a production of *Stop the World—I Want to Get Off*. Although I never claimed to have studied at the college, Harvard Black Community and Student Theater Group, an impressive credential, was added to my résumé.

In fact, Boston generally turned out to be a great place to express my childhood love of showing off. The acting school I began attending held about four showcases a year. In them, I performed scenes from classic plays like *The Children's Hour* and *The Women*. A gut-wrenching scene from *A Raisin in the*

Sun, in which I played the stern matriarch Lena Younger opposite a fellow student named Maxwell—who was memorable for his performance and his unabashedly nappy hair—got a gratifying ovation from the mostly white audience. Later, I got a paying role in an industrial film, and worked as an extra in the sequel to Ryan O'Neal and Ali MacGraw's *Love Story.*

Mercifully, my shot ended up on the cutting room floor; that sequel, *Oliver's Story,* may be the worst film ever made. That didn't stop me from having a campy "premiere" party. The invitation, designed by a New York art director friend, looked like something from a John Waters movie. Featuring a hand-tinted photo of ultra-skinny me, with hair in curlers and a long cigarette holder, it announced: *A Star Is Bored. That's why I'm throwing a premiere party for my latest film.* Today, you might recognize the fabulous, funky visual style of jewelry designer Gerard Yosca, but back then he was just Gerry, who had become an instant best buddy while he was working a freelance gig at Kenyon & Eckhardt. The festivities began at the theater, where Bill snapped photos of my guests and me as I emerged from the white Rolls Royce I had rented for the occasion. Everyone knew I had only been an extra, so the fact that my scene was cut just added to the joke. The party was a big success that was attended by almost everyone at Kenyon & Eckhardt.

I wasn't the only one who got to sparkle that night. Bill struck up an intense acquaintance with an attractive, stimulating friend of Shelagh's. I was only a little surprised that I didn't feel jealous; over in Boston, my relationship with Bill had mellowed into a friendship that could easily accommodate his having a new girlfriend.

Another amusing anecdote from the night came from Shelagh's fourteen-year-old daughter and her friend who were sent home after the movie in the splashy white Rolls Royce rental. They happened to pass a group of their school's mean girls and cheerily waved hello as their driver pushed a button that played "Jingle Bells." It was my party, but a good time was had by all.

I did another play, Alice Childress's *The Wedding Band*, at Harvard. We received nice notices in the *Harvard Crimson*, which described my portrayal of a Southern black mother who feared for the safety of her outspoken young son as "poignant." My conviction that I belonged in a city that offered creative opportunities was stronger than ever. Unfortunately, at the same time, the Kenyon & Eckhardt agency was becoming someplace I no longer fit in.

I should have started hunting for another job as soon as I met with the new boss. Reviewing my contributions, this executive creative director thought *Waking Up Is Hard to Do* was too soft. I thought his idea of the alarm clock waking up a hibernating bear was a very funny joke, but not too motivating in the real world. I don't think either of us was wrong. "Lifestyle" commercials like *Waking Up . . .* dominated the industry for at least a decade, featuring realistic situations beautifully shot and often set to music. Coke's *It's the Real Thing* and Chevy's *Like a Rock* are examples of the style. The boss's "Bear" commercial reminds me of today's attention-getting Super Bowl ads, some of which stuggle to get into regular rotation.

The boss and I might have found common ground if he hadn't been sleeping with an agency producer who had never liked me. Knowing I was dealing with that kind of handicap enraged me. A friend from the department later told me I was "like a caged animal," constantly angry and not trying to hide it. Being pissed off with the boss and his girlfriend was not a smart career strategy. The boss began giving me less and less to do, especially after he hired a very talented senior writer whose work even I respected, and whom everyone, including me, liked very much. The clients were happy with my work, though, so I continued on at the agency while planning my exit.

A holiday visit to Michigan took my mind off the war at work. I was always glad to see Brian, though he was entering the monosyllabic early teen years. Alvin Bessent, visiting home, invited me out for New Year's Eve, but I had another date. My New Year's Eve escort was considered quite a catch. A black microbiologist, he was head of the laboratories at a local hospital and owned a lovely house in Bloomfield Hills, the formerly all-white enclave that had formed my early image of wealth and privilege. He drove a new Cadillac, which earned him cool points with Daddy, who had long since traded his "deuce and a quarter" for a Coupe de Ville. As I had met this man just as I was moving to Boston, I had always been nonchalant about our relationship, even after he came east to visit me. Chemistry is a funny thing; he was a perfectly good guy who treated me like gold, but that spark just wasn't there.

Alvin Bessent was another matter. When I ended up staying in Pontiac longer than I had planned, I called and asked if he still wanted to go out. He did, and over a four-hour dinner at a local pizza and pasta emporium called Pasquale's, I fell completely in love with this brilliant, handsome man I had known most of my life. Alvin was moving back to Detroit after spending a year discovering that medical school and the long grind of internship and residency were not the life he wanted. He had been invited to medical school after Howard University saw his scores on the Medical College Admission Test, which he had taken simply to see how he would do. Broke, alone in DC, and studying twelve hours a day, he had looked at seven more years of the same and changed his mind about becoming a doctor.

My years working in the hospital gave me a lot of empathy. We both felt that while medicine was a noble calling, we lacked the necessary commitment to hospitals, sick people, and the constant company of other doctors. We laughed at the idea that I might be the only black woman in America who would be glad he decided not to be an MD. I was instantly so infatuated with him that it baffled me how I had ever let him get away. I think he felt it too, since we both got up to leave without realizing we had never asked for the check.

I spent the next few months getting closer to Alvin—who had gotten a job working as a financial aid administrator at a Detroit college—mostly via letters and postcards. I hoped my misadventures might be read as interesting footnotes, and my fallibility might allow me to be more approachable and lovable. My heart fluttered the first time Alvin answered a phone call to his office with a warm, "Hey, babe." I promised myself never to do anything that would remove that welcoming tone from his voice. Writing to him about my life as an independent That Girl in Beantown, I vowed to live up to the image.

Simultaneously, I was working out an amicable plan to get the hell out of Dodge. I requested a transfer to Kenyon & Eckhardt in New York, the formerly intimidating city where I sometimes hung out on weekends with my pal Gerry. Gerry introduced me to gay New York nightlife at amazing spots like the Paradise Garage, a semiunderground club that pioneered the concept of the celebrity deejay, was a frequent haunt of Andy Warhol, and featured a fantastic assortment of habitués from outrageously garbed transvestites to flamboyant gays and hip straight folk.

This crowd partied like it was a crusade—exuberant dancers gyrated shoulder-to-shoulder; some fueled by ecstasy or cocaine, getting down like it was the law. Those nights were the beginning of the end of my fear of the daunting Big Apple. I remember thinking that every concern a parent could have about life in Manhattan was on display every weekend at the Garage. I was just as certain that savvy offspring like myself could make the right choices, navigate the underground shoals, and handle it all. The club opened about four in the morning and was on blast until about eleven a.m., though I was usually zonked out on Gerry's sofa long before then.

When Boston needed my office space, I agreed to vacate early if they paid me while the transfer was arranged. Their compliant attitude was probably an indication of the apprehension agencies felt, in the affirmative action era, about letting black employees go for reasons like "creative differences." Free to visit Alvin in Detroit, I planned a weeklong trip. It lasted a month, interrupted only by a brief interview in New York. By the end of the visit, we were professing our love and shopping for a ring. I put New York on hold and went back to Boston to break up with the city of my rebirth. Almost unbelievably, I was engaged and headed back to Detroit.

CHAPTER 10

Marriage, Maturity, and Making VP

The summer I moved in with Alvin, an earthquake shook Detroit. Violent summer storms knocked out electrical power and felled giant trees. As we struggled to bring two independent, headstrong identities together, there was golf ball–sized hail and freaky weather of every kind. The turbulence in Detroit mirrored our stormy clashes over how we handled money, the need to set a wedding date, and Alvin's unsolicited opinions about how much skin my wardrobe should show. For one thing, Alvin hadn't been planning on getting engaged. My month-long visit had simply bonded us so tightly that it was impossible to imagine living apart. Before I jetted back to Boston to move out of my dream apartment, we'd had a marathon come-to-Jesus talk about my need to have an engagement ring on my finger before moving back to Detroit. My man was 100 percent ready to share his home and bed, but the prospect of a marriage—his second—was a big, scary specter that was daunting for him to confront. I was terrified of giving up my new life in Boston and ending up back in Michigan with nothing to show for it. For all my feminist beliefs, I was also a fan of marriage, that giant expression of faith in another person. While I celebrated my generation's gift of freedom from the obligation to snag a husband, I still saw a marriage proposal as the highest compliment a man could pay a woman. Engagement was what I personally needed to quiet my nerves and, adulthood not withstanding, stave off the disapproval of my parents.

Mama and Daddy had just begun to acknowledge the wisdom of my move to Boston. In their eyes, coming back to Michigan to live with "some man" would be a singularly foolish act. Coming back to move in with my fiancé, however, would be an unexpected step in the right direction. Regardless of their reaction, engagement would be my tangible evidence that this love of mine was requited. A female comedian once riffed on the subject of engagement: "Every girl dreams of the moment when that special guy will look at her and utter those magic words, *Oh, all right, for God's sake*." That scenario might have been a little bit too close for comfort, but I didn't care. On July 4, when I moved into Alvin's place, he put a tiny, near-perfect diamond on my ring finger. In a lovely bit of irony, on the day most Americans celebrate independence, I joyfully surrendered mine.

Our love, with its passionate physical compensations, turned out to be strong enough to withstand the onslaught of adjustment. Eventually, we learned the meaning of compromise: nobody gets exactly what he or she wants; everybody gets something they can live with. It was the beginning, though not the end, of my struggle to harness my incredibly strong will and accommodate another person's wishes.

This period was the first time I would appreciate my future husband's upbringing as the only boy in a house full of strong females. He was secure enough not to be intimidated by me, and shrewd enough about women not to try and dominate me. Bonding with a man also reminded me how much is lost when a girl is raised without a father. Once, as I prepared dinner, I laughingly recounted fending off an unwanted bear hug from Bo, our building's resident jovial drunk. I turned around and was surprised to find myself alone in the kitchen. When Alvin came back, I found out that he had immediately gone downstairs to confront Bo. "I told him he better keep his damn hands to himself." I was stunned. Every man who has heard that story tells me that he did this as much for himself as for me, but the unfamiliar experience of being protected by a man endeared him to me even more deeply. Snuggled next to Alvin, with Miles Davis, Thelonius Monk, John Coltrane, and Betty Carter serenading us, I felt safe enough to surrender my heart as I had not since I was a teenager. Betty Carter crooned, *I don't know where my man is. Where can he be? What is he doing?* but I knew, with the irrational certainty real love confers, that my man was finally right next to me.

Living with Alvin, I fell in love with him in new ways every day. I had known my future husband since he was an undersized boy in oversize specs, full of curiosity and questions. In 1980, as a handsome, bearded, full-grown man, he was transformed enough to keep me fascinated. His youthful physique had just the proportions I liked: average height, broad shoulders, narrow waist, strong legs that were on muscular display when I cheered him as he ran up and down the court playing guard for his fraternity alumni basketball team. Long before Steve Harvey gave us *Act Like a Lady, Think Like a Man*, Alvin became my guide to the land of men and their way of viewing the world. One important lesson I have passed on to many young women: if you want to know how a man feels, just watch what he does. "Men hate it when women start that, *Where is our relationship going?* stuff," Alvin told me. "We're more like, *I'm here, aren't I?* Men don't want to hear all that stuff women love to talk about at three o'clock in the morning. We show how we feel, we don't talk about it."

When I worried over Brian's seeming aimlessness and lack of interest in anything other than sports, Alvin calmly offered, "That's pretty normal at his age. What you really should focus on is teaching him responsibility and discipline. He's being raised by a lot of women who cater to his needs instead of helping him learn to stand on his own two feet." These ideas were simple, but in the intervening years their profundity became clear. How much pain would women be spared if we accepted that men tend to do what they feel? How many hours would we not waste agonizing with girlfriends about why "he" didn't call if we faced the obvious truth that "he" didn't feel like talking to us? How much better off would black male youths be if we females acknowledged that, no matter how phenomenal a single woman is, she is utterly unqualified to teach a boy to be a man? Perhaps because there had been no real adult male presence in my home until I was thirteen, these glimpses into the thought processes of the opposite sex struck me as newsworthy insights.

"*Alvin says, Alvin says, Alvin says . . .*" my mother teased me during my engagement, taking note of how his perspective had become embedded in my conversation and point of view. Even in the days when her deference to Daddy's opinion had annoyed me to no end, I had never doubted my mother's ability to form her own opinion; I was startled that she might be questioning mine. I didn't miss her subtle warning to think for myself, but I was confident I was quoting someone worth paying attention to. Now, all these years later, she is more likely to say, "What does Alvin think?" The man I fell in love with is a quietly surprising, curious person who delights me with his brilliant and interesting mind, effortless cool, devotion to family, and unself-conscious comfort in his own skin. I have never known anyone not to like him.

Until Alvin, the odds of my finding bliss with the boy next door would have been next to nil. Since the days of Dr. E., I had been attracted to men most likely to take me away from my roots. Since black was familiar, white was attractive; plus, my idea of success was attuned to wealth and fame. I was the type who had daydreamed myself appearing on *The Tonight Show*, chatting with the host about some yet-to-be-envisioned creative enterprise. My background in a factory town was a fact of life I couldn't change fast enough. Then, suddenly, there was a man in my life who was part of that hometown reality yet still an aspirational partner. The color we shared was something that bound him closer to me. Although he didn't have money, he was rich in potential. What also hadn't occurred to me was that a solid nuclear-family background like Alvin's could be exotic to me. "It bothers me when black families are stereotyped as being fatherless and dysfunctional," Alvin griped. "My parents and most of my family got married, stayed married, and raised families with both a mother and a father. My father worked hard, took care of his wife and kids, and taught me how to be a man by his words and by his example, and I know I'm not the only black man who can say that."

Even the romantic in me, the part that believed marriage is an agreement between two people to become one, hadn't yet considered that in marrying Alvin, I would gain the elusive intact family that I had unconsciously longed for. Becoming part of the life of a famous rock star had actually seemed like a more attainable goal. Looking at it from Alvin's point of view, I began to see durable black families all around me, especially if I included second marriages like Mama and Daddy's, which had survived its early battering and was by then headed toward its twentieth year.

Spending time with Alvin even opened my eyes to another way of seeing Pontiac. Amazing myself, I discovered that leaving my hometown didn't have to be an endless sprint away from how I had grown up. Although we had both started life at Lakeside, Alvin's father had moved their sturdy nuclear family to a leafy South Side neighborhood by the time he was five. Alvin's positive boyhood memories of roaming the woods that bordered the city's black neighborhoods, picking wild strawberries, catching crickets and garter snakes, and digging worms for fishing trips with his father on the area's ubiquitous lakes made me remember my own childhood good times. Thanks to my hometown husband-to-be, I began to recall the rich, earthy springtime scent of Mud Lake's squishy surroundings, and the lake's reflection of the sapphire Michigan sky as I ate my cornflakes and gazed out the window. Later, rather than being something to escape, that shimmering recollection inspired a Michigan tourism campaign, *Water. Wonder. Land.* It was the first time Mud Lake was allowed to touch the career that was designed to help me escape it. Inside Alvin's love, I learned that I could be outside Pontiac and still be of it.

Life settled into a rhythm as we spruced up Alvin's charming but underdecorated Detroit apartment. In the living room, we showcased the extravagant Boston fern my green-thumbed fiancé had cultivated. I slipcovered his hand-me-down sofa and we dressed up the space with a small handwoven Oriental rug, a hand-thrown pottery vase, a Haitian painting from Shelagh, and bamboo blinds that framed an open closet into a stereo enclosure. We haggled for cheap vegetables from the vendors at the bustling outdoor Eastern Market, lived on homemade soup, and daydreamed our future together. I uncovered a nurturing, domesticated part of myself as I cooked, cleaned, and made the most of our poor-but-creative circumstances. Alvin reintroduced me to classic jazz, reignited my teenage love of basketball, and encouraged me not to fear "the 'hood," but to discover its charms.

Our neighborhood was on the edge of a mansion district but well on the other side of what was considered desirable. My friend Ruth Ann's father, a native Detroiter, laughingly said, "You don't know where you're living, do you?" I laughed right back. I'd been around enough to know, for instance, that the barbeque restaurant around the corner was a hive of petty criminal activity. The tough-looking but respectful proprietor had the blackened, scar tissue–laden hands of a long-term heroin user, and it was impossible to stop by his joint for take-out chicken without being hit on to buy stolen bus tickets or boosted clothing. But I also picked up side dishes across the street at Aknartoon's, a Muslim buffet restaurant that was a model of Islamic decorum, frequented by respectful brothers in kufis and modest, veiled sisters.

An imposing and lovely limestone church on the corner of Woodward Avenue, with its towering steeple and compelling chimes, was the sentinel of the Detroit historical district, Boston-Edison, which began at the next block. In the salad days of Motown, the glorious early sixties, the extravagant residences of Boston-Edison had been home to many of the Motown pantheon. Until its sale in 2002, the grand Gordy mansion was a civic treasure that was sometimes used to host elite Detroit events.

Shortly after I moved to the neighborhood, as I walked to the corner store with a cardboard box of empty soda bottles to cash, a rough-looking guy walked up on me and gruffly demanded, "Gimme those bottles." I handed them over without argument and he walked on. As he approached the corner he turned back to me and said, a little impatiently, "Well, where we taking these?" That paradigm-shifting encounter demanded that I give my people and the neighborhood the benefit of the doubt. That instinct never betrayed me, and colorful strands of life on Glynn Court are woven into the tapestry of my early life in Detroit with Alvin.

I soon landed a job at Ross Roy Communications, a venerable, slightly fusty local shop that handled accounts like Kmart, Detroit Edison, and a regional piece of McDonald's. Once we had money, Alvin and I hosted dinners and brunches to introduce our families and let old friends know that we were a couple. At work, I was a reliable contributor, but my real creative enterprise was planning a wedding and making a life with Alvin. Wary of repeating my own stepfamily drama, I did not try to persuade my teenager to live with us. Alvin and I simply became more involved in Brian's life and assumed responsibility for his support. Alvin and Brian got to be friends and developed their own relationship without having ill-fitting roles thrust upon them, and my relationship with Alvin was free of the added stress.

We pooled and saved our money and upgraded from Alvin's battered Pontiac Astre to a used but classy Audi Fox. Unable to make a career choice between law and journalism, Alvin applied to both University of Detroit College of Law and Columbia University School of Journalism. While we awaited their decisions, we continued revving up our life in the Motor City. Alvin's job as financial aid administrator at Detroit Institute of Technology could not fully occupy his agile mind. My impatient future husband, probably already mentally exploring life as a journalist, had resurrected the university's long-dormant student newspaper, and while considering feature ideas for Black History Month, he began recruiting others to stage events. Over dinner one evening, he said, "I was wondering if you might want to create some kind of performance for Black History Month at DIT? Let me know if you think of anything."

Almost immediately, I latched onto the notion of directing a production of Ntozake Shange's Broadway hit *for colored girls who have considered suicide/when the rainbow is enuf.* I had seen the show—described as a choreopoem—on Broadway and been utterly entranced. The spare, intense production had seemed like an intimately public recitation of my late teens and twenties, as the anonymous characters furiously tried on different identities, wrestled with poverty, had compulsive misadventures with men, and feared being stuck and never gaining the creative lives that they craved. When I had first learned that the play's creator was exactly my age, I was gripped by a visceral jealousy. I actually got a cramp in my stomach eating lunch at my BBDO desk reading about Shange in *People* magazine. *This*, I thought, *should be me—dazzling the public with my artistry, the toast of Broadway while still in the infancy of a meteoric ascent.* In those befuddled days before I moved to Boston and hit the reset button, I was jealous of anyone my age who was accomplishing major creative feats. I had envied Janis Ian since her hit song "Society's Child" earned her a TV appearance with Leonard Bernstein when she was only fifteen. She had resurfaced to torment me with another hit, "At Seventeen," in 1975. Closer to home, and more painful because of proximity, advertising star Cathy Guisewite, a twenty-six-year-old vice president at W. B. Doner & Co., Detroit's hottest creative shop, had syndicated a wry comic strip, *Cathy*, about the neurotic reality of women our age. That comic would go on to be syndicated for thirty-four years. *Why them and not me?* I had obsessed, never letting in the thought that my nightly hanging out was not only drowning my sorrows but also suffocating my ambitions.

Still, when I had had the chance to catch *for colored girls* . . . while on a road trip to retrieve a divorced girlfriend's kids from a visit with their New York dad, it never occurred to me not to see it. While watching it—an unadorned examination of young, black womanhood, of the battle to reconcile one's circumstances with one's dreams, of the desperate clutching of men to create the illusion of happiness, of the torturous paradox of talent as torment—my jealousy evaporated into a feverish determination to benefit from these tribulations, not be consumed by them. Although I had already made up my mind to move to Boston, *for colored girls* . . . was the starch that molded my resolve to catapult myself into a second chance.

Now that I was loved and seemingly past the career struggle, directing that work would be a chance to atone for my former churlish jealousy. As usual, I relied on "see one, do one" overconfidence to carry me through the experience. Having been directed, I could direct. Right?

The Lady in Blue was looking at me like I had lost my damned mind. A few seconds earlier, I had directed her to walk center stage, recline resting on her elbows, and assume pretty much the same position she would at the gynecologist's office.

"I'm not doing that!" she declared, with the finality of a courtroom gavel. Her tone carried no hint of the deference an actor might generally give to a director. This inner-city college production of *for colored girls* . . . was undoubtedly her first encounter with the theater and its conventions. In any case, at this moment, she probably wouldn't have given a damn about the protocols of the proscenium arch. Like her fellow cast members, she had almost certainly tried out for the play as a lark. In fact, the entire troupe was pretty much comprised of any girl who hadn't collapsed in a paroxysm of giggles just trying to deliver a few lines of monologue. This run-in with being directed was probably the cast's first inkling that this adventure might be less fun than they had thought. As their director, I was beginning to feel the same way.

I guessed that not one of the girls assembled for our first table read had been onstage since grade school. Looking around at the cream of my untrained crop, I wondered if my appetite for theater was too big for my directorial stomach. My last experience of college theater had been with Harvard students. Though I had recognized their exceptional gifts at the time, my first encounter with the DIT cast drew a startling contrast between the focused, confident black youth of the Ivy League and the ingenuous strivers of an inner-city technical college. Facing financial hard times, Detroit Institute of Technology now hosted a student mix that included large numbers of diligent, serious Middle Eastern future engineers and Detroit natives attending college with help from state and federal programs. Many of the black students were the first of their families to attend college. The good news was that only the most adventurous of DIT girls would have taken a flyer on something as frivolous as trying out for a play. I felt connected to their foolish daring, and obligated to open their eyes to possibilities beyond the current horizon.

Getting the Lady in Blue to open her scantily draped legs in front of an audience would require a higher magnitude of persuasion.

"Why do you say you're not doing it?" I asked gently.

"Because it's embarrassing!" she yelled back at me. "I would be humiliated to be in that position."

I saw my opening. "Of course you would, and that's perfect. The title of your piece is, 'once i waz pregnant & shamed of myself.'" I motioned the rest of the girls into a circle around us to make sure they all could hear. "Take those feelings of shame and humiliation and give them back to the audience. The anger and hurt you feel at being so vulnerable and exposed are exactly what your character is struggling to express. If we see the tension in your muscles, if you yell, lash out, even cry because you genuinely hate being in that position and are ashamed of being there, the audience will feel what the writer intended and you will be doing your job as an actress."

I looked around the circle at the other young women. "Every one of you is going to have a moment like this, when you are called upon to do something you wouldn't do but your character would. Take what you feel and put it into portraying your character, because that's what acting is. I know this is more than some of you bargained for, but I need you to act, not playact. The only way I know to approach acting is to be committed and serious, even if the piece is comedic. And I believe you can do it. If you trust me I will never make you look foolish and will always support you. I believe you will amaze yourselves and each other with what you can do." At that moment, I was acting too; acting like the confident, serious director I aspired to be. Equipped with my observations of the teachers and directors who had been in charge of my fledgling acting efforts, I resolved to give these young sisters the benefit of whatever I had learned.

I thought back to one day when I was about five, playing outside with friends. My mother called me inside to scold me: "You stop telling everyone else what to do!" Confused and chagrined, I didn't talk back, but I honestly didn't know how *not* to be the leader. To myself, I thought, *If I don't tell them, who will?*

By the time I reached adulthood, Mama's directive had at least led me to discern the difference between a leader and a bossy know-it-all. Working with these untutored but audacious girls was a chance to be the former.

We rehearsed every unintended giggle out of our little production. I taught them for free what I had paid to learn at the Actors Workshop in Boston. "Energy is exciting!" I shouted, urging them to make their movements large and intentional. "Project your voice to the back of the theater. When you think you are yelling, you are doing it right." Sometimes, while Alvin patiently waited at home for a dinner of greasy Church's fried chicken, the girls and I sat and talked about the meaning of the verse they were delivering. Gradually, they began to share personal experiences that helped them empathize with the characters they were bringing to life and discovering they already knew.

We practiced several nights a week, breaking into groups small enough that I could drive them all home if need be. Shy Sherry, Too Cool Carolyn, Cautious Carrie, and the rest of the crew that had finally begun to distinguish themselves in my mind started to blossom right in front of me. I had one of the art directors at my ad agency design a T-shirt and printed a dozen as a surprise gift for the opening-night party. Yet, because I had never seen these new actors perform in front of an audience, I was still unsure of how much of what we had worked on would survive their inevitable stage fright.

When our saxophone player, the lone addition I had made to the Broadway production, was missing in action at the dress rehearsal, my own nerves became a factor. Though he later explained that he'd had a gig with his paying job as a sideman for the renowned Winans family, I didn't know this at the time and could only pray that his horn would be on hand on opening night to provide the soulful punctuation I hoped for.

On the night of the performance, I operated the lone spotlight from a perch facing the stage. My assistant director, Celeste, a student who had wanted to be involved but could not bring herself to appear onstage, also served as stage manager. From the first plaintive wail of the saxophone, when the ladies, attired in bright, chromatic dance gear, ran gracefully onstage, I could feel something remarkable happening. As if they had developed a sense of responsibility to do justice to these characters they inhabited, my newly minted thespians hit every mark, brought meaning to every line, and worked as an ensemble with an intensity and unity of purpose that made my chest swell and my eyes fill.

When the play ended, there was the briefest moment of silence as the audience, a full house of friends, faculty, and relatives—including Alvin and my mother—registered the caliber of performance they had just witnessed. Then, their sustained applause accompanied by hooping, hollering, and a generally raucous display of appreciation, they rose to their feet. A significant number rushed to the edge of the stage, screaming, "That was beautiful!" "Yeah!!" And the ultimate black accolade, "G'on y'all!" As a few audience members tossed small bouquets onto the stage, I handed the cast their commemorative T-shirts, which they donned on the spot. This was truly a peak moment: the audience did not want to leave; the cast wanted the adulation to go on forever.

As I stood with my mother, I watched this band of players who had not known this was in them as they autographed programs for those who had come out to support them. Taking in what we had achieved, I experienced the single proudest moment I have ever felt. Standing next to the woman who had advised me to "stop telling everyone what to do," I felt the difference between that and, "Share what you know," a revelation that has stood me in good stead as a creative leader.

As often happens with college productions, we were asked to perform our show at other schools and venues. Most performances were just fine, but none compared to the magical occurrence that was our opening night. The final performance was a fundraiser to help keep the doors of struggling Detroit Institute of Technology open. The college closed right on schedule, in a move designed to protect the integrity of the institution while it moved to a new suburban location. I was gratified that our young ladies had at least received one valuable piece of higher education—self-knowledge—in down-but-not-out Detroit.

Naturally, Alvin was accepted to both the University of Detroit and Columbia. U of D wanted him to start right away, in the summer session, which he did.

Ultimately, however, Alvin decided on journalism and Columbia, and I was back in the hunt for a job in New York. Our year in the city would be our honeymoon. After Alvin completed his master's degree, we planned to come back and live in Detroit until Brian was safely in college. I thought it might be amusing and productive to spend my year in New York educating myself on the nuances of a specialty that should come naturally to me: creating advertising targeted to African Americans.

Big brands like Coca-Cola and McDonald's had finally awakened to the loyalty that could be cultivated by advertising to black people. My instincts were telling me that paying attention to black consumers would pay big dividends for these companies. American advertising had taken the black audience for granted for so long, the first companies to pay special attention would almost certainly get a lot of love and loyalty in return. In time, that educated hunch would be borne out for brands I personally worked on. AT&T, for instance, as early as the 1980s ran an ad featuring a black family that had been employed by AT&T for three generations: from the janitor grandfather to his granddaughter the executive. Viewed through African American eyes, the ad not only acknowledged our existence and our value as customers, but also celebrated our struggle to better our circumstances through hard work and education. In the 1990s, an era of cutthroat competition for the long-distance dollar, a decade of ads and campaigns like those gave AT&T a rock-solid share of the African American business and a durable history of treating us with respect. This would later benefit them during an uproar over the stupid use of a gorilla as a symbol for the African region of the AT&T market.

Back in the eighties, when the big corporations were finally getting interested in the targeted advertising game, I thought that I shouldn't sleep on a perfect opportunity to acquire some niche agency experience without permanently leaving the security of the general agency world. At the time, I thought of this only as a shrewd career move. The realization that advertising to people of color would profoundly change me and my concept of my profession would only come years later. In 1981, I was mostly looking to acquire some unique chops that would make me more marketable to a white industry in a browner America. Ironically, years later, as the "general market" agencies of 2014 seemed determined to take over multicultural assignments, I would once again recommend that strategy to minority creatives. Backing up a lifetime of being a minority with experience in both general and multi-cultural agencies is an effective way to become a formidable commodity in a more colorful America.

I had read an article about UniWorld Group and its founder Byron Lewis in *Ebony* magazine. *Ebony* was the first place I had ever seen a black person featured in an ad for a big brand. When I was a child, those ads were exact replicas of the general ads, only recast with black models. Byron Lewis, while selling ad space for a different publication, had become aware of the need for an agency to create black advertising that would be more robust than what he called "Man Tan" advertising. In 1969, he founded UniWorld with early clients like Smirnoff, Avon, and AT&T. One of the agency's first Smirnoff ads featured a drink called the "Main Squeeze"—at the time, this was African American slang for a person's prime love interest. The drink, made with Smirnoff vodka and grapefruit juice, became a minor sensation in the black community.

By 1981, the idea that there might be value in speaking to black consumers using cultural insight was firmly taking hold. In that era, UniWorld, a Chicago agency named Burrell Advertising, and Mingo-Jones in New York were the major players. Ross Roy's sole black senior VP, a booster and confidant of mine, made an executive brother-to-brother call to Byron, who immediately granted me an interview. After a short trip and a long meeting in New York, I had a job offer. My interview at UniWorld had been going so well and lasted so long that I had to cancel my next appointment: a meeting with Caroline Jones. Caroline was New York's most prominent African American creative, executive vice president and creative director of Mingo-Jones and author of KFC's classic line, *We Do Chicken Right*. Although I later sent flowers and an apologetic note, I don't think she forgave me for a long time after I joined her competitor. Except for that small glitch, everything in New York had fallen nicely into place.

Alvin and I got hitched on July 25, 1981, in the Commandery Asylum of the Masonic Temple in Detroit, an imposing space that featured one of North America's largest pipe organs and a splendid stone floor. The irony was inescapable; marrying Alvin Bessent was the sanest decision I had ever made. The wedding itself was a simple but elegant ceremony. Brian and a young cousin, looking sharp in white dinner jackets, lit the altar candles to start the ceremony. A local R&B singer crooned the rock-and-roll standard "When We Get Married" as Alvin and his groomsmen took their places. Three attendants, Ruth Ann and two other girlhood friends, wearing gowns I had designed, made their way to the altar accompanied by a song that Al Jarreau wrote for his own wedding. Daddy, wearing his first tuxedo as if he had been born in formal attire, walked me down the aisle as brass instruments and a grand piano played the traditional wedding march.

The wedding was a vision I once thought I had forfeited by having a child. But times were changing and any bride could wear a white dress. My ivory silk gown was more than appropriate for a world that had learned to accommodate even maternity bridal gowns. When the pianist surprised me by playing the recessional on the asylum's majestic pipe organ, I felt as regal as Princess Diana, who would be married a few days later. For much of our wedding day, I was enveloped in the "wedding blur" friends had warned me about, but the ceremony that bound me to the love of my life was the lucid manifestation of a longtime dream.

I guess if you get married in an asylum, something crazy

is bound to happen. The Commandery Asylum was included with the rental of a catered ballroom in Detroit's Masonic Temple. Singer Stephanie Mills was performing in the auditorium a couple of floors above us. Her equipment overloaded the electrical circuits and caused a total blackout two hours into our carefully planned reception. While the crowd upstairs went wild, our guests calmly lit the candles on their tables and continued to celebrate as one of our friends played jazz on the piano. It felt like a sign that as long as we were together, everything would somehow work out.

It's been said that man plans and God laughs. Two weeks before our move to New York, I received a small check from UniWorld, along with a letter explaining that due to the loss of an account, they would no longer be able to offer me a position. I fought back some ugly thoughts about dealing with a black business. Alvin and I had just drained our savings to pay for the wedding. The day the letter arrived, Alvin had taken the final exam of his summer law course. When I picked him up, he was beaming ear to ear, knowing he had aced the test. I could hardly stand to break the news that would wipe the smile off his face. I had the unpleasant thought that I could keep my position at Ross Roy while Alvin went ahead to New York and I tried to find another job. I couldn't let the thought gel; I was the kind of newlywed who felt a thrill whenever Alvin said the words "my wife."

The notion of being separated from my new husband was unacceptable. It was quickly nudged out of mind by a plan that would finance our move. With the help of my friend the black VP, I negotiated a freelance assignment to create radio spots for Ross Roy, fee payable in advance. Solving our financial dilemma in that way was a robust reminder that having a marketable talent or skill can turn a disaster into an inconvenience. Right on schedule, with high hopes and very little breathing room, we set off for the big bad city.

When we got down to our last sixty dollars, I wrote a poem and said a prayer. We had arrived in New York in late August, a perfect time for school and the worst time to reach anyone in advertising. My VP friend at Ross Roy came through again, putting me in touch with an old colleague who could see me right after Labor Day. I calmed my nerves by unpacking and arranging furniture in the huge loft-style studio that Alvin had scored through Columbia housing. Our building, atop lovely Riverside Drive, was highly coveted despite its proximity to sketchy 125th Street and a truck-stop diner under an overpass. The apartment's only drawback was the lone, high, barred window that spanned its rear wall. Late at night, we were alarmed to sometimes hear women screaming, until the neighbors informed us that this was the sound of hookers stealing the wallets of truck-driver tricks, then running off screaming to discourage their customers from following.

September came not a minute too soon. My Detroit connection led to an interview at J. Walter Thompson. It had seemed to go well, but I didn't hear a word for a week. Alvin and I knew we would be getting a financial aid check, but we didn't know when. So far, we hadn't asked our families for help—it was the last thing we wanted to do. After our wedding, Alvin's grandmother had sent us home-canned vegetables and chow-chow relish—a zesty mixture of pickled cabbage, onion, and peppers—from her garden. I had packed them with the rest of our kitchen, appreciating her loving gesture but doubting we would ever taste them. On the night that we ate Big Mom's black-eyed peas with brown rice and homemade lemonade, I wrote about our situation, then dropped to my knees before climbing into bed. The next morning, I received a telegram from JWT, offering me a position as copywriter at a salary that would more than cover our family's expenses while Alvin was in school. The first thing we bought was telephone service.

I loved everything about my year in New York. I arrived at JWT just as the agency moved to gleaming new atrium offices on hectic Lexington Avenue. I could almost hear Gershwin music as I emerged from the subway stairs in Grand Central Station, amidst the hoi polloi of Manhattan. It all felt like a movie about a small-town girl out to make her mark on the indifferent metropolis. One such movie was *The Best of Everything*, and in those days I felt like I had it.

My new partner turned out to be a cute, friendly woman I had met in the ladies' room on the day I interviewed. Vicky Lee, incongruously Chinese and Texan, was funny and talented. Our complementary personalities made us a great team and we remain friends all these years later. New York advertising introduced me to the gold standard I had expected. Ideas that might have been good enough in Boston or Detroit were challenged in New York. James Patterson, who later became the world-class author of the Alex Cross crime novels, was a creative director who had huge influence on the agency's creative product. His taste ran to modern, believable but original advertising, and away from the corny or overblown. I kept some of my JWT scripts for years to remind me to keep my thinking sharp. Vicky and I were considered a hot team. We won an Art Directors Club Award for our print work on Nestea, and created two of the three campaigns in the agency's Nestea television presentation. One of those ideas was born after a crazy, spontaneous break one night with a piano-playing colleague, during which Vicky and I blew off steam in a beatnik interlude, banging on the creative department's bongos and reciting corny poetry as we shimmied around the room. This was not unexpected late-night behavior from a bunch of advertising creatives, and that's something I love about the business. Compared to the routine clerical shuffle of my hospital job, being a copywriter was a fantasy gig that more often than not justified the aggravations and anxiety that came along with it. Getting paid for making things up was far from the monotony of the Michigan assembly lines that had rescued my great-grandparents from backbreaking farm labor. To them, it would hardly have seemed like work at all. If our boss had stumbled across our nutty break—though that was unlikely to happen at ten o'clock on a Sunday night—he would likely have smiled and tossed a few encouraging words into the room. Right in the middle of spouting some trite verse about the sun shining down on me, I had the bright insight that I was living a reality I had fantasized into being, and I had the good sense to feel gratitude. *Do something you love for a living and you'll never work a day in your life,* the saying goes, and in that moment I knew I was living its truth.

Having had fun coming up with the concepts is sometimes the most satisfaction the creative team gets out of the process. This was fated to be one of those times. When the Nestea client later chose the only campaign not created by us, we were as deflated as a balloon with the air let out.

Our group creative director decided that partnering Vicky and me with different people might bring our spark back. I was paired up with a wildly inventive and eccentric fifty-something guy with Albert Einstein hair. His favorite outfit was saggy jeans, a well-worn cotton shirt, and ancient, scuffed boots, in which he looked as cool as some famous artist who had stumbled in from a Soho studio. He was a vice president whose big talent and equally large disdain for authority kept him on the staff but away from clients. This was fine with him. I thought he was a hoot. Our ideas for Shield deodorant soap ran the gamut from *Clean Getaway* featuring off-kilter comedian Jonathan Winters creating soap-bubble disguises, to *Give Me Strength*, a gospel-tinged celebration of life's little everyday challenges, and *The Clean Goes On,* a breezy lifestyle campaign featuring a Carrie Bradshaw–esque girl about town, to the tune of "The Beat Goes On." My reputation at JWT was secure.

In our free time, Alvin and I enjoyed our yearlong newly-wed sojourn in Manhattan, leaving our uptown digs for downtown breakfasts and taking the whole day to wend our way home. In those days, the city bus line ran a tour route that began practically outside our front door on Riverside Drive. Riding this bus, we became familiar with the distinctive neighborhoods and buildings of upper and lower Manhattan and nearby parts of Brooklyn. We heard the history of majestic Riverside Church and the Cathedral of St. John the Divine. Touring the ravaged streets of early-eighties Harlem, we heard the narrative of its fabled glory days, when downtown swells and their glamorous ladies filled nightclubs that showcased the talent and pulchritude of Harlem's black population. In Brooklyn Heights, we discovered the captivating promenade, where one could gaze back at enchanting, intimidating Manhattan from vintage cobblestone sidewalks that reminded me of Boston.

In the short time we were in New York, we hosted family, friends, and fifteen-year-old Brian. The grit and graffiti of 1980s New York inspired in my son an endearing protectiveness of his mom. As we strolled the streets of Morningside Heights, he closely monitored every male passerby for signs that he might be dangerous. He carefully counted the subway stops that I knew by heart, making sure we would not unexpectedly miss our station and end up in the notorious South Bronx. "Take care of my mother, Alvin," was my man-child's stern parting advice to my husband. That warning, along with his observation that he and his peers at the Macy's Thanksgiving Parade "were only there for their mothers," was an urgent reminder that my little boy was gone and a young man would soon displace my teenager.

When the time came to go back to Detroit, I had a big decision to make. My boss at JWT wanted me to transfer to the Detroit office. Ross Roy, which was attempting to shed its dusty old-school image, had held my job in anticipation of my return. With trepidation, I decided to go back to Ross Roy—out of loyalty, but also out of the belief that it would offer more opportunity for advancement. Walking away from my job at internationally known JWT was a big risk, but risk-taking was becoming as natural to me as dreaming. This move was a crapshoot, but the dice rolled my way.

The next two and a half years were a career growth spurt. The new creative director at Ross Roy liked my work and was enthusiastic about my being part of the "new" Ross Roy that he was charged with creating. Happily married, I was free from the distractions that had tugged at me in previous jobs. I was given a roomy office with no window, but a sofa and two guest chairs. More importantly, I got choice assignments like a public safety campaign for Detroit Edison, working with Detroit Pistons star Isiah Thomas, a shy young man who seemed to appreciate having a fellow person of color on the creative team. I wish I could say that the ads we made for the campaign, *Keep Your Guard Up*, were wonderful, but I was still refining my craft, and "credible" would be a more accurate descriptor. My TV spots for Kmart, Blue Cross, and the Yellow Pages were better-realized productions.

As my creative judgment matured, the agency also entrusted me with the Michigan Tourism account. I learned to navigate the troubled waters between industrial Detroit—whose confrontational and often-profane black mayor, Coleman Young, had once faced down the McCarthy-era House Un-American Activities Committee—and the rest of our agribusiness- and tourism-driven state. I admired Mayor Young's feistiness and race-conscious approach to his job, but lacked the power to bring those qualities to my own work situation, instead continuing to produce "mainstream" work. My team's campaign for the state, YES M!CH!GAN, even inspired a good-natured editorial cartoon in a Detroit publication of Governor James Blanchard's wife wishing the state were M!ss!ss!pp!.

In my first management position at Ross Roy, I learned and settled into the rhythm of being a creative director, the biggest challenge being that for the first time I was responsible for the work of others as well as my own. Every day in the life of a creative director was different. Some days were spent meeting with clients and account management, working through the strategic elements of selling a brand. Brainstorming with my team and attempting to inspire the best work from the copywriters and art directors also occupied a large portion of my days. Planning and delivering presentations of ideas to our clients was an area in which I happened to be very strong, thanks to countless performances in school plays and Baptist Easter Sunday extravaganzas. I began to spend many hours in recording studios and on locations where those ideas morphed into radio and TV commercials, a learning experience that required me to acquire a set of filmmaking skills that I still don't claim to have fully mastered.

Luckily, the real responsibility for the finished product lay in the hands of experienced directors, audio and video engineers, and producers. Helping them realize the vision of the creative team meant learning to speak their visual and audio language—understanding the filmic relationship between a lens and a "look," and learning to hear the sonic nuances that are obvious to a sound engineer or an actor who is asked to put more of a "smile" into a reading. I have a vivid memory of once feeling so overwhelmed that the word *OVERLOAD* literally flashed across my mind in bright neon colors, but as a young creative professional, I was also in my glory. Gradually, I began to feel less over my head, and one day, after a few months, I suddenly realized that I had become comfortable with my new level of responsibility. With subsequent promotions, that learning curve became a reassuring road map as I navigated my way up the organizational charts of the agency world.

Durinng this period, my son was trying to materialize some unlikely fantasies too. Brian was a sports-loving boy who had played away years of long Michigan summer days swatting baseballs, snagging footballs, and dribbling his way home as the streetlights popped on at dusk. Physical education was the one class where he could be counted on to make straight As. Though his father's diminutive physique and my exactly average height predestined that he would be short of stature, he had chosen basketball as his sport of choice. Brian, who avoided most types of physical confrontation, was fearless about getting shaken up while taking the ball to the hoop or fighting for the occasional rebound that caromed within his reach. At Magic Johnson's summer basketball camps, he developed the fundamentals of the game. Playing with great focus, he acquired a set of skills that gave him the confidence to try out for the varsity basketball team at Pontiac Central. That school, also my alma mater, competed in the tough Saginaw Valley Conference and had a history of excellent teams on which two members of our family had been stars. I worried about how Brian would handle the reality check that was certain to come his way. The night before tryouts, we had a long conversation about the merits of having tried one's best, no matter what the outcome. I assured him that Alvin and I were proud of his determination and that merely making it to the varsity tryouts was a major accomplishment.

The next day, I was the one who got smacked by reality. When the varsity roster was posted, Brian had earned a spot as backup point guard; he would be the smallest player in the team's history. Now that he had made the squad, Brian was convinced that he could defy the greater odds of making it to the NBA as the next Spud Webb or Muggsy Bogues, two tiny players who had found places among the giants. On one of the rare occasions when the coach gave Brian the nod, he bounced off the bench, stole the ball, sank a twenty-foot jumper, and the crowd went wild—though the game's outcome had long been decided. The Coopers told me that he lay awake for hours the night the local paper wrote up his exploits.

I, who had come to a very good place in life by keeping faith with unlikely dreams, was uncomfortable trying to convince my son that his were impossible. I argued, instead, that it was wise to use college as a route to the pros, and also as Plan B in case of a career-ending injury. The requirement for Brian to have decent grades in order to keep his place on the team worked with me, keeping him an average, if uninspired student. While I fretted about his lack of motivation in things unrelated to sports, Alvin and I pondered how to guide him toward a career that would mesh with his obsession.

At the same time, I was focused on taking my own game to a higher level. At Ross Roy, I had my first production experiences in California and New York. This was my first taste of the fine hotels, expensive restaurants, and Broadway theater tickets that fat production budgets made possible. After a while these things became routine, but as a young woman from the projects of Pontiac, I was in quiet awe of the life I was living. On my first California shoot, James Ingram sang my Kmart jingle, and Walter Matthau jokingly asked if we needed any extras as he walked his dog past our Pacific Palisades location. Now that I was fully focused, it wasn't just the assignments that got better. I was given generous raises and a promotion to associate creative director. Ross Roy also enrolled me in the company car plan: a discounted price on the Chrysler of my choice, and a monthly stipend that covered the cost of my vehicle and insurance. Life and career seemed to be on cruise control.

In 1984, I became one of three African Americans who had been elected Ross Roy vice presidents, the level at which creatives began to participate in agency perks like a four-figure line of credit and annual stock options. Bombing down I-75 in my free hatchback, sunroof open and radio blasting, I was indisputably "going places" and "getting somewhere." At last, I was living up to the expectations of every church lady who had ever chucked me under the chin and encouraged me to succeed. I was so busy patting myself on the back, I didn't notice that pothole dead ahead.

When the local press covered my promotion, Wayne State University sent me a letter asking for my date of graduation. I quickly sent them a letter explaining that the press release had been inaccurate; I had spent three years at Wayne but did not graduate. That solved the immediate problem, but I knew if I didn't correct my agency profile, my false claim would be repeated. I lay awake at night, wondering what action the agency would take. Would I merely be stripped of my new title and have my car taken away? Might I lose my job entirely because of a lie told so long ago I almost believed it myself? Whatever the cost, I knew it was time to put an end to the last desperate lie in my life. Dreading the consequences, I scheduled a meeting with my executive creative director, and steeled myself to take the punishment.

The boss literally shrugged off my confession. "It doesn't matter. Just tell the PR department so they can correct the profile." And that was that. It was the first time I realized that a college degree is sometimes as much about getting a foot in the door as getting an education. Some of the most important positions, like president of the United States and Supreme Court Justice, don't require a degree. Those jobs are too important to be tied to a piece of paper. It's just damn hard to get an interview if you don't have one.

CHAPTER 11

Big Pimpin' in the Big Apple

B rian's high school graduation also commenced a new chapter in my own life. The combination of Alvin's natural abilities and his Ivy League journalism training had helped him progress quickly at the *Oakland Press*, reporting on the county courts. My husband's brilliant grasp of legal concepts had even led a prominent African American attorney to offer to foot the bill if Alvin wished to attend law school. By that time, he had firmly decided on journalism as a career, but the boundaries of small-market journalism were beginning to constrain his talents.

Driving back to Detroit after settling Brian at Wilberforce University in Ohio (a historically black college where we hoped he would discover some interests other than sports), we both confessed a sense of not being done with New York City. Always having a dream to work toward had become essential to my happiness, and success in Detroit rekindled my desire to find accomplishment on the larger stage of New York. Remembering the sight of my gregarious son as we left him on campus, turning to a total stranger and saying, "How ya doing, man? My name is Brian," I had the feeling that it would be safe to move back to the East Coast. For two hundred miles, Alvin and I spun a fantasy of shedding cars and square footage in order to afford New York and Brian's college tuition at the same time.

Shortly after that conversation, we attended a journalism job fair at Howard University, where Alvin focused on talking to New York papers. Almost like magic, the general manager of UniWorld began seriously courting me. During our year in New York, UniWorld had hired me for a lucrative freelance job that took the sting out of our failed first attempt to work together. Not only had they paid me handsomely, but the campaign, for AT&T, consisted of high-profile, full-color, double-page magazine ads (called "four-color spreads" in agency lingo). The ads featured towering African American artists like Harlem photographer James Van Der Zee and Arthur Mitchell, founder of the Dance Theatre of Harlem. The visual impact of those beautiful spreads in magazines like *Ebony* and *Essence* was staggering.

Byron Lewis had hired me to write the campaign because he couldn't inspire his staff to explore photography and dance—both of which AT&T sponsored—as metaphors for communication. For me, product of dance school recitals, producer of *The Little Rascals*–style backyard talent shows and Personality Week at Jefferson Junior High, any situation that involved an artist and an audience was as much a conversation as a telephone call. Once I had executed Byron Lewis's vision, he was more determined than ever to recruit me. He directed his general manager to contact me with a job offer once a month. Now, in 1985, she approached me at a time of amazing synchronicity. Over an elegant dinner at Le Cirque on Manhattan's East Side, Byron Lewis displayed considerable charm and charisma as he smilingly delivered a pitch I could not resist. "To recruit talented black people like you from general market agencies, I have to make them understand that I offer an agency with no glass ceiling, where their talent and intelligence is assumed, and where they will do what I do: travel, work on America's top brands, and meet everyone who is anyone in African American culture."

It was hard not to feel beguiled. By coffee and dessert, the prospect of joining UniWorld was as sweet as the crust on my crème brûlée. I was far from immune to Byron's flattery; I felt pressure to prove my worthiness again and again at my general market job. I had come to the meeting with a sense of the hovering glass ceiling at Ross Roy, where I was expected to be overjoyed and probably forever satisfied with having achieved the level of vice president. The VP title in New York had a luster that Detroit could never match, and the UniWorld job came with a twenty-thousand-dollar raise and a bonus to compensate for the loss of my car plan. Leaving the security of general market advertising was another big risk, but every risk I had taken up to then had proved to be worth it. I assured Byron I would find a way to make things work, and flew home to ask my husband to quit his job.

Alvin was ready for a bigger pond too. The reactions he had gotten at the job fair made him confident he could find a spot in New York. In fairly short order, we were headed for the Big Apple again, this time with all expenses paid by my new employer. Like the Jeffersons, we were movin' on up to the East Side, to a deeluxe apartment in the sky, albeit a one-bedroom less than half the size of the lovely, rambling Detroit floor-through we'd left. Since it would take awhile for the moving van to deliver our belongings, we drove our sports car along a meandering route that took us to picturesque Montreal, the rolling green mountains of Vermont, and bucolic New Hampshire. Life was good and our future seemed as open as the highway in front of us. I only hoped that UniWorld would live up to its CEO's big promises.

In the New York advertising industry that I entered in 1985, casual cultural apartheid was the order of the day. Venerable agencies like Young & Rubicam, BBDO, Saatchi & Saatchi, and J. Walter Thompson dominated the landscape and the lion's share of the budgets of the nation's biggest brands. Enjoying the euphemism "general market," these giants created messages aimed at so-called mainstream Americans. In fact, there was little that could be called general about these agencies. Their work in those days spoke to white America, specifically white Americans mostly age nineteen to thirty-four, and that focus was reflected in the selection of concepts to produce, music, casting choices, and media buying. At best, their attention to diversity tended toward a tokenism without insight that is still too often reflected today.

Comedian Seth Meyers once joked, "Thanks to advertisers I've learned that every fourth person in a group of friends is a black guy in a cardigan." Some huge brands like Burger King, Avon, Coca-Cola, KFC, and McDonald's, knowing that a significant share of their sales came from African American and Hispanic consumers, were influenced by retailers and franchisees who had actual contact with consumers of color. Those brands with hands-on purveyors had become frustrated by the lack of attention to black and Hispanic customers and became the earliest and biggest accounts of African American–targeted agencies like UniWorld, Mingo-Jones, and Burrell Communications in Chicago, as well as several agencies dedicated to reaching Hispanic American buyers. Because our budgets were a tiny fraction of the total, the big agencies generally ignored our existence, as long as our work carried the campaign tag lines that they, as "lead dog," created. I had discovered back in junior high school days that segregation often provides fertile ground for growth and self-expression, if not equality. The intimidating world of New York advertising proved to be no exception to that rule. If I had liked my job before, I was besotted by the prospect of creating advertising for black audiences.

UniWorld fit me like a comfortable pair of slippers. Inside its walls was an environment that no general market agency could provide. Although a walk through the halls would reveal white, Latino, and Asian faces, UniWorld was unapologetically rooted in the African American experience. The agency's client roster was blue chip: AT&T, Burger King, Seven-Up, General Foods, Ford Motor Company, and Kodak, among others. All of these companies also had at least one general market shop to handle the lion's share of their business. UniWorld existed solely to help them connect with African American consumers. Instead of the ads that generally decorate agency walls, UniWorld was adorned with important art from Byron Lewis's Afrocentric collection. His reasoning? "Clients don't come to UniWorld for advertising. They come because they think we know something about black people that they don't. I want everything about UniWorld to validate that feeling."

He had come to the right woman. Back when I was at Jefferson Junior High, a black English teacher had given us an assignment to write our feelings about the civil rights movement. After he had handed back our papers, he looked at our 100 percent black class and said, "I wonder how it is that none of you are personally affected by the many problems and issues facing Negroes today. Not one of you wrote in the first person. It's all, *They are denied their rights,* and *They must continue their struggle.* Does that strike you as strange?" Still haunted by my girlish rant at the NAACP meeting, I felt so miserably ashamed that I never forgot the lesson, and never again referred to my people as *them* or *they*. The UniWorld agency was my first chance to bring that respectful *we* to work.

Byron Lewis was as good as his word. A typical day at UniWorld was my career fantasy fulfilled. I was paired with art director Aaron Bell, son of a well-known jazz bassist who had been part of the Duke Ellington Orchestra. Aaron, like me, was a product of the black consciousness movement who was fervent about bringing our rich cultural experience to the agency product. My first day on the job, we met with Arthur Ashe, who was looking to promote the game of tennis on inner-city courts like the ones that later produced Venus and Serena Williams. Aaron and my first campaign for Kraft Foods featured Earl "The Pearl" Monroe, Jesse Jackson, and Ronald McNair, a black astronaut who, sadly, would soon after perish aboard the space shuttle *Challenger*. Within the year, we did a Kodak TV spot with Patti LaBelle and radio ads with vocalists Cissy Houston, Patti Austin, and jazz legend Jon Hendricks.

Just as I arrived at UniWorld, my advertising career got made. *Advertising Age*, the industry trade bible, named me one of the "100 Best and Brightest" in the business. That national honor, for which Ross Roy had nominated me, upped my standing in Byron's eyes and cemented my place as one of his top executives. Byron, far from being a typical adman, was a trailblazing entrepreneur who had been locked out of the white advertising industry and had formed his company as a way in. He harbored no illusions that the real power in advertising lay anywhere but within the larger general market world and had great respect for any recognition it conferred. After the *Advertising Age* honor, Byron sent me as his surrogate to industry associations like the Advertising Club of New York, where I was able to make my own industry connections.

My previous jobs had prepared me well for occupying the

black seat at mostly white tables. Over the years, I have encountered African American advertising professionals who rail against being singled out in this way, but I have tried to use those seats as a bully pulpit to bring attention to the concerns of African Americans and other minorities. Strikingly, I have rarely seen a black or brown face in the room that was not there to provide expertise about minority consumers. In a country where so many advantages have been doled out to whites because of their color, it baffles me that any "colored" person would devalue a situation in which not being white actually made one more desirable.

Thriving inside a black agency brought into play a whole other set of skills. Everything I had gleaned from the Lakeside projects, Les Jeunes Filles, General Hospital, and scary Laverne was the key to getting along at UniWorld. Like the people I had grown up with, the African Americans of UniWorld were seriously looking for respect. Unlike the sacrosanct hierarchy of the general market, at UniWorld respect was accorded to people, not titles. Chairman Byron Lewis was respected because he had built the agency and signed everyone's paychecks. The agency president, on the other hand, had a hard way to go after he endured a loud and profane dressing-down from a white creative director who technically reported to him. The other black men of the agency felt he should have demanded respect and resorted to violence, if necessary, to get it. His "Now, I don't think we need to sink to the level of that kind of language . . ." response guaranteed that he would never be deferred to by African American subordinates. Such deference would imply that we were subordinate not only to the black CEO, which might have been a matter of protocol, but also to the white creative director who had hurled epithets at his face. That would not do.

At UniWorld, you were given the respect you commanded, a version of the Lakeside code I had understood since I was three. Our black CEO was actually from a background similar to mine, but his reaction to it was different. His relationship with the ghetto was complex and absolute at the same time. In some respects, his profile was almost a stereotype: he was a fun-loving brother who constantly flashed a toothy smile, danced well, had gone to a historically black college on a basketball scholarship, and continued playing until his playground games generated too many scratches and bruises to explain to his colleagues at Procter & Gamble. He was also a buttoned-up suit-and-tie guy, a graduate of the Wharton School of Business, and a black man who chose to live in the white Connecticut community that Martha Stewart called home. By his own account, he and his family received an appraising once-over in every store and restaurant they entered.

This man refused to be dragged back into behavior he considered ignorant in any aspect of his life, including the African American agency world. I, having seen and heard of profane altercations in the same white agencies he came from, was not worried about being thought to be a product of the ghetto if I responded in kind. I was actually happy that Mud Lake rules had provided me with useful skills for surviving in the aggressive realm of Madison Avenue. Although I denied it when the white creative director asked me why I didn't seem to like him, I harbored a real animosity for this boss who had disrespected my brother. When he very publicly asked me to dance with him at the agency Christmas party, I accepted with a smile, but our relationship as colleagues was forever blighted by my vicarious indignation. Disrespect my brother and you have disrespected me. And rightly or wrongly, to attack one of us in an agency founded by one of our own seemed doubly odious. When this guy later lost his job after overplaying his hand with Byron Lewis, the chairman was heard to say, "I knew after he got away with cursing out the president that it was only a matter of time before he would try me." In all fairness, for that particular creative director, acting out at a big white agency had probably landed him at UniWorld in the first place, but he had almost certainly been booted out before he got in the face of a general market agency president. It was no mystery why he took his behavior to that level at a black agency. Race relations experts like the late Charles King, founder of the Urban Crisis Center, have documented that it is difficult for many white people to take orders from blacks. At UniWorld, we didn't need an outside authority to verify this.

UniWorld as an agency was also looking for respect. As the Supreme Court famously noted in *Brown vs. Board of Education*, separate is inherently unequal. UniWorld was never given budgets that represented the size of the African American audience. Our project budgets were consistently smaller than the general agency, though we were expected to deliver high-quality work. Then, as too often now, our general agency counterparts created campaigns for brands without an apparent thought about African American, Hispanic, or Asian consumers. Agencies like UniWorld were expected to shoehorn our work into campaigns that often had no intrinsic connection to our consumers. Our challenge was often to even be allowed to create for the all-important medium of TV. In 1984, UniWorld had broken through with a classic Burger King commercial, *Great Balls of Fire*. That rollicking rendition of the Jerry Lee Lewis classic featured Broadway star Ken Prymus playing a flaming grand piano and was the perfect mnemonic reminder of the chain's iconic flame-broiled burgers. The spot was hugely popular with all audiences and emboldened Burger King to make targeted TV spots a component of their general TV rotation. In 1986, my partner Aaron and I gave them *Fashion Statement*, a hip-hop–driven celebration of African American creativity. Our commercial featured an original Herbie Hancock track and a memorable appearance by young, unknown Cuba Gooding Jr., with a large parrot perched on his shoulder. The spot indelibly underscored Burger King's *Have It Your Way* message. The national TV audience ate it up, young black consumers loved the spot, the commercial dominated the airwaves, and I had a fabulous time collaborating with one of the world's most creative musical talents. Despite the segregation of agencies and the disparity of resources, I remember the mideighties as a time of growth and personal transition into someone who could have real impact on my agency and my industry.

By this time, being a college dropout had helped transform me into someone who took pride in finishing everything else. Struggling to overcome my psychological deficit of not having a degree, I became the "go-to guy" in the agency. Byron Lewis, an innovator who never lacked for ideas, came to know that he and his clients could count on me to bring a high level of effort to his special projects and any assignment that came my way. My direct boss, the senior vice president of creative services, a skeptical guy by nature, slowly made me his right-hand person and began to teach me the nuances of management and dealing with outside suppliers. Now, I would hardly have been recognizable as the tardy, talented screw-up who had vexed my first bosses at D'Arcy and BBDO.

The biggest changes inside me happened far away from the world of Burger King and AT&T, as new lines of communication were opened to the deepest parts of my being. Shortly after we moved to New York, I morphed from an uncommitted, lapsed Baptist into a student of new age metaphysics. The roots of the change lay in a life-altering conversation and the reading of a book, two events that were separated by almost seven years.

The fateful conversation had seemed anything but at the time. Back in the Boston days, an art director and I had been working on a life insurance ad. In one of those rambling exchanges that creatives often get into as we amble toward an advertising concept, we digressed into a discussion of death itself. I mentioned a high school classmate who had died of a chronic illness.

"It's weird to think that she knows what happens when you die," I said.

"Oh, I know what happens when you die," said my collaborator, who had always struck me as a cute, happy-go-lucky Alfalfa look-alike who happened to have a gift for making ads, rather than a deep thinker.

"You do?"

"Oh yeah," he smiled, "I read this book called *Seth Speaks*, and it explains why we're here, what happens when we die, all that stuff. When we die, we return to a higher plane, but we still have work to do. We look over the life we lived here on earth, review the lessons we learned, look at what we did well and what we could have done better, decide on what to do next, and continue to grow in consciousness of our true nature, which is to be loving, unlimited beings."

I asked if the book talked of reincarnation.

"Well, you might choose to come back and live another physical life as a human, but human life is really limiting. After we die, time takes on a completely different meaning, so you might choose to take a vacation and live a hundred years as a tree."

What he was saying struck me as a little crazy, but his demeanor was calm and pleasant as he spoke those off-kilter words. After experiencing years of marijuana-laced, Age of Aquarius musings—some of them emanating from me—on the nature of life, I didn't find it necessary to judge the conversation; it was simply interesting idle talk. I do remember thinking that whatever this guy knew—or thought he knew—he was a person who genuinely seemed to enjoy his life and work and get along with everyone. By 1985, I would have thought I'd forgotten all about his provocative perspective. Then, in the midst of a lively party at a friend's home, I came face-to-face with the book in question.

Discovering *Seth Speaks: The Eternal Validity of the Soul* was like meeting an intriguing person who you suspect knows something you don't. I pulled the book from my friend's bookshelf and began to read the first few pages as the good times swirled around me. People were getting down to whatever mideighties R&B or early rap tune was keeping the party going. Almost immediately, I felt that I should put the paperback down, buy my own copy, and give it my full attention. Seth somehow captivated me right away. I was anxious to give his words my full focus.

Seth Speaks was densely worded, written in an unfamiliar style, and full of ideas that were entirely new to me. I sometimes read a page twice in an effort to comprehend the material, and even then, I often read on without being sure that I truly understood. In those days, it was hard for me to learn from anyone unless I believed they were smarter than I was. Today, I smile at the wisdom of a universe that sent me a new way of believing wrapped in complicated explanations of the nature of consciousness, time, and the manifestation of physical reality. My new book presented a God that was the loving, sum total of all consciousness. It challenged my childhood religion's picture of a judgmental old man on a heavenly throne; it denied the very existence of evil, and exhorted me to become more consciously aware that my beliefs were attracting the reality I experienced. I was introduced to the crystal-clear reality that everything man has created was once just an idea that someone believed in. My reading encouraged me to have faith in a God that gives me the power to express my unlimited, loving nature, create abundance, and abandon fear; to view myself as a unique expression of the divine consciousness we call God, no matter how infinitesimal a portion.

The more I absorbed, the more I accepted that the world I believed in was the world I experienced. Best of all, metaphysics was not a religion; it did not require me to observe any ritual, judge anyone else's beliefs or behavior, or recruit anyone, though I found it hard not to share my newfound way of believing with anyone who seemed interested. Alvin, who thought my new belief system was interesting but not as compelling as I did, offered this advice: "Right now, you're not over the top, but just make sure that people really want to have these conversations you're having. You don't want to sound like a fanatic."

As usual, I took Alvin's words to heart. Still, people seemed to start spiritual conversations with me even when I was careful not to bring up the subject. It was as if new age thinking was in the air, and my circle of friends and acquaintances were taking it in. Ruth Ann, still my best friend, read *Seth Speaks* and was as taken by these new notions as I was. Out of nowhere, a makeup artist sat down next to me at a shoot and said, "I just read this book called *The Celestine*

Prophecy. Have you heard of it?" I hadn't, but a few minutes of conversation made it clear that the book was in the same vein as the *Seth Speaks* material. As the saying goes, *When the pupil is ready, the teacher will appear*.

During this time, new spiritual teachers and material began to cross my path almost daily. *Creative Visualization* by Shakti Gawain provided spiritual underpinnings to my life-long habit of "pretending" the life I wanted into existence. Shirley Maclaine and even Oprah Winfrey put famous faces on the belief that our creator grants us the power to shape our own reality. Deepak Chopra, a medical doctor, lectured on the spiritual power of intention. His simple book *The Seven Spiritual Laws of Success* laid out most of what I had found in the dense *Seth Speaks* material in a few simple principles that can guide us to the lives we want.

Most influentially, I began to see the results of my beliefs in my physical life, past and present. No matter what turns my life had taken, my unwavering belief that I would have a creative career had come to fruition. The hopes and dreams that Alvin and I had expressed for our life together had come true, despite very real challenges, because we believed they were possible. Looking back at the conversation that had led Alvin and me to return to New York, I could see that our reality had unfolded exactly according to what we had envisioned while driving home from Brian's college. Even the factors that seemed out of our control were exactly as we had discussed them. Our combined salaries totaled exactly the dollar amount we had said we would need and believed we could command. Supported by my newfound faith that it is God's plan for us to live in love and abundance, I vowed to dream bigger dreams. Seemingly without effort, our life moved in an upward direction.

The ultimate gift of metaphysics—also known as new age thinking—was that it put conscious control of my life in my own hands. Nowadays, I can hardly remember what it was like to believe that life just randomly happened to me. Today, I routinely meditate, take stock of my belief system, and try to assess the experiences I do not enjoy by looking at why I attracted them. If I lose a job, I look at why I no longer believed I should have it, and what lesson I was trying to learn. I am far from a perfect practitioner; blaming others for what happens to us, self-pity, and the inability to believe in our own power are habits of a lifetime, and sometimes I lapse into all of them. At the same time, it is a short journey back to the teaching I believe: *The world I live in is the world I believe in.* That is my truth, and I cannot unknow it. Luckily for my career, one thing I undeniably believe is that black creativity fuels the culture of America.

Over the next several years, our creative department joyfully drew from an endless wellspring of black culture to deliver the advertising messages of UniWorld's clients. Owing, I suppose, to the competitive nature of the industry, UniWorld's modest budgets seemed to always be under siege from our general market counterparts, who tried to convince clients that they could appeal just as effectively to African American consumers. If I believed anything, it was that no white agency would ever "out-black" me. A lack of cultural knowledge forced general market agencies to rely on superficial cues from hip-hop nation as it enraptured the country's youth. UniWorld's messaging sometimes reflected that hip-hop aesthetic, but also celebrated the whole of black culture. As we shone a light on the soulful, creative ways of African Americans, we black creatives tapped insights from the black psyche—what we loved and believed about ourselves—and in department brainstorming sessions, we dug deep in an effort to compete with each other and inspire confidence in our clients.

Black inventors, painters, cowboys, mathematicians, civil rights leaders, and heavyweight champions played prominent roles in UniWorld-created Black History Month campaigns. Even before I joined the agency, Lewis Latimer, the draftsman who drew the plans for Alexander Graham Bell's first telephone, was the subject of an award-winning national AT&T ad. A black rodeo champion, Charlie Sampson, rode a bucking bull in a TV spot I wrote about Coors's efforts to help the African American community stay on top of tough social issues. A poignant Kodak commercial done by UniWorld was inspired by the little-known propensity of African Americans to adopt children. Our African American AT&T commercials featured the lustrous voice of the great Ruby Dee. Miss Dee was a delight to work with: disarmingly eager to please and inexplicably jittery in the recording booth as she created artful, inimitable voice-overs. We also featured Miss Dee in a Black History Month print ad after a wartime photo of her as an AT&T employee turned up in the company archives. The headline, *At AT&T, Black History Wasn't Born Yesterday*, addressed the longevity of the corporation's commitment to a community accustomed to here-today-gone-tomorrow marketing. Jazz great Oscar Brown Jr. lent his baritone announcer voice and classic composition "But I Was Cool" to an award-winning campaign for Coors. When he called me at home to discuss a couplet he was writing for our commercial, I was pleased to realize I was now his collaborator. George Clinton of Parliament-Funkadelic, flamboyant in appearance but with a surprisingly low-key personality, hawked "a wild new breakfast" as he piloted a big brass bed to the local Burger King; and newcomer actor Michael Jai White sported a muffin carved into his haircut for the same spot.

In one of my favorite spots, Evander Holyfield agreed to "pop a buddy in the mouth" for Burger King's Breakfast Buddy promotion. When a crewmember asked how he felt about having to fight Mike Tyson soon, Evander said, "Way I look at it, he got to fight me." I took his lesson to heart and used it in my quest to become a more confident creative leader of our underdog squad. Like an athlete in training, I took filmmaking courses at New York University in order to refine my skills as a creative director, and became a keen observer of the top talents in the business, including multicultural agency stars like Caroline Jones, who taught me the importance of staying visible in the industry as a whole.

As UniWorld and I grew in confidence, our agency team fended off general market challenges and became a champion in the arena of cultural advertising, much of it created for Burger King. Figuratively and often literally, my career was on a roll.

Just when I was tempted to believe I might have this life-and-career thing figured out, the universe decided to have a few yucks at my expense. In 1988, twenty-two-year-old Brian and his steady girlfriend made me a grandmother while I was still in my thirties. Anticipating the birth of his baby, Brian followed in my footsteps and didn't return to college for his senior year. Although I was ashamed of the feeling, I couldn't shake the sense that no matter how enviable a life I had built—loving husband with Ivy League degree, high-paying New York job, corner office, and tony Battery Park City address—the tacky consequences of having had a baby at sixteen were like toilet paper stuck to my shoe, trailing behind me wherever I went.

My New York life sometimes felt like *Breakfast at Tiffany's*, with the ghost of Mud Lake standing in for the hillbilly husband.

I was genuinely sad that Brian would extend the cycle of unmarried parenthood that I had brought to my generation of our family. I was also feeling frustrated that he had foiled my attempt to retroactively "legitimize" our nuclear family. A glance through photos of my extended family would reveal four generations of married folk. Once I was wed to Alvin, I had hoped we would take our place among them, with Brian in the picture. Two generations from now, who would question my son's parentage? I felt the frustration every parent knows—that Brian couldn't learn from my missteps as if they had been his own.

Because I was the vessel through which Brian had entered the world, I felt the false entitlement of unexamined parenthood. My son was my property, or at least my project, to mold according to my ideas of what was best for him. Too often, that may have been some flawed notion of what was best for *me*.

Like my mother, I fell instantly in love with my infant grandson on first sight, but in those disappointed days before his birth, my only grandchild's imminent arrival was simply a problem that Brian had presented to be handled. I was reluctant to tell my New York friends what was going on, yet, except for the truth about Brian's father Bob, I have never been the type to try and hide my life. So, perhaps still acting on my friend Laverne's advice, I told people a lot. And like a good adwoman, I was adept at casting things in their best light. Lately, it had been a lonely enterprise; my son was not cooperating and my husband was an unpretentious *It is what it is* kind of guy. He matter-of-factly created a life that reflected who he was and what he thought was important. If someone mentioned that he looked too young to have a twenty-two-year-old, he was likely to say, "Yeah, well, my wife had a child when she was a teenager." Only I was concerned with the image I was trying to paint. Although I had long since evicted the Cleavers in favor of the Cosbys, my ideal picture of life was still a screen-grab of a made-for-TV family. Alvin was a real-life Cliff Huxtable, my advertising success gave me artsy entree into Claire Huxtable's league, and Brian sometimes acted so eerily like Theo Huxtable, they might have been separated at birth. In some ways, the Cosby parallel was quite legitimate. But the Huxtables didn't have out-of-wedlock babies, whereas my line of Graveses was making it a trend. If my life were a TV program, it seemed the show might never be ready for primetime.

Years later, in the mid-1990s, I worked on a project with the wife of a very high-ranking black executive at a Fortune 500 company. Over lunch at the Waldorf, she confided that she had framed several James Van Der Zee photographs of well-to-do Harlem couples, placed them on her mantel, and told her children that these were their ancestors. Her husband was bemused, her mother appalled, but neither contradicted her in front of the children and the pictures remained in place. Such is the need of some of us first-generation black "successes" to reconcile history with our reality. To own one's actual life takes a certain courage. In those days, I was finding it a challenge and a complication to my spiritual growth.

As dismayed as I was by the prospect of Brian being a college dropout, I was impressed by his decision to "man up" and face his responsibilities to his child. My beautiful grandson bore my son's name and an unmistakable resemblance to our family. I was moved by Brian's determination to be a constant presence in his son's life, and felt guilty when I admitted to myself that the absence of his own father was what spurred his commitment.

Brian moved into an apartment a block away from my great-grandparents' Houston Street house with his little family and struggled to make ends meet. Though part of me was proud of him, I feared that my branch of the family would never master the knack of finishing college and establishing oneself before taking on the burden of raising children. Both of my brothers had avoided this pitfall. Gary—whose conviction and sentence had mercifully been reduced on appeal, leading to his release after less than eight years—had had a college degree in hand long before his son and daughter were born. Spurgeon—now known as Isa—had converted to Islam, was working on a master's degree in Arabic law at the University of Michigan, and was firmly in the embrace of wedlock before he and his wife began producing their brood of five. Before long, though, I would realize that far worse things could happen than not completing a college degree.

In hindsight, I should have known when my son got into trouble with drugs. As someone who supervised a creative department, I had seen those signs firsthand. What I hadn't counted on was how strong the parental impulse toward denial could be. When my grandson was a toddler, two men attacked Brian, robbed him, and broke his jaw. It wasn't entirely implausible that Brian might have been the victim of a random attack, but street muggings were a rare occurrence in car-friendly Pontiac, where there was little foot traffic. I gave Brian the benefit of the doubt because my hometown had become more crime-ridden as the city grew poorer and the occupants of its rented houses less and less connected to each other.

When I flew to my son's side in Pontiac, getting him quality medical care and pain relief for his wired-together jaw were my priorities. Warning signs like Daddy's skepticism—"I keep wondering why Brian isn't interested in pressing charges or even getting revenge"—were too subtle to catch my attention. Later, when Brian lost his job with the Sports Authority, a chain-store retailer of athletic gear, for missing too many days, I mentally sped back to my own frustration as an ambitious young parent in a dead-end job. I promised myself to help Brian plot a course to a professional career. It took the Coopers, still close enough to see Brian stumble off the straight-and-narrow, to pull my coat and make me face what was really going on in my son's life. When Mama Cooper called, as she almost never did, and said, "Val, they're saying that Brian didn't get jumped on the street. They say he was up in one of those houses smoking that crack," I knew she was convinced that "they" knew what they were talking about. She was too protective of Brian to pass on some idle gossip that would disparage him. The moment the unwelcome truth assaulted my ear, I recognized it for what it was.

This was a devastating realization. For the next couple of years, my family and I dealt with the reality of my son's drug addiction and its consequences, including the general downward trajectory of his life and the eventual breakup of his nuclear family. Brian did avoid one common pitfall: unlike many addicts, he never stole from his family—or anyone that I know of—so people were glad to see him whenever he could break away from the embrace of drugs.

One Christmas, while Alvin and I were visiting Pontiac, Brian made an appearance at dinner only after I pleaded with him to come join the family that loved him too much to judge him. Catching sight of him, my grandson's face lit up as he yelled, "Ooh, Daddy!" and ran to the arms of the father he hadn't seen in far too long. I fought back tears and wondered how I would save my child's life. The answer, of course, was that I couldn't. Brian would have to save himself. Still, convincing him to come to dinner might have been a first step. Seeing that his disappearance into drug addiction was leaving a hurtful void in his son's world seemed to get through to him as nothing else could.

A few months later, with the help of a young men's leadership group and its founder, Brian began to find his way back. The founder of the group even demonstrated his faith in Brian's abilities by introducing him as a speaker at a youth meeting where Brian thought he would only be sitting in the audience. "Today, we're going to hear from a young man who is overcoming some big challenges and has a powerful story to share." This man had sensed that Brian had a great gift for communication, which has since been demonstrated again and again. That day, Brian began to see his own potential and the gloomy curtain of drug addiction started to lift. I tried to persuade him to augment the group's support with therapy, but he was certain that he could conquer the addiction with the help at hand. Though I was not convinced that he understood the underlying reasons he might have turned to drugs—including my inability to be a responsible parent—I felt hamstrung. I could only hope he was right, and be grateful to the organization that had brought him this far.

As a token of appreciation, I purchased a few tickets to a banquet that the leadership group was holding. At the most fortuitous time possible, Brian met the keynote speaker, Rex Nelson, a community relations director for the Detroit Pistons, and through him, was able to apply for the team's internship program. Given the opportunity to spend his days in the pro sports world he had once only dreamed of, my son quickly became the impressive intern every organization wants: eager, thorough, and uncomplaining. I desperately hoped that the prospect of a full-time job in pro sports would prove more alluring than a crack pipe and a cocaine rock. For the duration of Brian's internship, at least, I felt I could catch my breath. When he ultimately landed a job with the Pistons' sales team, I thanked God, from the bottom of my heart and a kneeling position.

Brian's sobriety wasn't all I had to be thankful for. By 1992, reality had overtaken my dreams. I had a thriving, lucrative career in New York. Back in 1985, during Alvin's tryout week at *Newsday*, he had left the editors gobsmacked when he mapped a route around a historic traffic jam and quickly got the story he was after. They offered him a job pretty much on the spot, and my intrepid husband had been labeled a comer ever since. I was now traveling constantly and working with celebrities like Danny Glover, Vanessa Williams, and Bill Cosby. My experience with Cosby turned out to be especially memorable, though not necessarily in the ways I would have expected.

It was the end of a long day, and I had spent it all waiting for Bill Cosby. UniWorld was doing a campaign for historically black colleges. Kraft General Foods was the sponsor, and snagging Cosby, the Jell-O Pudding spokesperson, for our print ad was a huge "get" for us. In order to make things most convenient for Cosby, our print shoot was piggybacked onto a Jell-O Pudding commercial. Cosby would get to us when he felt like it. That could be during a lunch break, some other pause in the commercial shoot, or at the end of the day. If we wanted him, we would just have to hang out and see what happened.

If we wanted him? We would have pitched tents on the sidewalk outside the studio to have a chance to work with Bill Cosby. His show had redefined the television sit-com, saved NBC, and lit the way for television in the 1980s. His positive portrayal of a black upper-middle-class doctor and family man had caused African Americans to stand a little straighter and puff our chests out a little farther. Long before that, I had had a mad crush on him as a teenager, watching his character Scotty on *I Spy* traveling the world playing tennis and keeping us safe from international bad guys. Like the rest of the country, I had split my sides laughing at his stand-up routines about life with his wife and kids. Bill Cosby was a giant, an icon, and a hero of mine. Now, I was not only to meet him, but also to work with him on a project as an advertising creative director. Remarkably, I approached the encounter with a lot of apprehension.

I had heard horror stories of sessions where Bill Cosby had been highly critical of the creative he was given. Ours was a simple print concept, but I was terrified that the man might crumple our layout, toss it onto the floor, and stalk out. I thought our idea was good, but I'm sure the copywriter who heard a disdainful Bill Cosby bellow, "Who wrote this garbage?" had been just as confident. Now, taking into consideration that Cosby had spent the entire day shooting a TV spot with a herd of rambunctious kids, I was bracing myself for an exhausted star who might have a very low tolerance for anything not to his liking. When the door swung open and Bill Cosby strode into the room, sans entourage or even his assistant, and said, "Okay, so what are we doing?" I had no idea what would come next.

What followed was a revelation. From the moment he walked over to the photographer—who had been selected at the actor's request—took a brief look at our layout, and said, "Where's my costar?" Bill Cosby put on a display of professionalism and creative mastery that was a graduate seminar even for an experienced creative director like myself. He understood what we were after with one glance at the concept. He took care to put his starstruck young coperformer at ease before even a Polaroid was taken. When that teenager wasn't delivering the on-camera commitment Cosby felt was required, he told the young guy, "We're going to shoot a Polaroid, and I'm going to be you, and you be me." He then transformed himself into a college student in a dorm room, shocked and amused to see "Uncle Bill" carrying in cases of the Jell-O Pudding every college student can use. Cosby took that instant photo and patiently went over it with the young model/actor, explaining his expression and body language and nudging the guy to find his own interpretation and fully give himself to it. The young man did a much better job from that point on; Cosby went back to giving the impeccable performance he had been delivering. Then he gave me something even more important.

One of my challenges as a female creative director was to command respect from the males on my team. On the Cosby shoot, where everyone jockeyed to look important in front of the most important person in the room, my art director aligned himself with the photographer, making it necessary for me to insert myself into the creative process. Although I was irritated at having to get between the two white men and stand on tiptoe to look at the shots I was ultimately responsible for, I said nothing in order to avoid making our agency look silly in front of such a huge star. When the two of them tried to get Cosby's approval of the approach they liked, he didn't look at it, then nodded in my direction and said, "Show it to her first." He appeared to feel that I must have earned my job, and saw to it that I was accorded the respect that went along with it.

When we went over the film later, every shot of Cosby was a keeper. Our only job was to choose the best performance of the other guy. Once we were done shooting, Cosby posed for individual pictures with every member of the agency and crew. Mine, entrusted to my mother for safekeeping, shows me with an ear-to-ear grin, my reaction to a surprise smacker on the cheek that Cosby planted after I said, "I've been waiting for this for twenty years!" He cracked a few more jokes, collected his gift—a sweatshirt from a historically black college—and left us all grinning like a bunch of schoolgirls.

"See?" my mother smugly chided me after I told her that the fears I shared with her had been groundless. "I knew Bill wouldn't be mean to you." She'd practically put her fingers in her ears and said, *Lalalala, I can't hear you,* when I had shared my concerns. In light of recent devastating allegations of drugging and rape by a small army of women, it's possible that the whole country had done the same thing, but you certainly couldn't prove it by my experience of Bill Cosby on that day.

I loved it that I sometimes received letters and notes from African American consumers telling me that they felt proud or touched to see and hear our race depicted in such a positive light. A Coors Black History Month radio commercial, saluting the Tuskegee Airmen of World War II and offering a free calendar with their image, shut down the Coors switchboard when the calendars did not arrive in stores on time. Fresh assignments poured into the agency from new and existing clients. Professional life was so good that it almost seemed wrong to hunger for new challenges. Yet, a certain restlessness was whispering to me that I could not be content simply to continue doing what I was doing forever.

One thing I hadn't done enough of was give back. Although I accepted every opportunity to speak to students about careers in advertising, I was less than convinced of the lasting value of my words. My cheery description of the dream job of my own youth didn't seem to impress the young Tashondas and Daequans I met in urban high schools. UniWorld's creative reel, authentic to their parents' culture, looked unadventurous and corny next to splashy music videos that featured their icons. Back in junior high, my doctor's wife's Personality Week visit had mostly left twelve-year-old me wondering how I could get a powder-blue Lincoln Continental convertible, and all these years later, kids seemed to set the same priorities. "How much money do you make?" was invariably the first question from the inner-city students who had watched me arrive in a chauffeured Lincoln Town Car. Even though they were impressed by the ballpark salary range I gave that could keep them in new Jordans and enough bling to impress the block, it depressed me to think of the hurdles they would have to overcome to find themselves anywhere near that pay scale.

My own herky-jerky ascent was owed to an obsessive childhood love of words and books, a loving mother who was involved with my education, teachers who went above and beyond to help me, a supportive community and church family, friends who would only let me fall so far, a belief in my own dreams, the sweeping social agenda of the Kennedy and Johnson administrations, the civil rights and black consciousness movements, my name that sounded like an author of romance novels, above-average intelligence, and several of those divine lightning strikes we call good luck. While I talked the talk of the good life an advertising career can provide, I hungered for a way to help erase some of the deficits that would keep most of my listeners from walking my walk. But what could I do about undereducated parents, failing schools, burned-out teachers, an indifferent federal government, high dropout rates, "thug-life" culture, and the dream of upward mobility by "blowing up" into rap or NBA stars, as opposed to the reliable but unglamorous route of education? As usual, my spiritual resources were not without answers. *What can you do?* They responded: *Do what you can.* I didn't bother asking how. I was finally learning that the answer is always contained in the question.

In a way that I was beginning to accept as the divine universe at work, I was given the chance to make a difference through public service advertising. Almost from the moment I hatched the thought that my career was lacking when it came to pro bono work, opportunities to contribute began to flow into my life. First, because of connections I had made standing in for Byron Lewis at the Advertising Club of New York, I was invited to be a judge of the club's annual International ANDY Awards competition. This was certainly easy lifting; three days at a four-star hotel in Miami's South Beach, with mornings and afternoons spent evaluating advertising and nights filled with elegant meals and glamorous outings, spouses welcome.

At the very first judging, I felt the need to be a strong advocate for a stereotype-busting commercial. It featured a black man who was presumed by most viewers to be a criminal until he was revealed at the end to be the arresting officer. When the spot was played at the awards show, there was loud applause from the audience. Several of my fellow judges came up to share that they had underestimated the potential impact of the spot and that my passionate defense had caused them to take a second look. Despite my reluctance to be seen as the "angry black woman" during the judging, my roots in the black consciousness movement had spurred me to speak on behalf of that work, in hopes of seeing more like it. That experience was a potent reminder that it is important to stand up for what I believe, even if it involves discomfort or being accused of playing "the race card."

Shortly after the ANDY Awards, I was invited to become a member of the board of directors of the Ad Club, and to cochair its diversity committee. Contacts I made through the ANDY judging also led to my being recruited to the Campaign Review Committee of the Advertising Council, a group that produced the most important public service advertising in the nation and addressed many of the problems facing those young students I had been speaking to, as well as their families and neighborhoods. *Do what you can*, is such a simple and profound answer that when I think of it, I smile. Advertising and writing happen to be what I can do. When I look at it that way, I see that we all—from Bill Gates to the person who sweeps the streets—can do something to help solve the problems of the world.

The Clinton campaign was another answered prayer that fell from the sky. I was in Los Angeles to attend the taping of a Burger King–sponsored TV special. The messages in my voice mail included a call from a former colleague I'll call Tiny. Tiny had once been senior VP of client services at Uni-World. He was a small, bright man who projected the savvy and confidence a prep school scholarship and general market advertising career can instill. I was happy to have a counterpart in management who was not simply a yes man to the clients. Unfortunately, Tiny's outsized ego couldn't coexist for long with Byron Lewis. I had been sorry to see him leave the agency before we accomplished much together. Now, back at the general market agency he came from, Tiny was calling me with a big idea. "I wrote a letter to Bill Clinton's campaign, telling them that they need to make sure their ad team has diversity, and guess what? They want me to assemble a group of people for them to interview. There's probably no money in it, but it would be a lot of fun and a great credential to have. Are you interested?"

I was beyond interested. Before long, Tiny, two young white creatives, and I were meeting with Mandy Grunwald, a high-level member of the Clinton team. Bringing two white men, no matter how talented, to a diversity recruitment meeting was exactly the kind of tone-deaf move I would later associate with Tiny. Mandy, a tall, handsome woman, was an all-business member of the campaign team. She chatted with us all, then asked that we provide the Clinton campaign with samples of our work. I sent in some campaigns I had written to help AT&T bond with the African American audience. *Is There a Doctor in the House?* was created to publicize a scholarship program for medical students. It was illustrated with a charming photo of a little black girl with a stethoscope pressed to her doll's chest. *Pro Material* was a stereotype-fighter that highlighted AT&T's internships for promising minority science students. I included *Deal with Your Kids,* an antidrug TV spot my team had done that featured a black father role-playing with his kid how to resist drug dealers.

Within a week, Mandy offered me a spot on the Clinton national ad team. About five seconds after I enthusiastically accepted, Mandy asked whether Tiny was someone I really needed. I told her that while I couldn't say I needed him, I also wasn't willing to dump the person who'd gotten me this opportunity. "Oh, okay then. Don't worry about it. We'll call you about next steps." I never told Tiny about that exchange, though I would later wish I had.

Like a case of synchronicity gone wrong, my big break put Alvin's career and mine on a collision course. What were the odds he would win the coveted assignment of covering the presidential race just as I got the opportunity to work for a candidate? It was the kind of quandary that can test a relationship to its core. We spent our evenings in the usual way, reading and watching TV in the same room, but we hardly spoke about the problem. Our mutual dilemma was like an open wound that was so tender we dared not touch it. The tension in our home was palpable as we waited for word from *Newsday* on whether there was a way to work things out. There wasn't, and in our hearts, we knew our situation was a conflict of interest.

In the end, Alvin reasoned that while he might have another opportunity to cover a race, the Clinton campaign might be a once-in-a-lifetime event for me. Then he did the single most generous thing he could ever have done: Alvin relinquished his assignment so that I could join the Clinton team. My heart ached for him. For days, our spacious duplex apartment was hardly large enough for the two of us and the huge, invisible presence of his disappointment. The fact that we never turned on each other, or wasted time pleading our cases to each other, strikes me as a testament to the strength of our love and commitment. Our marriage came through all this intact, and Alvin has never spoken of that sacrifice in anger. The saving grace of the whole affair was that it led him to move to the paper's editorial board, a situation he loves, where his opinions and journalistic gifts help influence the public policy of the nation.

"Beginning with George Washington and all the way to Bill Clinton, there have been almost no little guys elected president," Chicago columnist Mike Royko wrote, noting the superficial proclivities of the American voting public. Bill Clinton surely was tall and good-looking as he entered the room at the Arkansas governor's mansion where I first met him. His height, his elegant hands, and the muted swagger of a man who is entirely comfortable being the big gun in the room impressed me. But at that meeting, it was his mind that truly engaged me. Our gathering was a freewheeling session in which we were encouraged to ask the candidate any questions we liked. I had two. The night before, on *The Arsenio Hall Show*, where Clinton would later make a memorable appearance, Eddie Murphy had shocked me by petulantly advising the viewing audience not to vote. His suggestion seemed to have been evoked by some petty Hollywood struggle where Eddie had been made to feel his opinion didn't matter. He extrapolated this to the upcoming presidential election, saying that he was not voting because his vote didn't matter, and suggested that the audience follow his lead.

My question to Clinton: "What can you say to a young black voter who looks up to Eddie Murphy that can counteract a message like that?"

He rested his chin on one hand, bit his lower lip in that now-familiar manner, and slowly replied, "This country doesn't have to work . . . in order for Eddie Murphy's life to work. But if you're like most of us ordinary people, you need to get out and vote for a government that's going to fight for the things that are in your best interests." As simple as it sounds, without attacking Murphy, he was offering a message that young voters could relate to: *Well, Eddie's got it like that. If you don't, voting is your only shot.*

My other question concerned a vexing conundrum that I had heard discussed for years, without a satisfactory answer: "Why do you think it is that immigrant groups like Koreans and Chaldeans are able to operate thriving businesses in African American neighborhoods where black owners so often struggle and fail?"

Clinton didn't seem to need to think much about that one. "I really think black people need to stop being so hard on themselves about that." He pointed his finger at nothing in particular, accentuating the statement. "That Chaldean store owner might be coming from a family of shopkeepers that stretches back a thousand years. Why should an African American from an industrial or agricultural background be better at it? Put them both in a factory or on a farm and it's a whole different story." His uncomplicated remedy: stop expecting yourself to know how to do something before you've learned how to do it. In a culture of families splintered first by slavery and later by two great waves of migration, the power of education handed down from father to son outside of a classroom might have lost much of its vitality. Perhaps Bill Clinton had tumbled to something about us that we ourselves were largely ignoring. Coming from a white, Southern, centrist politician, it struck me as a potent sound bite in the post-Reagan era. One thing was certain: he had come up with a response that flattered me as an African American and assured him my vote.

Bill Clinton broke out his abundant charisma for our entire team, but he took a special shine to me. I actually believed this until I found out that most members of the team had exactly the same impression of their relationship with the future president. We could all point to evidence that supported our feelings: Once, when a senior advisor interrupted a brief one-on-one conversation between Bill Clinton and me, I started to move away in deference. The future leader of the free world reached behind his back and clasped my wrist as if to say, *No, don't go.* During a commercial shoot, I ran over to speak to the director and Clinton between takes. That action quickly took the entire secret out of the Secret Service. Thrown off by the sudden appearance of armed men rushing my way, I tripped over a cable and stopped in a near curtsy in front of a smiling Governor Clinton.

"Nice feet," he drawled. I tried to play off my clumsiness.

"Oh yeah, I'm a real Grace Kelly."

"No," he said, pointing to my peep-toe sandals and fresh pedicure, "nice feet."

On another occasion, after a couple of takes of a TV commercial I had written, Clinton suddenly asked, "Who wrote this script? I really like this copy." When his advisor Frank Greer informed him that I was the author, he looked me in the eye and said, "I really like this commercial."

I replied that he was a quick study who was doing a great job of delivering the lines.

"That's because you understand my message," he said. "This is it, you got it."

It turned out every member of the team had a story of his or her own connection to Elvis, as the Secret Service code-named him. Linda Kaplan was amazed when he sought out and greeted her cousins after seeing a sign bearing her name at a campaign rally. My art director friend Vicky, whom I had subcontracted to work with me, was especially pleased when our candidate noticed and complimented a colorful silk art deco top she wore. "I love, love your vest," were the words that won her affection, and not even her husband's teasing, "He really meant, *I love, love your chest*," could stale the moment.

Tabitha Soren, MTV journalist and driving force behind Rock the Vote whom I met a few years after the campaign, recounted going into an interview with Clinton determined to resist his vaunted magnetism. She was quickly thrown off when he asked, "Now that color, would you call that salmon or peach or what?" When she gave him a blank look, he continued, "Your dress. That's one of my favorite colors and I never know what to call it."

As she launched into a description of the particular shade, she suddenly thought, *Damn. He got me.*

On a TV shoot, our very professional young director of photography handled her equipment with particular élan whenever the candidate happened to be watching. At one point, a female makeup artist, in an incredible breach of professionalism, rushed into the shot in the middle of a take and began powdering Clinton's nose. "I couldn't help it," she was later heard to say, standing in a corner trying to compose herself with a glass of wine. "I saw this little shiny spot on his nose, and I just wanted him to look perfect." Years later, after watching Clinton's address to the 2012 Democratic Convention, I remember thinking that we the enchanted should cut ourselves some slack. When it comes to winning people over, "Bubba" got skills.

The Clinton campaign was the perfect remedy for my restlessness. Working on a national presidential ad team was something entirely new. Driven by the results of almost nightly focus groups, we created work as it was needed, and on candidate Clinton's schedule. One day I might be joking with him while shooting a commercial at the governor's mansion in Little Rock, or eating vanilla wafers and finger sandwiches at Clinton's aunt's house in Hope, Arkansas, while his uncle Buddy and a few cousins shot the breeze under the carport. Dinner might find me chatting with James Carville and our team over steaks at Doe's, a Little Rock insider hangout. The next day I could be a spectator watching with the rest of the country as the campaign played out on CNN.

Donny Deutsch, now an MSNBC contributor, was a dominant presence on our team who actually managed to travel with Clinton and Gore on their bus tour. As much as Donny, with his big personality and trademark cowboy boots, sucked all of the air out of the room, I also learned a lot watching him run circles around the rest of us when it came to garnering access and media coverage.

Taking a cue from Donny, I once made a call to Mandy Grunwald, asking for the opportunity to do more for the campaign. That call resulted in my being asked to write a commercial that would appeal specifically to the African American audience. The pitch would be made by the Democratic Party, rather than candidate Clinton, a decision most likely designed to protect the governor's fragile support among white, blue-collar males. The commercial used gritty footage of actual inner-city residents to address urban blight, violence, and lack of opportunity in their communities. Much of it was shot on Harlem's 125th Street in front of what would later become Bill Clinton's postpresidential office. It was an uncanny foreshadowing of the man's impact on Manhattan's most downtrodden neighborhood. I was able to funnel the job to a deserving young black director, Steven Connor, and bring a plum assignment to my longtime music collaborator Bernard Drayton. Both delivered outstanding work despite a tight budget and crazy time constraints.

Squarely in my creative comfort zone, I loved showcasing the genuine concerns of African Americans who were wrestling with tough conditions. Here, finally, was success on my own terms: doing my thing on a big stage, to an audience of millions, selling them a product I believed in my heart was worth buying. I should note that even though the campaign had never tried to pigeonhole me into doing "black" work, playing to my cultural strength paid the highest dividends to my clients and to me. The dignity of those Harlem spokespeople was undeniable, especially the natty octogenarian in a beret, who memorably capped the commercial as he leaned forward on his cane and said, straight into the camera, enunciating each word, "There . . . must . . . be . . . someone . . . that . . . can . . . try . . . to . . . do . . . BETTER." The spot pleased the Democratic Party and the Clinton campaign. It aired nationally on BET, generated positive buzz among African Americans, and turned out to be my most impactful and gratifying contribution to the 1992 election.

I made some lasting friendships working on the Clinton team: David Angelo, future founder and chairman of David & Goliath, among them. Advertising star Linda Kaplan-Thaler and Hollywood director Michael Apted, one of the producer/directors of the successful TV series *Masters of Sex*, who shot some of our commercials, also became more than acquaintances. We spent hours scouting locations and chatting about film, advertising, metaphysics, and life while we traveled in the production van. Bill Clinton, who pledged to have an administration that "looked like America," had easily assembled the diverse and talented creative team that the country's leading ad agencies still find so elusive. Young and older, male and female, black, white, Asian, and Latino, we brought our various perspectives to one unified campaign: *For the People. For a Change.* Best of all, our candidate won.

As the Clintons headed for the White House, I went back to my full-time job as executive creative director of UniWorld.

The inauguration, gala, and ball were an eventful coda to the campaign interlude. Soon, though, that restless feeling began to stalk me again. In my daily meditations, I asked the universe to send an interesting opportunity my way. Some Clinton-related prospects, like an invitation to interview for Deputy Assistant Secretary of Labor or White House Fellow, were unexpected and flattering offers that were too far outside my creative wheelhouse. I was becoming frustrated, but then a big opportunity suddenly came from where I least expected.

Remarkably, UniWorld was to be given a chance to create a campaign for the entire Burger King audience. Burger King, known for changing agencies like hats, had sometimes relied on UniWorld as its only agency while they auditioned new shops to handle the bulk of their account. This time, we would be given the chance to officially speak to the white audience as interim general market agency. Of course, they would not simply award it to us in recognition of our past good work. We and Saatchi & Saatchi, the agency for their advertising targeted to kids, would compete for the assignment in a head-to-head pitch. UniWorld was also given the strangest parameter I have ever received: our new campaign must reintroduce Burger King as a top hamburger restaurant and reinforce its core benefits of flame-broiling and *Have It Your Way*, without being so distinctive that a new general market agency could not abandon it. In other words, *Be good, but not too good.* To this day, I wonder if I should have ignored this directive, and what that course of action would have cost us. As our team's creative leader, I willed myself to step up my game. My group creative director and I facilitated brainstorming sessions where the team used our institutional knowledge of Burger King to come up with insights about the brand and its image. I read up on techniques designed to elicit great creative ideas. I prevailed upon Byron Lewis to pay for an offsite creative session at a New York hotel and exhorted the team to shock themselves and the ad world with the quality of their thinking. I visualized us as the winners and sent my intention deliberately into the universe. All of our efforts paid off when the UniWorld campaign, *We May Not Be Number One, It Just Tastes That Way*, was tapped for a $100 million media buy.

It soon became apparent that even when we kicked butt, we would not be allowed to completely win. A reporter from *Newsday* informed me that Burger King had no interest in publicizing our selection, though he wrote a story anyway. *Adweek* greeted our win of the assignment with the following lead: *In a sign that things have truly turned chaotic at Burger King, the general market assignment has been turned over to UniWorld.* Our campaign, an inclusive, all-American celebration of customers who preferred the flame-broiled taste of the Whopper over the mighty Big Mac, was truly multicultural and would only have come from UniWorld. It scored undeniable success as Whopper sales surpassed Big Mac for the first time in a decade. The industry press ignored both our success and the failure of Burger King's new agency to replicate it. I comforted myself with Burger King's historic sales results and a nice bonus check, but my desire to move on was certainly stoked by my industry's slap in the face. All evidence to the contrary, it seemed UniWorld would continue to be treated by some colleagues like the Mud Lake side of the business.

I remember this whole period as a time when every success also seemed to contain the seeds of disappointment and failure. "Rehab is for quitters," said singer Amy Winehouse, shortly before her final plunge into the abyss. Her next line might just as well have been, *But relapse is for everyone.* My mother, fearing that Brian was about to lose his dream job as a sales executive with the Detroit Pistons, called me to say, "There's no need for you to be thinking that Brian is doing well, because he isn't. He's using that stuff again." Sure enough, it wasn't long before the Pistons team, having exhausted every other option and inducement, let Brian go.

There was nothing like seeing successes go awry to make me "let go and let God." After Burger King finally selected a new general agency, I focused on UniWorld's day-to-day creative and management challenges to take my mind off my hurt feelings and the seeming futility of competing with the big boys. At home, after a period of trying to prop Brian up financially, I came to the painful decision that I could not be an enabler. By then, I had become a member of the creative review committee of the Partnership for a Drug-Free America, which showered me with useful information about drug abuse and behaviors that parents should look out for. "If drugs are going to ruin my life, I'll be the one getting high," I told Brian as I let him know that he was on his own with his addiction. "The one thing I can give you is this: I will never stop expecting something better of you. You will never be 'sprung' because you will always know that I am somewhere feeling that you are better than what you are doing."

As I gave up the illusion of control over two vital areas of my life, I was plagued by doubts and demons. Professionally, I pondered the unthinkable: might it be true that our work was just not good enough to compete with white agencies? Away from the office, I feared the consequences of deserting the battlefield against Brian's addiction. One night, sitting at dinner in John's Pizza in Greenwich Village, out of nowhere, a great whoop of fear passed through my whole body as I suddenly realized I had no idea where in the world my only child was. For all I knew, he was being duct-taped and prepared for execution on some filthy crack-house floor. I felt as if my heart would leap out of my chest when that image popped into my head. I dropped my chin to my chest, closed my eyes, and entreated God to watch over my son.

As the saying goes, *God may not be there when you want Him, but He'll always be on time.* Understanding that the answers to the challenges I faced lay in unwavering faith, meditation, and belief was the key to reaching a different reality. Denying Brian's actual situation, I pictured my talented son using his charisma and encyclopedic sports knowledge in another dream job. I consciously brought to mind my own recovery from the darkest days of my early career.

There was no single bright moment when things began to turn for the better, but gradually, green shoots sprouted on both the work and home fronts. UniWorld was asked to create the ad campaign for Lifebeat's Urban Aid, a music industry campaign against HIV. It was a relief and a respite from the constant competition of brand advertising, and an invitation to focus on people with problems greater than my own.

Brian, confronted with the full responsibility of keeping a roof over his own head, discovered that he wasn't addicted enough to accept homelessness. With the help of a Michigan advocacy group, he found work, though it was far removed from the glamour of professional sports. The universe has more ways of bringing us what we need than our puny minds can imagine, and in those days, providence was hard at work. Getting out of my own head and out of my son's way were two solutions that came from my surrender to a higher power. Once I let go of my need to map the route to a good outcome, or even to determine what that good outcome might be, the pace of favorable events picked up.

A research director at Burger King presented UniWorld

with a plaque documenting for posterity the success of our campaign. Brian found a therapy group, sobriety, and a better job. Ironically, though unconnected to me, this significant stop on his way back was Ross Roy, where my own career had taken a giant turn for the better. Visiting Michigan, I accepted an invitation from Brian to stop by for lunch. Ross Roy had become a one-client merchandising agency for Chrysler, and no one I knew was with the company anymore. Brian was the newest and only Graves in the agency, and he had already made his own mark. "He's just like a ray of sunshine that I look forward to seeing every day," his supervisor said when Brian brought her over for an introduction. It was a great analogy; Brian's ascent from addiction was like the dawning of a new day in my life too. That same sun seemed to be shining on all of us.

The anti-HIV campaign, from which I had expected nothing more than the satisfaction of doing good work without general market competition, paid the biggest dividend of all. Deepak Chopra calls this phenomenon the Law of Dharma—of service to humanity—by which we are rewarded for those things we do with no expectation of getting anything in return. I just called it an unexpected blessing.

CHAPTER 12

Motown Madness

When music mogul Andre Harrell called to invite me for a drink, I figured he must have another pro bono assignment for UniWorld. My team had totally rocked the work we did for Urban Aid 4 Lifebeat's anti-HIV fundraising concert, right down to the stylized collage of condoms on the program cover. While I waited for Andre in the see-and-be-seen Royalton Hotel lobby, the waiter refreshed my tonic and lime juice twice, "with apologies from Mr. Harrell." A few seconds after Andre arrived, Tommy Hilfiger popped over to pay his respects. Sean "P. Diddy" Combs bounced into the chair next to Andre and joked, "Am I late?" Just being close to the music biz was already feeling like way more fun than advertising.

As Andre sipped a glass of merlot, he shared with me that he would be taking the reins of legendary Motown Records. He spun a beautiful vision of the evolution of Berry Gordy's legacy. In his scenario, with my help, Andre would harness the power of the Motown brand to make inroads into film, television, advertising, apparel, toys, and whatever else we could conjure up. He blew off my lack of experience in the music business, saying, "It's not brain surgery. You'll pick it up."

I floated home to the Greenwich Village condo my Clinton payday had helped finance, and told my husband, "Andre Harrell just offered me a job I can't think of a reason to turn down." Maybe I should have thought harder.

Motown was certainly a dope way to exit UniWorld. It was also a rare opportunity to move up and still work in an African American environment. It would make me the absolute envy of the creative community. Andre and his new job had made the cover of *New York* magazine—Motown was the hottest joint in town, and its celebrity CEO had drafted me. While my contract was being negotiated, the irritations of UniWorld, including Byron Lewis's hiring of a new senior creative without my knowledge, rolled off my back. *Sayonara, suckers*, was a phrase that often ran through my head. The moment I gave notice, the news shot through UniWorld like a nerve impulse in synaptic fluid. Those who knew me well enough called to ask, "Is it true?" I had begged the universe for an interesting opportunity, and interesting had been delivered gangbusters. At the time I wasn't thinking that *May you live in interesting times* is a Chinese curse.

The last few nights before starting my new gig at Motown, I could hardly sleep. One reason was pure excitement at becoming part of the historic label whose hits had been the soundtrack of my life. From childhood days until hip-hop bogarted "the sound of young America" in a TKO, Motown's R&B giants like Marvin Gaye, Smokey Robinson, the Temptations, Diana Ross & the Supremes, Martha & the Vandellas, and others had accompanied the hottest dances, deepest heartaches, and highest points of my days and nights. Making up our own dance routines, my playmates from Lakeside and I had performed a repertoire from "Please Mr. Postman" to "The Way You Do the Things You Do" at parks and recreation dances and school talent shows. Our little girl groups, made up of an ever-shifting roster of whoever was in the mood, were a worshipful homage to our heroines, the wig-coiffed, brocade-sheathed Supremes, Marvelettes, and Vandellas who set the music and fashion trends in black enclaves from Detroit to Dallas, and their male counterparts who first embodied our idea of cool black manhood. At about age twelve, I had practically swooned when four ninth-grade Jefferson Junior High guys, looking equal parts Marvin Gaye and the Temptations, introduced a slick new dance called the Skate as Mary Wells crooned "The One Who Really Loves You." (My teenage brothers later showed off these same moves in a juke joint in Mama's hometown, tiny West Blocton, Alabama, and became instant "celebrities" from Detroit.) Then, as now, I can pretty much sing the Motown discography of those early groups. For me, Motown was more than a great job offer; it was the ideal position I never knew I always wanted.

For all the nostalgia that the Motown name conjured, I harbored no illusions that I would be joining the record company of my bouffant-and-bop teenage days. Andre Harrell was one of the pioneers of a new style, "New Jack Swing," an R&B-tinged evolution of hip-hop that broadened the harder-edged rap genre to include more melodically driven artists like Al B. Sure!, novel acts like Heavy D & the Boyz, and soulful singers like Mary J. Blige and guy group Jodeci. Even before the advent of hip-hop, Motown had had to introduce another generation of stars like the Commodores with front man Lionel Richie, and new voices like Rick James, to keep itself relevant.

As I had grown up, so had the Motown brand, into movies and new imprints like Mo'Jazz that spoke to changing and expanding tastes. It was precisely the opportunity to help evolve

Motown into the next new era that had set my creative juices pumping. Based on my initial conversations with Andre Harrell and synchronicities like the opening of the Motown Café on West 57th Street, my head was almost spinning with ways to expand the empire. A revival of the fabled Motown Revue, sponsored by a big-name soft drink company? A natural. An urban clothing line carrying the coveted Motown logo? TV shows, animated young urban characters in the vein of *Fat Albert and the Cosby Kids*, even young adult books, based on our new girl groups: all these things—some of which have since come to pass—seemed eminently possible, especially with the support of the CEO who had handpicked me. With the media momentum and excitement that surrounded Andre's take-over of Motown, how could we miss? How could I fail?

"Well," one of the successful woman buddies I consulted before accepting the gold-plated offer had said, "you could find yourself just being a department head at a record label. That would actually be a step down for you." Another schooled me: "The record business is really more of a hustle. You'll pick it up in no time, but you might not like it." Though my friends offered me their best advice, what was missing was a friend who was actually in the game. I once read that Gladys Knight told a young hopeful, "Don't just think about whether you want to be a singer. Ask yourself if you want to be in show business." As a casual reader, it was enough just to sense the meaning of her advice. As someone who was about to enter the every-man-for-himself wilds of the music biz, I could have used a sit-down tutorial on what I was getting myself into and the art of survival in an unfamiliar world.

Right from the start, Motown was a hot mess. Andre Harrell, a true visionary, had surrounded himself with too many people, many of whom had street credibility but little useful talent. Although Andre captivated all of us as he laid out his vision for our artists and label, lassoing his recruits into an organized team was a tough assignment. Posing, flexing, and jockeying for Andre's attention, many of them talked loud and fast, drowned out more sober team members, and outnumbered the senior staff that had both street smarts and music industry experience. Motivated by Andre's desire to avoid "wackness" and its by-product, "wack juice," Motown made too many bad decisions, reversed good ones, overpromised, underdelivered, and went through alarming amounts of money without producing either hits or lasting new stars.

For the first year, as I learned the business through observation, I wrote and produced commercials for Andre's popular Motown Talent Search and our less-than-stellar lineup of new artists. Though I struggled to define my job, using the client contacts and skill set I brought from advertising, I was able to secure marketing relationships with the Clairol and Coors brands, trading on Motown's iconic stature and pointing out our shared target audiences. I ran Andre's special projects like a youth mentorship program for Harlem kids, and developed project ideas like the New Motown Revue, involving giant brands I had worked with at UniWorld.

Despite the things I loved about my position—autonomy to create and execute my own projects, my large office with the panoramic Hudson River view, first-class travel, hotels and rental cars, a place on the VIP list of every hot event, and the satisfaction of being a doer in the land of talkers—the music business just wasn't for me. Its more questionable conventions—a devotion to pecking order and ruthless dedication to moving up in it, what seemed to me to be outrageous conflicts of interest, the awarding of lucrative assignments to friends and lovers—were foreign to me. I kept those feelings to myself, but I was a corporate type who didn't participate in the game, and that made me a jerk and a threat in the eyes of some of my counterparts. By the end of my first year at Motown, it was clear to me that my status as a fish out of water wouldn't be changing.

Our differences often made it difficult to respect each other. "Silly" and "corny," two descriptors that had been used to attack me since childhood, were sometimes invoked against me. So be it. Learning from my role model, Maya Angelou, who had been laughed at by more experienced Broadway performers and dismissed by a classical conductor whom she later inspired, I had come to believe that creativity requires the willingness to be both silly and corny. There was ample evidence that everything cool was corny first, and I cheerfully chose to agree.

Despite rough sailing, I managed to stay afloat in the uncharted waters of Motown. Andre's regard for me and my senior VP title shielded me from most outright attacks. No one else at Motown had my kind of relationships with blue-chip marketers like Burger King and Pepsi that could help promote our artists and save us a marketing dollar or two. The BET commercial I created for Andre's Motown Talent Search—a comical spot that depicted Andre scouring the church choirs and home shower stalls of America looking for the next great voice—had helped create a national buzz about the new regime at Motown. The kick-off of our summer program for Harlem's youth was attended by former governor Mario Cuomo and was written up in the *New York Daily News*. My wonderful and meticulous assistant, a savvy young Filipino named Gerry, was ingrained with the ins and outs of the culture and had an unerring instinct for the all-important VIP environment that executives of any importance were expected to seek out at any event. Gerry had been smart in seeking the job as my assistant, where he sensed we could be helpful to each other. His presence on my team kept me from looking any more clueless than I already did, and in return, I went out of my way to give him opportunities to demonstrate his value.

Despite my difficulties feeling at home in the music industry, I did have some great relationships with several of my Motown colleagues, including the affable and knowledgeable general manager, producer/artist Al B. Sure!, our very professional senior VP of publicity, the director of radio promotion, the label's tasteful, image-making stylist, Andre's powerful personal assistant, and a number of people in less exalted positions. But, like the auto factory workers I had grown up with, I began to live for Friday and dread Monday morning's return to the battles of my job. I made a personal commitment to rise above most of the petty confrontations around me, though I walked into a few dust-ups I wish I had avoided.

After a career of opportunities that had come my way based on speaking my creative mind, it took awhile for me to relearn the lesson my mother's friend had taught me at that first hospital job: sometimes, it is simply smarter to keep one's big mouth shut. One good example was my suggestion, in the face of the rise of the music-sharing site Napster, that Motown begin marketing its music online. "Right," scoffed the general manager, usually an ally of mine, "and put our biggest customers, the retailers, out of business!" Today, if you go looking for an actual record store, it's easy to see that the retailers did indeed go out of business in the age of iTunes, and my instincts were right on point. Unfortunately, back in the day, my comment was about five years ahead of its time.

My lack of music industry history didn't help. Clarence Avant, the powerful, irascible godfather of the black music business, was Motown's chairman emeritus, seemingly there at the label to look after the financial interests of the parent company. He once yelled at me, "Who ARE you?" when I dared to offer a differing point of view. The truth was, I was an outsider who didn't know any better than to challenge some-one of his stature in the business. Thankfully, the big corpo-rate names and six-figure opportunities I brought to the table earned a grudging modicum of respect even from this formi-dable giant. If, indeed, money talks, in the music business it shrieks like a fourteen-year-old girl at a Justin Bieber concert. Andre once told my son Brian, "Your mom is professional, but she's down." It was high praise under the circumstances.

Spiritually, Motown was a seminar in my continuing course on surrendering to a higher power. I could no more control Motown than I could control the weather. I had lost my innocence, but I clung to my good intentions, did my best to promote our artists and earn my salary, and watched as most of my foes blew away in a hurricane of chaos and mass layoffs.

As the confusion at my new situation continued unabated, I tended the relationships I had developed with New York "Mad Men" like Stephen Frankfurt of Y&R and Stanley Becker of Saatchi & Saatchi, as well as organizations like the Partnership for a Drug-Free America, the Ad Council, and the Advertising Club. I knew I might soon need their help find-ing a way back into my previous industry. Ironically, in the ad world, my Motown position gave me a new level of youthful-ness and urban credibility. It opened doors to interviews with the CEOs of major advertising agencies. In a stunning testa-ment to the power of the Motown brand, I am still grateful for the two years I was associated with the label. As frustrating as my sojourn there felt, and as far out of my comfort zone as I had been forced, it had also brought a breadth and sheen to my career and résumé that few other jobs could have.

My husband's next foray into elite academia turned out to be the source of my salvation. Marriage to Alvin has always given me the benefit of almost having another self—another brain to think with, a different set of skills with which to accomplish things—and twenty-four more hours in every day. This time, my better half inadvertently rescued me. Six months before my two-year Motown contract expired, Alvin was awarded the prestigious John S. Knight Fellowship for a year's study at Stanford University.

On a whim, I asked Andre Harrell, who by then was under siege and negotiating a golden parachute himself, if I might finish my projects and contract while living in California. Amazingly, he agreed. With four months left on my contract, Alvin and I packed up and set off for a paid adventure in Northern California. He felt like a lottery winner. I felt like a runaway slave.

CHAPTER 13

Stanford: "If We Catch You Working, We'll Have to Let You Go"

Safe in California, I slept off Motown like a drunk coming off a bender. Palo Alto was a sunlit, flowery Eden where pollen drifted on the air like fairy dust and made me dizzy, sneezy, and constantly drowsy. As soon as we arrived, we were swept up in the whirl of Alvin's fellowship. The program's directors, seeking to make life as stress-free as possible, included spouses and partners in all activities, and the doors of Stanford were open to us as well. In the first days of the fellowship, we were constantly thrown together in a calculated effort to create bonds among twenty people who had been strangers on arrival.

Sitting on the huge leather sectional in the fellows lounge, we all told our life stories. Most of the American tales were of successful academic careers that led from good schools to famous newspapers and big stories, with interesting detours and stumbles along the path. The international fellows told harrowing stories of being educated and doing their reporting amidst revolution and political turmoil. For the noble cause of bringing the truth to the people, they had endured harassment, arrest, and even the deaths of colleagues or family. Although I wasn't naïve about geopolitical reality, meeting these extraordinary reporters brought home the fact that we Americans lead a charmed existence in so many ways. Some of the spouses were also journalists and writers with stories to tell. One notable spouse participant would go on to bona fide literary fame. Tabitha Soren's husband, Michael Lewis, would write several hugely successful books, from the Silicon Valley saga *The New New Thing* to the baseball story *Moneyball*, which became a Brad Pitt movie that was nominated for an Academy Award, to *The Big Short*. Only one of us was a former teen parent who had traveled from the gritty industrial middle class to glitzy Madison Avenue. That novelty appealed to these journalists who always appreciated a good story. Michael and Tabitha were the stars of the group; Alvin and I became a popular couple.

Stanford was the latest chapter in my academic experience that never included actual university enrollment. After almost two years in the stressful vortex of Motown, I was ready to earn a BA in the art of renewal and relaxation. Although I scoured the Stanford course catalog for classes that would challenge my intellect, I found myself completely disinterested in auditing classes in literature, philosophy, art, or psychology. My experience at Stanford paralleled my days of performing in theater and music at Harvard or working on an as-yet-unfinished play in the library at Columbia while waiting for Alvin. There have been times when I have chastised myself for being lazy or not having "the right stuff" to attend those schools under legitimate circumstances. Other times, I am content to know that I got from academia what I most wanted: to hold my own in the lofty circle of elite university graduates. From a distance of years, I see an unorthodox sequence to my educational life: I skipped a grade early on, missed a semester of high school but still graduated a year early, left college after three years but found success in my chosen field. For years, guilt—a truly useless emotion—gave me a recurring nightmare in which I was sent back to junior high to make up the time. When I am charitable with myself, I feel that I simply did what my second-grade teacher had allowed me to do: skip over the parts that I could pick up on my own, and learn from teachers when I really needed instruction.

While Alvin studied macroeconomics, the global food economy, and the nature of genius, I learned things that were truly enjoyable to me, brushing up on conversational French, improving my singing voice, getting into better physical condition, and finally learning to swim under some of the best instruction in the country.

Although Alvin had had to propose a project and go through a rigorous competitive process in order to win "our" fellowship, he was completely at liberty to pursue his subject area or not. Because it truly interested him, he read and studied his proposed course—macroeconomics and the world food economy—with vigor. My own journey was all about self-discovery; contrary to my assumption of a lifetime, I learned that I did indeed have physical gifts like a natural ability at weight training, and that with perseverance, I could manage to stay afloat and even propel myself through deep water.

Both of us were grateful for the gift that a year without nine-to-five jobs could be. Thankfully, fellowship advisers had warned us newcomers that freedom from our high-intensity positions might be accompanied by a slightly untethered feeling at being severed from our former responsibilities and titles. Unlike most of the fellows, I would not be returning to my previous job when the fellowship ended. It was the first time in years that I had not been senior VP of something or other, and though I was elated to be out of the maelstrom of Motown, and even the stress of UniWorld, I did feel something of a loss of identity. I had left my job as advertising creative director in a blaze of glory; now I had been propelled out of Motown into an ephemeral cloud of choices that I had not encountered since high school graduation.

Still, after more than twenty years of working, I was determined to push aside anxiety and enjoy my liberty to the fullest. I reassured myself that life since high school graduation had been an adventure, that even the low moments had been the source of valuable lessons about myself and my ability to recover from setbacks and self-inflicted wounds. If unwed teenage motherhood, unemployment, and brushes with career failure had not taken me down, why should I fear a year in which I would be free to meditate, soul search, and plan the next stage of my life bathed in sunshine and surrounded by the natural wonder of California?

In a week or two, I noticed that I had relaxed into the blessing that I had been given. Alvin, who is not a worrier by nature, had slid right into the flow of being a carefree midlife scholar. Together, we would often stop to glory in the sight of the golden hills that ringed the campus and the sun-washed Spanish arches and cool shadows of Stanford's buildings. We sipped coffee in the sidewalk cafés of downtown Palo Alto, dined from their organic food–laden chalkboard menus, and drank in the unfamiliar pleasure of being without jobs and without money worries at the same time. When not pedaling around on his bike, Alvin could drive his beloved BMW M3 on twisting, scenic roads. Instead of navigating rowdy Manhattan streets with their passive-aggressive pedestrians or the grinding commuter creep of the Long Island Expressway, his challenge was to keep his vehicle from zooming above eighty miles per hour.

For once there were enough hours in the day. Even with classes three days a week, free from the demands of tests and papers, life at Stanford left plenty of time for afternoon movies, day trips to surrounding towns, and excursions to nearby San Francisco, the place Ronald Reagan must have had in mind when he described that "shining city on a hill." In the Northern California sunlight, the buildings of San Francisco appeared like a shimmering white magical realm. At street level, the city was a bustling urban echo of home, an idealized mini–New York, complete with skyscrapers, harried businesspeople, and relaxed-looking bums who seemed right out of central casting. "It's a theme park for yuppies, where nothing significant has ever taken place," said Bill Schneider of CNN, a visitor to the fellowship who had once lived and worked in San Francisco. I couldn't argue, but after the do-or-die seriousness of Manhattan and the thrill ride of Motown, a kinder, gentler playground was very appealing.

The sight of the Golden Gate Bridge, its rust-colored magnificence splayed across the blue San Francisco Bay, filled me with emotion. I had sensed this beauty from my earliest days on the shores of a murky lake, and finally I was living it. During the fellowship, time itself took on an elongated, unfamiliar but welcome shape. The two-hour drive to Monterey and Carmel seemed like a reasonable jaunt for lunch, let alone being acceptable traveling distance to dazzle Alvin's visiting parents with the majesty of Big Sur and Nepenthe, a few miles farther south. Their elderly eyes were unclouded as they took it all in, hurtling along Route 1 clinging to the edge of North America. "Now Jim," my father-in-law said, using Alvin's family-only nickname as the road dipped and curved between voluptuous hills that towered over our heads, "you're planning to drive us out of here before dark, right?" Despite apprehension at the lack of streetlights, both of my in-laws were obviously excited by unfamiliar sights like the seal-covered rock outcroppings of Pebble Beach. Seeing it all through their eyes, and knowing that we had been able to give them an entirely new experience, I was as elated as when I first saw those extraordinary sights.

On New Year's Eve, we walked out of a mountaintop restaurant after dinner with our houseguest Ruth Ann, and were confronted by stars that appeared as big as low-hanging fruit on a backyard plum tree. "Oh, this is wonderful," she had exclaimed. I silently echoed her sentiment and pondered whether New York would ever be the same after a year in such awe-inspiring environs. For our entire time in the fellowship, my biggest worry was that we might become like the former fellow we had met at a local movie theater. She had simply been unable to return to normal life in the workaday world of journalism. I chose to make peace with that concern. *Life is good*, that wise voice within me whispered, quieting the part of me that was ungrateful enough to worry at such a moment. *Trust that you are always where you are supposed to be.*

One of the two requirements of the fellowship was attendance at a weekly seminar where the fellows and spouses conversed in an intimate setting with eminences such as Bob Woodward, Condoleezza Rice, former Secretary of Defense William Perry, Christopher Hitchens, Jill Tarter, the former director of the Center for SETI (Search for Extraterrestrial Intelligence) Research, Carl Djerassi, an enigmatic combination of chemist and screenwriter who invented the birth control pill, and other assorted geniuses and near-geniuses. Those enlightening weekly encounters were enough of an in-

232 W PRESSURE MAKES DIAMONDS

tellectual exercise for me. At close quarters, surrounded by the fellows, our impressive guests were unintimidating and accessible. Much like the conversations the Clinton ad team had had with our candidate, we were free to ask any questions we chose.

Bob Woodward might not have been fully prepared for what came at him. After fielding a few softball questions about his latest book on Bill Clinton, *The Choice,* and declining the one fellow's de rigueur request for the identity of Watergate whistle-blower "Deep Throat," Woodward seemed surprised by my question about a fifteen-year-old scandal: "How do you think an undistinguished reporter like Janet Cooke was able to hoodwink a prestigious newspaper like the *Washington Post?*" In the intimacy of the Knight Fellows Lounge, I was comfortable enough to ask for a horse's-mouth explanation of how a not-particularly-brilliant black woman without a strong reputation was able to walk into the fabled *Washington Post,* snag a job, ensnare world-class editors in a sticky net of untruth, and create a sensational journalistic scandal.

In 1981, Cooke won a Pulitzer Prize for what turned out to be the entirely fabricated story, titled "Jimmy's World," of an eight-year-old heroin addict. Top editors Ben Bradlee and Bob Woodward were revealed to have been duped not only by her made-up news account, but by her almost equally imaginary résumé, which included a nonexistent course of study at France's Sorbonne, among other things. Conversely, Janet Cooke's black colleagues, with whom she was not popular, were skeptical of her child-addict story from the beginning, and some encouraged Woodward to look deeper into Cooke's sources and reporting. Although Cooke dismissed their doubts as the product of jealousy, the paper was attempting to verify her story—something many felt should have been done before it was published—at the time she won the Pulitzer. After Cooke was unable to provide the names of "Jimmy's" parents and could not identify the building where they lived when driven around the neighborhood, the tent pole of her flimsy fabrication collapsed and she finally admitted to making up the entire story. The *Post* at last got around to checking her résumé and found it was padded with fictional academic and professional achievements. Far from having attended a prestigious French university, she could only answer haltingly when Bradlee spoke French to her. In the Knight Fellows Lounge that day, it was Bob Woodward himself feeling the heat.

"Well," he sighed, "I've thought about it a lot, and I'm still not sure." Savvy enough to know that a black woman who would bring up this incident likely had a hypothesis of her own, he asked, "What do you think?" There was zero chance I wouldn't swing at that pitch.

"I think when she presented herself—articulate, beautiful, well-dressed, and confident—she was so far out of your belief system that you were eager to think that only the Ivy League or the Sorbonne could create this black woman who could handle herself so well in front of you and Ben Bradlee. On the flip side, I think she used your low expectations to sell you a tale about an eight-year-old junkie and the scummy parents who fed his habit. The other black reporters immediately thought the story was fishy, and that makes me feel even more strongly that this is the case."

I didn't tell him that I had relied on similar assumptions to get my first job in advertising. The conversation wasn't about me, and personalizing the insight would have made it less impactful. It would, however, have let him in on something he might have found useful to know. Black Americans have spent hundreds of years trying to figure out how white people think; our survival has depended upon it. Janet Cooke wasn't all that wily, she just made it her business to understand important white folks, while important white folks had to create room in their belief systems for the mere existence of a person like her.

Woodward didn't deny my hypothesis. "We didn't ask the right questions," he said, "and we paid a price for that."

I wondered if he even knew which "right" questions had never crossed his mind. Leaving out Cooke's fib-filled résumé, her prize-winning story raised fundamental questions that would have been answered in a heartbeat by anyone who had ever seen the desperation of drug addiction up close. I imagined my friend Laverne reading Janet Cooke's story and dismissing it out of hand: *That's some bullshit right there. Hard as junkies chase dope, they don't be giving it away to nobody.* In fact, this had been one of the arguments of the more streetwise black reporters who had leaned on Woodward to check out the story. Then again, Bob Woodward probably never had a friend who was married to a born-to-die junkie.

"There's probably truth in what you're saying," he admitted, and I had the almost guilty feeling that I was only the latest black person to hit him with this conclusion. I wondered if those before me had been wary of winning the point but losing a job for the next smart black applicant to come Woodward's way.

Still, like a journalist at a high-level press conference, I couldn't resist a follow-up question: "How can you keep something like this from happening again?"

With that question, the whiff of accusation dissipated and Woodward seemed reenergized. "It's easy enough to be rigorous about checking out a résumé," he replied, "but I think there will never be another 'Jimmy's World' for me, because this story changed me. What Janet Cooke's story said was happening was no different than if someone had been holding a gun to the head of a little boy. If I had looked at this story as a human being first and a journalist second, the lies would have been uncovered right away. Some of the right questions that didn't get asked were, *Where is he, so we can send the police there right now? How can we save this eight-year-old child who is being injected with heroin by his parents?* I should have been worried about saving that kid, not getting the story. That's the lesson I took from this, and that's why I believe it could never happen to me again." Then Woodward looked at me directly and asked, "What do you think?"

I was thankful that forty-plus years of life had taken away the temptation to try and skewer him simply to show off in front of company. I told him the truth: "I think that was a really good, surprising answer, the kind that makes me think of you differently." I was glad to be able to let Woodward off the hook and still feel good about our exchange. I was also grateful to the Knight Fellowship and my talented husband for giving me the opportunity to ask questions of an important thought leader that might have a chance of shifting his paradigm when it comes to black people. I felt I had learned something real about him from his last answer. I guess if you go to Stanford, you're bound to be a little more educated when you leave, even in ways you don't expect.

The Knight Fellowship required that Alvin do no professional work during the school year, and he happily complied. This tickled the hell out of Daddy, who paraphrased it this way: "Now, Alvin, if we catch you working, we're gonna have to let you go."

PART FOUR

MAKING IT BIG, MAKING IT WORK, AND MAKING IT MATTER

CHAPTER 14

New York, Part III

As we descended from heaven back to Manhattan, I was hoping for a soft landing. After a year among the big-brain people, I was feeling smart enough to make a living off my talent and experience. My long-distance work for Motown had culminated with a public service campaign against teenage tobacco use. It featured superstar group Boyz II Men and was a collaboration involving the Columbia University School of Medicine and the Centers for Disease Control and Prevention. The campaign kicked off with a press conference at the offices of US Secretary of Health and Human Services Donna Shalala. She greeted the Motown crooners with a hip-hop fist pound that was covered by news outlets and entertainment TV shows nationwide. As the architect of a campaign that brought youth and music culture together with government and public health advocacy, I felt I could successfully market myself as a consultant.

Working on my own buoyed my confidence but brought back the economic insecurity of my youth. My consulting business took off right out of the gate. Clairol, a company I had worked with at Motown, enlisted me to introduce Textures & Tones, an entire product line created for women of color. Agency giant Young & Rubicam came to me for expertise on young African American male beer drinkers. They also hired me to assist in the search for an agency to handle the African American US Census account. My public health work led to assignments fighting the spread of teenage HIV infection. The Robert Wood Johnson Foundation invited me to be a "creative catalyst" at a Sundance Institute conference of scientists. I never lacked for work, but I could never quite get comfortable not knowing where my money would be coming from.

One day, after witnessing a creative presentation I made in Washington, DC to the Centers for Disease Control, the CEO of a major health-focused advertising company asked if I would change my flight and accompany him from DC back to New York. At the end of the trip, I had an offer to start an African American division of his company. The allure of another guaranteed six-figure salary was too compelling to turn down. Despite my post-Motown reservations about making another wrong choice, I took a top position in an executive role.

Cue the Gershwin music again. The view from my office on the executive floor of Nelson Communications, through a twelve-foot wall of windows, impressed even me. The variegated skyscrapers and glistening domes of Midtown Manhattan stretched east to the river and north to infinity, an immutable kingdom of money and power. I placed a framed photo of myself with President Clinton on the credenza behind me to remind myself that wherever I had come from, I belonged here now.

I needed all the reassurance I could get. Despite my warning to the CEO that I was a creative, not an entrepreneur, I was expected to solicit opportunities from within the various units of a billion-dollar enterprise. Nelson Communications was a collection of many independent companies, and there tended to be a competitive attitude even from those that could use African American expertise most. My magnificent office was also just around the corner from the company chairman, a pragmatic self-made multimillionaire who was keeping an eye on the company's experiment with me. Even the corporate ally who had introduced me to the CEO became exasperated when, accustomed to a brainstorming environment, I gave a prospective client an idea they could use without hiring us. As a businesswoman, I was clearly out of my element.

Just as I was about to become discouraged, imagination came to my rescue again and I sold a big idea. My multicity, satellite-downlinked World AIDS Day conference with controversial former Surgeon General Joycelyn Elders garnered a nice fee from a major pharmaceutical company. It also gave me a bit of daylight. I then created a promotional piece, *Black America: Living in an Unhealthy State,* to make the case for my area of expertise and, in an effort to give myself a base of operations, suggested that Nelson acquire an African American agency I had heard was in play.

Showing up with a buyer who had twenty million dollars to purchase a stake in UniWorld got Byron Lewis's attention. Byron's advisers were dead set against the deal. His trusted lawyer convinced him that selling to Nelson—a little-known billion-dollar enterprise—instead of a major holding company would be an act of folly. The biggest result of our bid to buy the agency was that Nelson's advances brought me back into Byron's orbit. He began a campaign to get me back to UniWorld. He wooed me with a free trip to his newest endeavor, the Acapulco Black Film Festival. In Mexico he introduced me to celebrity guests and potential advertising spokespeople like Robert Townsend, Isaac Hayes, and TV Judge Greg Mathis, and plied me with the message that he knew had the best chance of working: "Come to UniWorld and you'll spend your days working on Pepsi, Burger King, and Ford, not hypertension, heart disease, and HIV."

Over breakfast with Alvin on the terrace of a luxury beach hotel, as the tropical breeze rustled palm trees overhead, I contemplated returning to my comfort zone: the place of my greatest accomplishments and most encouraging prospects for the future. Even though I had it on good authority that Byron's enthusiasm was intensified by a potential holding company partner's demand for a different and more well-known creative leader, I was flattered enough to forgive him for not having tried to dissuade me from leaving for Motown in the first place. I realized that whatever I might achieve at the Nelson agency would never be as satisfying as working among my own people and showing the ad world what a black-led company could do. There is success, and there is success on one's own terms. In that moment, I knew it was time to come back home.

UniWorld offered me a good deal, and my aggressive lady lawyers turned it into a great one. When I had left UniWorld for Motown, a solid contract had been the insurance I insisted I must have in order to leave advertising and take the new job. In the music industry, contracts are common and it was no problem. In advertising, mostly because of the compensation they provide when employees are let go despite good performance, contracts are not as prevalent. When I landed the Clinton campaign, Byron Lewis had referred to me as "our superstar." I'm not sure I ever allowed myself to fully believe him, but after having seen how some of my colleagues' stints at UniWorld ended, in contrast to my experience at Motown, I decided I would never take another position without a contract, a resolution I have never regretted.

On the day I signed my UniWorld contract, I gave notice to the CEO of Nelson. He seemed both disappointed and relieved. Six months wasn't long enough to know how things would have turned out, but it was long enough to tell that it wouldn't have been easy. He wished me well and we both walked away with clear consciences.

CHAPTER 15

On Top of the (Uni)World

The 1990s movie *Boomerang* was loosely based on Uni-World, and movie star Halle Berry was playing me. Her fabulous new job at the end of the film, giving critiques to creatives waiting for approval, is a spot-on slice of my gig as UniWorld creative chief. Taking the reins, I was grateful that I was equipped with ten years of insight about the potential pitfalls of dealing with Byron's troops and how to navigate the agency's complex dynamics. I knew, for one thing, that Byron almost always recruited staffers from general market agencies as potential saviors who could teach black employees how a "real" agency should do things. Ironically, the person who knew least about the day-to-day workings of general market agencies was visionary entrepreneur Byron Lewis himself.

Byron, a shrewd businessman, had seen the need for African American agencies and founded one without ever having spent a day in traditional advertising. It was a challenge to cope with his employees' disillusionment when they realized that his little black enterprise—with its deeply ingrained notions about authority and respect—was as likely to change them as they were to overhaul it. His recruits were almost always unprepared for the fact that clients expected general market quality for a fraction of the budget. It was also vital to know firsthand that, given a semblance of the structure where they had learned their craft, and the opportunity to rise as high as their abilities would take them, these former general marketers probably wouldn't leave the bosom of black advertising. Most of the people looked like them, their intelligence was a given, and here, they would find a comfort that few of us had ever known in the American workplace. One feature that had made Motown so attractive was that it offered a rare opportunity to move up while still working in an overwhelmingly black setting. In the first departmental meeting I convened as creative chief of UniWorld, I danced a delicate boogie between the role of boss with years of experience, not only in the business sector but also at UniWorld, and that of sympathetic fellow player in Byron Lewis's troupe. *I am not here to fix you, but I am here to lead you*, was my message. Although I soon replaced my very formal male temporary assistant with a laid-back and savvy young woman from Motown, one of the writers told me that the first time he heard that stentorian, "Ms. Graves's office, how may I direct your call?" he took it as a signal that there was a new sheriff in town. At the same time, there were still people in the department who were happy to see me return and reassured their nervous colleagues that talented creatives had nothing to fear from me.

I had come back to a bigger and better UniWorld. The booming Clinton economy had been good to the company and its clients. My immediate predecessor, a better producer than creative director, had improved the production values of the creative product. I promised myself and Byron to build on the gains he had brought to the agency reel.

My reputation as a tough cookie when it came to dealing with account management had the account staff concerned and chattering among themselves. Miss Gwen, an audacious, fast-talking, and successful account supervisor who ran the Pepsi and Burger King businesses, came straight to my office, five-inch stilettos clicking and bracelets jangling, to offer me a brightly manicured handshake and an open mind. I assured her that the only account people who had problems with me were the ones who didn't do their jobs or made unreasonable demands of the creative team. Proactive, capable account managers had found me a cooperative partner, and together, we had achieved great successes. "Well," Miss Gwen quipped, flipping her Chaka Khan–worthy hair weave with her half-inch nails, "I definitely handle my business, and good creative gets me excited, so I don't see us having a problem." That was an understatement. With the help of our client, an African American woman who had actually been referred to Pepsi by me, our team bombarded the cola giant with good ideas and attracted the attention of consumers, the entertainment industry, and the media. I was sorry when Miss Gwen eventually left to start her own business in Virginia, but our personal friendship continues on to this day.

On the agency's important Ford account, a new female executive at the automobile giant gave us an opportunity we hadn't had since Burger King offered us a fair shot at creating a general market campaign. Just before I'd returned to the agency, the UniWorld team came up with a compelling print campaign, *Life in Focus*, for an important new vehicle launch. This futuristically illustrated effort, carrying headlines like, *Life Without Focus Is Just Existence*, looked like what Leonardo da Vinci would be drawing if he were working in 1999. This strong effort far outshined a particularly weak presentation from Ford's general market agency. Based purely on merit, as rarely happened in those days, Ford gave the nod to the UniWorld work to be the national print advertising campaign for

Ford Focus. Along with *Velvet Rope*, a simple, insightful, and gorgeously shot commercial aimed at the elusive, bling-friendly "hip-hop generation," these ads comprised a complete campaign that won the respect of our new contact at Ford. As I came back to UniWorld, this bonanza of trust fell into my lap, albeit with the weight of a boxing gym medicine ball.

"Production-wise, we can't slip back," Byron Lewis said to me as I retook the creative reins. Though the admonition stung just a little, I knew where he was coming from. During my first ten years with the agency, our television efforts, some of which were wildly successful, had included a few clunkers and near misses that were mostly the result of trying to execute ideas that were too big for our budgets. Technically, this was more the responsibility of the producers, but filmmaking is a collaborative exercise, and when the end result is less than excellent, the blame deserves to be spread across the entire creative team. I took Byron's remark to heart, and vowed to be vigilant in making sure that the work created on my watch was up to the level that had now been established. Before long, that resolve was put to the test.

The new Ford contact was an innovative woman who didn't seem to have received the "separate and unequal" memo when it came to allocating opportunities and resources to her agencies. When the Focus introduction was expanded to include sponsorship of short independent films for viewing on the Internet, she offered UniWorld the opportunity to produce one targeted at the American audience. The assignment came with very cool parameters: serving as executive producer, UniWorld would choose the director with the best idea for a short film that organically included the Ford Focus, manage the budget, and generally shepherd the project from concept to finished product. For me, and for UniWorld

producer and business affairs director Dana Offenbach, this
was a dream assignment. During my filmmaking studies at
New York University, I had written and coproduced a comedy
about AIDS testing, *Positive Thinking,* and for the Advertising
Club of New York, I had written and produced a short film on
diversity, *Mission Possible.* Dana was an experienced producer
of feature films who would later leave advertising to found her
own production company, CinemaStreet Pictures.

Taking the lead in Ford's forward-looking program and
providing an opportunity to a deserving black filmmaker was
a rare plum. We devoted ourselves to our little production as
if an Oscar might be waiting at the end of the process. We selected a script created by director/writer team Rolando Hudson and Julie Atwell. Their story was a sweet little homage to
films like *Heaven Can Wait* and Chris Rock's *Down to Earth.*
An elderly woman (played by renowned black actress Mary
Alice), whose vintage Ford Mustang is a beloved reminder of
her late husband, passes away suddenly. Reincarnated in the
beautiful but unfamiliar body of a young woman, she finds
comfort and a sense of connection through the new Ford that
comes along with her second chance at life. The resulting
short film was charming and moving, with wide appeal. It was
a delight to read the comments on the Atom Films website
where it was shown, and to receive kudos from our client at
Ford.

No feedback was sweeter, though, than Byron Lewis's almost grudging approbation: "Well, that's really nice. I have
to admit, I wasn't in favor of taking this on. I didn't think we
could do it. Congratulations." His reaction was yet another
reminder that the deepest wounds of institutional discrimination and prejudice are the gouges to our self-confidence. In
this instance, I could only be grateful that Ford had had more

faith in our team than our leader, who had apparently looked on with trepidation from the sidelines as we took our big risks.

When we shot a Pepsi commercial with Wyclef Jean in Brazil, it felt as if UniWorld and I had stepped up to the major leagues. There were solid, practical reasons to take our shoot out of the country; just the ability to use local extras in the crowded beach scenes meant savings in the high five figures, which delighted the client. The exotic locale brought added credibility with the young, jet set–friendly Pepsi target. Our glamorous Rio de Janeiro location would also help assure our celebrity talent that this commercial—for the brand that had featured Michael Jackson and MC Hammer—would be a fitting showcase for his musical star power. Despite all that common sense, though, two weeks in Rio at the end of Carnival felt a lot like a fabulous vacation with a star and film crew to capture the highlights.

The agency team was outwardly cool and professional about the South American trip, but to the insider eye, the signs that this was no ordinary shoot were everywhere. The director of broadcast production personally covered the shoot, a rare occurrence, and the producer, head of business affairs, was also responsible for wrangling the superstar and his entourage. Fortunately, the Pepsi client demanded my presence, because there was no way I would have let the copywriter and art director—two talented but unpredictable young guys—go on such a high-stakes shoot accompanied by just the producers. The group creative director on the account was a mature team player who voluntarily stayed in New York to handle the radio and print aspects of the Wyclef Jean campaign. Miss Gwen had just left the agency and the new account supervisor, whom we would meet for the first time in Rio, had never met Wyclef and was an unknown quantity when it came to the schmoozing that might be required to deal with an unpredictable celebrity.

Right from the beginning, Wyclef Jean was mad cool to work with. The company that handled celebrity talent negotiations on behalf of Pepsi had arranged a meet-and-greet before our deal was signed. As we chatted with Wyclef and his collaborator Jerry "Wonda" Duplessis at New York's Hit Factory studio, the show business chops that I had almost unknowingly acquired at Motown helped the meeting start off smoothly. In the music industry, relationships are everything, so I brought along a UniWorld producer who had been Wyclef's product manager at a record label. "That's my mother right there," Wyclef said upon spotting her. Before we talked about our commercial, Wyclef showed us a clip of himself performing at a recent White House Christmas concert. As he told the story of how he had selected "The Little Drummer Boy" for his performance, I knew, even though he was in the power position, that some part of him couldn't help auditioning for us. The conversation flowed in that creative and musical vein until it logically arrived at the business at hand: our concept for Wyclef and Pepsi.

Wyclef Jean happening upon a party of drummers on Rio's Copacabana Beach, draining his Pepsi, then kicking the celebration to the next level—*The Joy of Pepsi*. What's not to like? Selecting his own Brazilian musicians and composing the music for the commercial? Even more enticing. A million dollars later, we had our star, and the creative collaboration got underway. Working with great musicians was a very fulfilling part of my job as creative director, and the sessions with Wyclef were right up there with collaborating with George Clinton, Oscar Brown Jr., jazz great Jon Hendricks, Busta Rhymes, and Herbie Hancock. One quality all these giants had in common was an unbridled appreciation for good music. Watching 'Clef bring our ideas to life, directing musicians, playing multiple instruments, and swaying in the groove of what was being created was a joy and a rare privilege. The soundtrack for our Brazilian TV spot was a perfect combination of drums, exotic percussion instruments, and Wyclef's guitar. Even in the missteps, though, there were lessons. An up-tempo radio track, with lyrics I had written, initially came out as an uncool mishmash that satisfied none of us, least of all Wyclef. After taking time to work on the music alone, Wyclef presented us with a beautiful ballad version that inspired love at first hearing. He never blamed himself or us for the unsatisfying track; he simply relied on solitude and his own talent to fix it. For me, it was a reminder that belief in oneself is the key to achieving the results we desire.

By almost any measure, a two-week shoot in Brazil is a desirable endeavor. Rio turned out to be a startling mix of tropical surroundings, racial diversity, wealth, poverty, and unanticipated human beauty. Even in the United States, I had never seen such racial variety. Although there were more or less Caucasian Brazilians at one end of the color spectrum, indigenous Brazilian/Indians in the center, and black African types at the other, the vast majority of people we saw were some form of mixture. Outrageous beauty ran across the entire range. Coupled with a local fixation on physical loveliness, that diversity of appearance made for a perpetual parade of human pulchritude. Here were shapely, skimpily dressed blondes whose sun-kissed complexions and facial features whispered, in varying degree, of Africa. On the same streets and beaches, deeply tanned brunettes dotted the landscape, their Latin beauty a counterpoint to their golden sisters. During Carnival, the colorfully clad splendor of Rio's black-skinned women spilled out of the ghetto-like favelas and was also on full display.

For the duration of the shoot, our crew members' heads constantly swiveled to follow the latest passing beauty. At night, most of our guys crowded the clubs only to find that the time and attention of the girls in those bars was mostly only available for a fee. Still, the word was out that our big American production was in town, and there was no shortage of lovely female hangers-on looking to strike up an acquaintance with our bedazzled crew. There was also no shortage of male eye candy for the members of the Pepsi team. From the casting sessions where we looked at dozens of great-looking guys, to the beaches and our legitimate excursions to the Capoeira martial arts groups that we cast for their special skills, we were bombarded with the muscular male gorgeousness of Rio de Janeiro.

On our location scout we also saw fantastic parks, gardens, and, on Corcovado Mountain, the imposing and familiar statue Christ the Redeemer towering over Rio with outstretched arms. Standing at the statue's base at twilight, gazing upward as clouds and birds drifted around the head of Jesus, was a transcendent experience. My thoughts pingponged from the magnificence of the sight to the heroic effort and pain of those who had hauled this hundred-foot behemoth up a steep mountain and lifted it to a standing position so that I might enjoy this moment. Like so many aspects of my time in Brazil, it was a juxtaposition of splendor and suffering that left me both awed and confused.

Just as rewarding as the feast Rio offered us was seeing the bounty our production brought to Rio. While shooting in Brazil created savings for our client, the daily fees we paid were a huge windfall to the performers and extras we hired. Many of them were dark-skinned—chosen for their resemblance to American blacks—and lived in the poverty-stricken favelas of the city, hidden from the view of tourists and casual observers. One player, a child percussionist featured in a scene with Wyclef Jean, probably supported his family for six months on the pay from his two days of work.

On the beach, our big production was impossible to ignore. To begin with, our director had rented and trucked in huge palm trees to create an oasis-like setting for our main shot. Periodically, the helicopters we had hired would sweep over the beach, capturing aerial footage at different times of day. On the ground were white tents erected to shield us from the blazing sun as we watched the progress of the shoot on video monitors. Each morning, Wyclef and his entourage, accompanied by rap music blasting from an ever-present boom box, would make their way to our "video village." In the lead was Wyclef's bodyguard, an enormous man known as "Beast." Even in temperatures nearing 100 degrees, Beast wore a heavy, oversized military jacket, presumably concealing instruments of protection for his client, but since we observed a tacit *don't ask, don't tell* policy on the subject, that is pure speculation. Protected by his team, Wyclef joked with the agency personnel, did cartwheels and handstands with the Capoeira crew, conversed with the ever-present female members of his party, and delivered a joyful on-camera presence to every scene.

As we crossed shot after shot off the list of scenes to be covered, we all began to relax into the rare experience of this work. During a break, one of the young Brazilian brothers we had recruited from the favelas sat down next to me. "I have a dream," he said quietly but with great intensity, "that someday I will go to Brooklyn." It didn't seem like so much to ask. I wished I were in a position to make his fantasy come true.

For now, though, he would have to settle for the excitement, celebrity, and cash that *The Joy of Pepsi* had delivered to his doorstep.

Pepsi wasn't the only account on a roll. Early in this second stint at UniWorld, I realized that along the way I had actually mastered the job of creative chief. Leading a team of talented creative directors, I helped guide UniWorld to new creative elevations. My natural curiosity about consumers' attitudes and motivations tended to make UniWorld's work more strategically driven and robust than some of our multicultural counterparts. My belief in the power of celebrities to telegraph a brand's message—what I once heard advertising guru Phil Dusenberry call "the grandeur of scale"—resulted in highly visible campaigns. Cultivating relationships and negotiating deals, we brought the hottest celebrities of the day to UniWorld commercials, from Busta Rhymes and Wyclef Jean to Bernie Mac, Shaq, Steve Harvey, and Johnnie Cochran. *Mad Men* creative director Don Draper described celebrity ads as a crutch. As usual, this fictional observation had little to do with African Americans. Not only do we generally love seeing our heroes celebrated, black Americans appreciate the clarity that a known figure can confer. When Busta Rhymes, fueled by Mountain Dew, rolled his monster truck over a traffic jam to get to his goal, young black boys took away a message about energy and drive that no extreme sports vignette could match. Likewise, when Busta's billboard image towered over Times Square for Mountain Dew, I wasn't the only African American who felt empowered by his presence at the crossroads of the world. Silver-haired R&B star Sisqó refueled a Pepsi party in outer space and *The Joy of Pepsi* went stratospheric. Marlon Wayans's goofy comic excess removed the stigma from young black guys calling friends and family

collect. Laila Ali, a tough but tenderhearted beauty, personi-
fied the next generation of the best-selling Ford Explorer as
still "ready to go the distance." From Erykah Badu to Magic
Johnson to Bernie Mac to Wyclef Jean celebrating *The Joy of
Pepsi* on a Brazilian beach, our splashy campaigns racked up
successes and attracted new business. With that kind of impact, it was only a matter of time before some general agency
set out to obliterate us, but we were used to that. One big
blow, however, just couldn't have been predicted.

It must have been a slow news day at Fox TV. With little else
to rouse the rabble that make up his audience, professional
conservative Bill O'Reilly's staff seemed to have stumbled
across the *New York Times* advertising column about our new
TV campaign featuring the rapper Ludacris. Even O'Reilly
admitted there was nothing offensive about our ad or its spe-
cially written PG lyrics. Ours was a playful spot about the
search for a hard-to-locate party where Ludacris was rock-
ing the microphone. Instead, O'Reilly teed off on Pepsi's af-
filiation with the rapper himself, whose music was as casually
profane and misogynistic as hip-hop culture itself. As the media glommed on to O'Reilly's threat to make a daily call for
a boycott of Pepsi, the client crumpled like an empty plastic
soda bottle. They would later pay for this response when high-
profile critics like Russell Simmons pointed out the hypocrisy
of Pepsi running away from Ludacris while they retained their
contract with decrepit, profane, decadent Ozzy Osbourne and
his whole dysfunctional family. Eventually, O'Reilly moved on
and Pepsi made a generous donation to the Ludacris Foundation, but it was all too late for UniWorld. What should have
been a big success for the agency had become an embarrassing
takedown.

* * *

When Byron sold a 49 percent interest to giant holding company WPP, the move gave us some protection in the agency world and triggered a fat bonus for me. Alvin and I celebrated that windfall and a stock bonus of his own by hosting a two-week family vacation at an elegant Jamaican villa. As the lady of the house, with a staff of three and a driver, I gloried in sharing our blessings with my mother, my in-laws, my best friend, and my son's family. Sitting alone on the veranda of a Caribbean mansion, looking past the lush hibiscus, pool, and cabanas to the moonlit ocean, my forty-something self embraced the eight-year-old I had been. "Look where we are," I whispered in her ear. "The Crystal Lake side can't hold a candle to this." I could almost feel her hugging me back. Again, my reality had outrun my dreams. Life was unbelievably good.

CHAPTER 16

Owning My Life

Building a career, I had spent so much of my life trying to "go places" and "get somewhere" that I hadn't just aspired to a different future, I aspired to a different past. Loving the place I was trying to leave required an act of will, one I could not muster until well into adulthood at a "safe" distance from Mud Lake. Because I was too afraid of being exposed to lie outright, I became adept at simply acting like someone who came from more prosperous circumstances than I did.

In my idealized version of where I came from, the players would remain the same, but the script would be rewritten. My father would have been better educated, would have been a kind and generous man who provided an environment like Bloomfield Hills for his children, even if he was divorced from my mother. Mama would only have required only a little tweaking, to make her more dissatisfied with anything less than deluxe for her kids. My stepfather, Daddy, would have completely embraced the concept of upward mobility and insisted on a nicer street on which to park his Cadillac. My great-grandparents would pass muster as they were, solid citizens with a house, sumptuous draperies, crystal, china, and a collection of the great books of the world. My grandfather would never have seen the inside of a prison, and my brother Gary would have used his industrial management degree to manage industry, instead of doing time for murder. My son would have been fathered by my husband, the love of my life, and would have done me the favor of being born ten years later than he was, thus sparing me the explanations that come with having a ten-year-old at the tender age of twenty-six. Though I never put my idealized background into words, I lived as its product. I spoke like the daughter of a wealthier man. I favored the dancing school, piano lessons, and sleep-away-camp truths of my childhood, and mostly left out the occasional ghetto stabbings and run-of-the-mill bitch fights that had been facts of life in the projects.

I share with Maya Angelou and Oprah Winfrey, women who greatly inspire me, humble beginnings, the lopsided legacy of the missing-parent home, teenage pregnancy, and the distinction of not conforming to the popular notion of what someone from those circumstances should achieve. All of us had to find our way to personal authenticity. Oprah revealed the seamier details of her early life only after she was famous. As a young woman, Maya Angelou adopted an exotic name, and for a time, a silly accent. She married interracially, then internationally, early moves that blurred her connection to the cotton fields of Stamps, Arkansas. For many years after scary Laverne advised me, I practiced a version of her rough-hewn wisdom, telling everyone enough to banish curiosity about my life.

While I lived in Boston, my friend Karen's husband, working on a project, once spent a week in Pontiac. I thought, correctly, that he might appreciate having the name of another guy to look up while in town—particularly another Jewish person. I gave him the name and number of Stuart, a bright, slightly eccentric old friend of mine. Sure enough, they hooked up for dinner and conversation. What I never consciously intended was that their evening should include a tour of Seward Street and its environs that had seen better days. "So, Eric wasn't too impressed with your parents' neighborhood," my girlfriend indelicately shared after he returned home. Met with silence from me, she added, "He said, *I absolutely cannot picture that sophisticated woman that I know coming from this neighborhood.*"

Though she might have meant that part as some sort of compliment, I was thankful that we were speaking by telephone so she could not see my face. I cringed to picture her husband cruising past my parents' house, judging it, them, and me, trying to reconcile the person he thought he knew with his ideas about neighborhoods like theirs.

"Well," I bristled defensively, "there's nothing for him to be impressed by. It's a working-class neighborhood in a factory town."

She sensed that this was a topic not to be discussed between us, and it never came up again. In my heart, though, I am sure there was conversation with mutual Boston acquaintances about where I came from and what it said about me. After that incident, I slammed shut any door that might bring the East Coast to my Midwest doorstep. Today, decades removed, it is clear to me that I sent Eric to that street—accompanied by a friend who would inevitably reveal things I had chosen not to share—out of some need to be seen whole, to be appreciated for where and what I come from, what I have come through, and who I genuinely am. That moment of clarity, however, only came after a long and murky interval.

As soon as I arrived on the New York advertising scene, white colleagues had assumed that I must be the daughter or niece of Earl G. Graves, wealthy publisher of *Black Enterprise* magazine. I am proud that I never allowed anyone to linger under that impression, though it might have done me some illegitimate good. Still, I was quite pleased that the image I had spent my youth acquiring had given me the sheen I had hoped for. "No," I would reply, "I'm one of the Michigan Graves," as if they might also have heard of that branch of the family. In truth, my father was a big fish in a very small pond. He accumulated a respectable fortune for a man of his education and time. My maternal great-grandmother operated a Pontiac beauty shop, and Banks, Alabama, the rural farm town where my great-grandfather's family founded the local church and own property to this day, bears their name. My family has always been well-dressed, well-spoken, and generally well-thought-of. Still, in New York, the land of black millionaires and even billionaires, I had showcased my people like a beloved pair of well-worn but spit-shined boots: looking their best, with the scuffs buffed out. New York is a tough place to become somebody, and in the land of fake-it-till-you-make-it, allowing people some of their self-invented presumptions about my origins didn't seem like such a big deal.

One night, listening to the daughter of billionaire Reginald Lewis speaking the impeccably accented French a European boarding school education provides, I felt the gulf between a rich girl's childhood and the cracked concrete and crabgrass surroundings where I had dreamed up a life. Yet, it was also the instant in which I realized that, like the character Regine in the black sitcom *Living Single*, I am everything I pretend to be. There we were, in the same room, the girl who was born rich and the woman who had struggled to affluence, nibbling the same canapés. The author of the book about her father that we were celebrating was a close personal friend of mine.

Via several other channels, we were one degree of separation apart. And though a linguist could easily discern the middle-class origins of my public school French, I could converse with her in a language other than our native tongue. As humans, as females, as African Americans, we had commonalities no bank balance could erase. That revelation marked the emergence of a new authenticity. I started to publicly become myself. With that self-acceptance came a new level of relevance and impact in the advertising arena.

When it mattered, I began to tell surprising truths. In order to speak with credibility about an important issue, I shared in a meeting of the Advertising Council of America that I had been a teenage parent. My creative colleagues at the Partnership for a Drug-Free America now know of my son's struggle with drugs for the same reason. Disclosing those things was not a hard choice.

When I stopped protecting an inauthentic image, I suspect my peers wondered why I would reveal such personal information. My colleague, advertising star and author Mary Lou Quinlan, inscribed my copy of her book *What She's Not Telling You*, "To Valerie, who always tells her whole truth." What she may not have realized was that telling those truths didn't diminish me in any way that I cared about. The president of one of these prestigious organizations once described me as "our conscience." Another acquaintance brought me onto Senator Bill Bradley's primary campaign for president, saying that I represented a unique point of view. Having met the challenges of unwed teenage parenthood and my son's drug addiction, there was value in showing my colleagues that social problems not only affect some invisible "them," but that survivors might be sitting just across the conference table or in the next seat.

Living authentically has sometimes been uncomfortable. It has meant admitting to myself that I envy some of the "Jack and Jill" aspects of the childhood I did not have, and finally just getting the fuck over it. For one, I was not a member of Jack and Jill of America itself, an upper-middle-class organization whose alumni find instant kinship in their status as sons and daughters of the doctors, lawyers, and professionals of the African American community. Observing from the edges of their chatty reunions, I am reminded of long-ago days when I wished my mother would use her looks to snag a wealthy husband who would remove us from the projects and make me a once-removed Cinderella in a castle, or at least a single-family brick house. I may always feel like an outsider on Martha's Vineyard, where Barack and Michelle vacation, and many of my friends "summered" as kids. I do not ski because I hate cold weather and find the lack of oxygen at high altitudes suffocating, but I wish I were letting languish the skiing skills of Earl Graves's resort-raised children. I still feel a pang when I drive past a certain attractive brick colonial in a Pontiac subdivision. It was new when Daddy decided it was too rich for his blood. I wish the used piano, clarinet, and flute that my mother sacrificed to buy had come into our lives shiny and new. Past age fifty, the eight-year-old in me still longed for the top-of-the-line Betty Crocker Junior Baking Kit and the deluxe sixty-four-piece Crayolas that included silver, gold, and the strangely foreign pink-orange color that was labeled *Flesh*. My beloved husband long ago bought me a deluxe set of crayons as a tender joke. Otherwise, the lack of those longed-for trappings has become, like the absence of my grandmothers who died before I was born, just something about my life that couldn't be helped.

For all I know, every Jack and Jill-er my age secretly

wishes to have been in the Boule, an even more exclusive group. Their hip-hop offspring may long for the "street cred" a ghetto upbringing confers on a new generation. The secret of my comfort is now being grateful for the truths of my life. My father made money without a good education. My beautiful mother had the integrity to marry for love, not money. My appreciation for music is no less real because my flute case was scratched and our piano old and situated in the kitchen. Most importantly, now having acquired some accoutrements of the good life, I know that an impressive home, foreign vacations, and a Mercedes-Benz are lovely to have, but do not define me at all. "Some gets hair, some gets color," my friend Ruth Ann's grandmother told her when she lamented not having been given her cousin's long locks. Some also gets talent, happiness, and dreams come true, I have learned. I wouldn't trade my life for anyone's.

Like Maya and Oprah, I am from that unexplored place just the other side of the tracks: close enough to the good life for the lucky and determined to cross over, yet far enough away for any of us to be sucked into struggle and underachievement by the insidious pull of invisibility. At last I have made peace with that. Now that I have stopped wishing those circumstances out of existence, if I'm lucky, my hometown will stop physically disappearing before my eyes.

Last Thanksgiving, I posted on Facebook a video of our family gathering, shot in my mom's cozy, attractive little house—still the best on its tired block. I made the video for out-of-town relatives, but it could be viewed by anyone who visited my page. Looking at it myself, I realized that Mama's ability to unpretentiously brighten her own corner of the world, and to be happy with what she has, is a quality to be admired. I thanked the universe for giving me the good sense to stop obscuring my roots. They teach me to remember who I am, no matter where I am, and that the only limitations in life are those we place on ourselves.

As my authentic self, I have walked with a president, conversed with Henry Kissinger, given Bob Woodward my opinion of why Janet Cooke was able to hoodwink him and Ben Bradlee, and dared to differ with Jesse Jackson when I did not agree. At those moments, no one knew whether I came from Crystal Lake, Mud Lake, or Mars, but the memories are more precious to me because they belong to a girl from the projects.

My well-dressed, articulate UniWorld colleagues and I were sometimes told by overly familiar clients, "But come on now, you guys aren't really black," because we had equipped ourselves to succeed in the world of business. We no longer squared up with their notions of what black people could achieve. What they saw in our shiny corporate armor was not our true makeup or backgrounds, but a reflection of themselves.

"Well," an audacious colleague once answered for us all, "maybe I'm not really black, but for one brief and shining moment, I used to be."

CHAPTER 17

9/11 and Other Acts of Terrorism . . .

Byron Lewis saw the second plane hit the Twin Towers from the wraparound windows of his Soho office. Panicked UniWorld staff stood weeping in his corner suite as what were unmistakably bodies began to fall from the flaming structures less than a mile away. UniWorld workers abandoned the office and began trudging home, not knowing whether bombs would fall or planes would strafe them before they got there.

While terror and dread invaded my coworkers' lives, I sat helplessly watching from a cruise ship anchored off the bright blue waters around St. Thomas. It had been more than a year since our Jamaican vacation, and I had been inexplicably frantic for a getaway. I had scoured last-minute deals and come up with a cruise to Puerto Rico, St. Thomas, St. Maarten, and the Bahamas at a price not even Alvin could resist. After an exercise walk around the deck, we turned on the TV in our cabin and saw the news that we could not at first comprehend.

Returning to the city, I found it eerily quiet without its usual migrating throngs of visitors, and soberly communal in its new vulnerability and loss. As New York's much-boasted-about confidence and the sense of safety we had taken for granted lay buried in a smoldering pile of death, I wondered what would become of us in the postattack era.

The 9/11 attacks took a toll on the economy and client budgets and UniWorld quickly began to feel the squeeze. Whenever budgets get tight, multicultural dollars are the first to be cut. We lost the account of a major bank in a cost-cutting holding company consolidation. A series of small account losses led to layoffs at the agency, and then came the biggest hurt: we lost the Pepsi account, partly because of the surprise attack by Bill O'Reilly, partly because an otherwise talented art director/writer team idiotically placed the coded marijuana message 4:20 in one of our print headlines, and partly because of the machinations of a UniWorld senior VP I'll call Don Barzini. Like *The Godfather* character whose behind-the-scenes maneuverings nearly took out an inattentive Vito Corleone, this executive was a would-be back-channel career assassin. Fortunately, like Don Corleone, my career turned out to be hard to kill.

Barzini, a Texan, actually reminded me of my father in the oversized way he wielded power in a tiny kingdom. He was often seen shooting his cuffs, which were secured by gaudy solid-gold cuff links, after scoring some small victory over a weak subordinate. As I spent more time around him, he struck me as a man who would have preferred it if women executives would disappear from the workplace. Once, when he was moved to a large corner office, his stash of downloaded porn was rumored to have been so big it had to be disposed of away from the premises. Though I pretty much ignored his shady presence, I had to laugh when one of the copywriters did a killer impersonation. This guy shot his make-believe cuffs, adjusted his imaginary cuff links, then growled, capturing the essence of Barzini, "Pimpin' ain't easy . . ."

The rise of Barzini was the beginning of a treacherous end for me at UniWorld. A genius at marketing promotions, Barzini had hired a staff of promotions people who were unskilled at brand account management but loyal to him. I convinced Byron Lewis, who needed time off to deal with a health problem, to bring back Tiny, an agency guy, as a president who could make up for Barzini's lack of account management skills. I also hoped that Tiny could coax Byron toward the realization that UniWorld needed to envision what its role would be in the majority-minority country that America was rapidly becoming.

With that move, I outsmarted myself. Like President George Herbert Walker Bush, Tiny had a problem with "the vision thing." His return to the agency was more notable for the return of his big ego than for the reemergence of success. While I wasn't looking, Barzini, who had long since warned me, "I'm getting tired of you criticizing my people," convinced Tiny that I, not his staff, was UniWorld's problem. In his scheme, with me gone, he and Tiny could rule UniWorld, with Barzini set up in an out-of-town satellite office to service the agency's largest client.

When my contract expired, it was not extended, despite the fact that UniWorld's award-winning creative department was its most successful component and that Tiny owed his very job to me. After more than twenty years in advertising, I had finally encountered—in the form of a glowing letter that praised my accomplishments but ended my tenure—the cutthroat business I had thought existed only in cheap novels.

I spent a year meditating on why I had attracted these experiences into my life. Financially, I was not hurt; my airtight contract guaranteed that I would be handsomely compensated if my job ever ended without cause. The year I had to stay out of the industry was like a paid vacation. The leaders of UniWorld's holding company partner, while it was their policy not to interfere, promised to assist in my job search when my noncompete year was up. Spiritually, I didn't waste much time thinking about the putative villains in my story. I had to accept that my passionate criticism had made me complicit in the treachery. I had come to deeply believe that we are the cocreators of our experience, and I spent many hours looking inward to see why I had attracted this one. As usual, it wasn't long before the universe gave me a shiny new answer.

CHAPTER 18

Life as a Vigilante: Coming Back Smaller and Better

As soon as my year off ended, another satisfying career interlude began. A former UniWorld colleague, whom I'll call the Dear Leader, was CEO of the agency that created the historic Oprah Car Giveaway. Oprah's famous, "You get a car, and you get a car, and you get a car . . ." will echo in advertising's halls for decades to come. I called to congratulate this guy on what may be the splashiest single achievement of a multicultural agency. My call led to a visit, an extended freelance situation, and ultimately, a new job as creative chief officer of Vigilante, a hot young specialty shop with a kick-ass reel. Vigilante had been founded in the nineties as an experiment in big agency ownership of an urban-targeted shop. Like the parents of an alienated teenager who lives in the family basement surrounded by rebel artwork, loud music blasting behind a *Keep Out* sign on the door, Vigilante's parent company, the Leo Burnett agency, basically paid a lot of our bills and left our fledgling shop alone to find itself. One year after leaving UniWorld, I miraculously found myself working for the same salary in a smaller but much more visionary agency, with an inspired strategic planner, capable

account supervisor, and a staff of creatives I knew from Uni-
World. My corner office on Madison Avenue had a breathtak-
ing two-state river view, and the rest of our small, close-knit
staff was ensconced in smaller quarters with equally inspiring
vistas. The Dear Leader was a brilliant guy and in some ways
an easy boss. He also had his share of foibles.

Having worked with the Dear Leader at UniWorld, I
knew that he was prone to drop names, exaggerate accomplishments, and be evasive when the simple truth might do.
The Dear Leader was also wildly creative, beyond impressive
in initial client meetings, amusing to be around, and a not
half-bad musician. My stint at UniWorld had taught me to
focus on the positive, do my own job, and let the CEO handle
his.

For a couple of years, we had a terrific run. Our first campaign, featuring, of all people, rapper Ludacris, created a connection between the hip-hop audience and a tough-to-sell car
brand, Pontiac. Our gifted art director, whom I had imported
from Detroit, masterfully married special effects with the urban authenticity of Ludacris to create the commercial. Our
code-cracking spot for the Pontiac Solstice—*Two Miles an
Hour So Everybody Sees You*—was written up in everywhere
from *Billboard* magazine to *USA Today*. That whole affair felt
like a godsent vindication of the hurtful O'Reilly debacle.

As usual, the advertising trades ignored us, but the Buick
group at General Motors did not. They invited us to try and
connect them with a young black target. Our minicampaign,
Drive Recognizes Drive, was hard to ignore in our test market,
Atlanta. A hip young black male model was its face, and time-
lessly cool Isaac Hayes its radio voice. With only a million
dollars and the gasoline in our veins, we created a strategy and
campaign that evoked the heyday of a quality brand. When

an Atlanta Buick dealer donated the side of a building that
he owned, our handsome young face of Buick became a giant
presence that was visible from the freeway as affluent black
Atlanta cruised by. The *Wall Street Journal* ran an article about
Buick's bold young campaign. Our client, a smart and ambitious Asian woman, made Vigilante a valued resource on her
team. After our Atlanta success, she insisted we be included
in the development of the campaign for the new Buick Enclave. Enclave, a sculpted, luxuriously appointed SUV, was
the great hope to make Buick a relevant brand for the future.

Our Vigilante team quickly found a way to take the *ick*
out of *Buick*. Art director Vincent St. Vincent discovered that
the lead interior designer for the Enclave was a handsome African American man named Michael Burton. We Vigilantes
knew that a presentation featuring a real black executive with
impeccable taste would resonate more deeply with African
Americans than a celebrity or a hit tune. Vigilante collabora-
tively developed a whole campaign around this man. I wrote
the script, and art director Paul Osen suggested the anthem
"Feeling Good," made famous by Nina Simone, as the track.
I identified soulful singer Oleta Adams to cover the song, and
our agency producer steered the project through tough music negotiations and a joint production with general market
agency McCann Erickson. In testing, our commercial demol-
ished research records for changing a brand's image to the
black audience.

The *New York Times* labeled Enclave's good-looking designer "the Buick seducer." Michael Burton's handsome presence was felt in St. Vincent's bold print spreads that ran in
publications from *Ebony* to golfing and lifestyle magazines. Our
spot ran on prime network programs like *60 Minutes* and made
almost incessant appearances on design-centered networks

like HGTV. In an advertising competition for work from small agencies, our Enclave ads won seven awards. The campaign shot a shockwave through Ford's black agency—UniWorld—and inspired an obvious homage commercial from Toyota. During the National Association of Black Journalists' convention in Las Vegas, Buick hosted a fabulous Enclave party at the Bellagio Hotel. As the fountains outside splashed over a colorful bank of lights, a mostly black crowd of successful professionals partied, radio superstar Tom Joyner hosted, and Oleta Adams serenaded us with a song that seemed especially apropos, "Get Here." As I watched national TV commentator Gwen Ifill tearing up the dance floor, it seemed like my own personal party. I had the presence of mind to note how the universe brought together so many disparate elements to manifest my joy. It's a good thing I had that moment to hold onto. Very soon, it was clear that party time was over.

The general market guys hunkered down and determined that our understudy agency would never again capture the leading role. I guess from their viewpoint, they were footing the bill for our glory—though as our parent company, they could just as easily have laid some public claim to it. To be fair, the Dear Leader left us vulnerable. He was never effective at attracting the new business that would enable Vigilante to pay its own way. He had tried to emulate Byron Lewis's success at acquiring new business through relationships, rather than pitches, but he lacked Byron's longtime connections to black America. We also did not win the one or two pitches a year for which I led the creative effort. Sometimes, we just seemed snakebitten. Our hot campaign for the New Jersey (now Brooklyn) Nets was well liked but doomed because of part-owner Jay-Z's stake in a competing agency. An awesome global update for Heineken was only used to prod their general agency to do a better job. A fantastic deal we struck to make Beyoncé a spokeswoman for a hot Pontiac hardtop convertible was undone by a GM exec who wanted her for a smaller project, though he never closed that deal. With our abysmal new business record, the endemic antagonism of general market agencies to our successes, and a failed, interminable bid by the Dear Leader to purchase Vigilante, the handwriting was all over the wall.

Honoring the terms of my enviable contract at all costs, I hung in through Vigilante's painful slide into nonexistence. In May of 2010, the doors of the New York agency were closed.

Still, even the end of Vigilante didn't represent complete failure. Our last campaign, for the Partnership for a Drug-Free America, was favorably written about, praised by the federal government, and widely run on youth-focused networks like MTV. The centerpiece was a commercial in which a young black man has his lunch check picked up by a diner owner in validation of his choice to "hit the books" rather than join his buddies who are about to "go get twisted." That spot is not only a source of personal satisfaction, it is one of those that friends, family, and acquaintances remember as sticking out amid the visual clutter of television. The simple words, "Oh yeah, I saw that one. I LIKE that commercial!" are a healing balm to the sting of losing an agency that I loved.

I've always been proud that we exited with a bang.

CHAPTER 19

Puttin' My Foot in It

Just as Vigilante closed and I began a contractual noncompete year, the cofounder of a hip, young general market agency approached me about adding a multicultural component to his smart, forward-looking shop. He had sat across the table from me for years reviewing advertising for the Partnership for a Drug-Free America, and had been impressed when my team made a presentation that had made me proud.

The all-male Vigilante team—one African American, one white, and one white but de facto black urban hip-hop defector—had filed into the room to present to an intimidating squad of top New York creative directors. In their eyes and body language was the same determination to do well that had emanated from my young son when he smacked that home run long ago at the BBDO picnic. My creative "sons" took their places at the huge conference table, faced the panel, and explained that the setting of their commercial would be the inner-city street corners, schoolyards, and stoops frequented by young African American teens and feared by so many American TV viewers. The dialogue of the commercial would be delivered by the black teen males that those same Americans feared even more than the neighborhoods.

"I am a statistic," Vincent St. Vincent, the lone black

man, soberly began. "I am the one out of three black males who will go to college." One by one, his colleagues joined him:

"I am the four out of five who won't drop out of high school."

"I am the five out of nine who already have a job."

"I am the six out of seven who won't become a teenage father."

"I am the seven out of ten who don't do drugs."

For thirty seconds, their baritone chorus continued adding positive statistics, ending with the campaign-inspired line, "Statistically speaking, I am the majority who live above the influence." When they finished, the panel of white men, one white woman, and myself sat in silence. Those voices had resonated within all of us. Even in those pre–Trayvon Martin days, they conjured a rare empathy with what it must be like to have so much of the world assume the worst about you. Mentally rushing back over decades, I imagined my brother Gary's anguish at having lost himself to the trap of low expectations. Nurturing that commercial and its presentation out of my team was a personal moment of affirmation.

At the conclusion of their entire presentation, creative honcho Allen Rosenshine pronounced it "the best creative presentation I have ever seen." Almost poetically, Rosenshine was the newly retired worldwide chairman of BBDO, agency sponsor of that long-ago picnic where my son Brian's talent had risen over other people's limited expectations. My chest was barely large enough to contain my pride at the accomplishment of the Vigilante team.

In African American vernacular, when a cook has put her delicious stamp on a dish, we say, "You put your foot in that!" The funky, counterintuitive intimacy of that expression is black creativity at its most evocative. I have tried to put my foot in every creative department I've headed. The most sat-isfying evidence that I have succeeded is not measured in ads, but in ad makers like the group that rose to the challenge that day. Most of the obvious products of advertising—magazine ads, radio and TV commercials, and even more modern me-dia like interactive campaigns and social media—tend to be so ephemeral that only the very best of them live in our mem-ories for more than a few years. Almost none have the power to live on more than a generation. We remember campaigns like, A Mind Is a Terrible Thing to Waste, written by African American Harry Webber, but they are so exceptional in that regard that they prove the rule. Even a fine example like that one is remembered more for its great tag line than for any individual ad or commercial.

In the inaugural year of ADCOLOR, a twenty-first-century coalition addressing the twentieth-century issue of di-versity in advertising, the organization named me a "Legend." This honor came after I had survived being toppled from my post at UniWorld, dodged the bullet that a noncompete year can be, and enjoyed some successes in another highly visible job. It felt like a symbol of victory and is my favorite award—the statuette features the words, Rising Up and Reaching Back, with a graceful figure holding a star aloft in one hand with the other outstretched behind her. Being named an ADCOLOR Legend by peers was the most satisfying recognition of my ad-vertising career. It was also the big uh-oh, a signal to exit the stage before getting nudged in the butt by the next act.

When I look back, however, it's not the ads I've created—or even any award or recognition—that is most important to me. It's the careers I've helped shape that touch my soul deepest.

Ever since I was a child without the good sense to stop dreaming of a career no one I knew had ever had, the importance of role models and mentors has been clear to me. As much as I appreciate every relative, teacher, and church lady who ever encouraged me, elevated my standards, or just egged me on, I had to get my first advertising job before I found a mentor—a white supervisor at D'Arcy—who was eager and able to show me how to earn a living being my creative self. It is in my nature to pass on what I know, other than what should rightly be kept secret, and my professional journey has given me sharing opportunities galore.

Seeing my footprints in places where I have not stood, I understand something about the nature of power. At the top of one agency are the executive creative director and her second-in-command, both UniWorld alums. I helped the first escape an unfulfilling career in electrical engineering when I met her at a party and invited her to apply for a UniWorld internship. She wrote a few days later, *The more I think about it, this could be my golden opportunity.* It was, at least, the beginning of a sterling career. That internship, an ingenious concept developed by Byron Lewis and administered by me, placed our interns in general market agencies, thus removing what Ogilvy & Mather's white CEO had admitted to Byron was his real barrier to hiring blacks: "We're afraid we can't fire them if we need to." No one, I'm happy to say, wanted to fire any of our interns.

Byron Lewis had understood that using his access and influence to create opportunities for others would ultimately benefit him and his business. He made sure that lesson was not lost on me. Of our class of five "Uni-babies," two are now agency creative directors who became leaders at UniWorld. One, Reginald Hudlin, producer of the Academy Award–nominated *Django Unchained* and director of the Eddie Murphy classic *Boomerang*, left our program very early to make the first of several successful films. As a director, he later helmed UniWorld's popular commercials starring Steve Harvey for Burger King. The agency can forever claim a role in launching a major Hollywood career. A former UniWorld art director also went Hollywood as the screenwriter of the Arnold Schwartzenegger hit *Eraser* and creator of a successful graphic novel franchise. To paraphrase poet Nikki Giovanni, he and Reginald are evidence that even our errors were correct.

Other UniWorld alums are leading lights in their chosen fields. Two own their own small agencies. One is executive creative director of Spike Lee's ad shop. Even the white woman who left UniWorld to become a senior creative at a major general market shop feels better equipped than her peers to address the "true" general market because of the time she spent in our creative department. What I have tried to impart to all these people is belief in the value of black culture and their talents and abilities to share it. Also, when their work has not been up to snuff, I have not hesitated to tell them; unlike some white bosses, I know they can do better.

Jimmy Smith is a dreadlocked, unabashedly African American industry leader who gave Nike much of its street credibility with breakthrough spots like *Freestyle*, a rhythmic tour-de-force of basketball handling. Although he never worked at UniWorld, Jimmy long ago made my day when he called to say, "Thank you for telling me straight up that if I wanted a career in advertising, my work would have to come up to a different level." I gave him that critique with every confidence that he could respond. I believe that the black creativity that fuels American popular culture is absolutely applicable to advertising. I simply encouraged young people to bring their cultural reservoirs to the job. Their intelligence was assumed. All they had to prove was that they could conceptualize great advertising. In the process, they learned to conceptualize themselves not just as participants in the industry, but also as leaders.

When the engineer-turned-intern became convinced that her talent was not tied only to math, her right brain unleashed a lyrical flow of emotional ideas. Utilizing Erykah Badu and other cultural icons, she sold long-distance calling, financial services, and Kodak film. Later, as a creative director, she coaxed the copywriter out of a stand-up comedian named Macio, thus giving UniWorld a huge advantage on accounts like 1-800-CALL-ATT, which had a target audience of joke-friendly young black males. The work Macio delivered ranged from pitch-perfect comedy scripts for zany Marlon Wayans to a death-defying D.L. Hughley/Johnnie Cochran courtroom spot for which I dared him to invoke Cochran's OJ-trial rhyming skills. The Cochran commercial ranks among the most memorable and controversial advertising ever created for the brand. It also paid off for Macio when D.L. Hughley tapped him as a writer and opening act for comedy shows. But bringing Macio into the agency world had been no ordinary feat; the comedian had shown up for an interview with no résumé and no idea that he needed one. Our engineer-turned–creative director took careful notes throughout the meeting. At the end of the conversation, she handed him a sheet from her yellow legal pad. "Here. That's your résumé," were her parting words that day. It is impossible to imagine any such thing happening in a general market agency, and it would certainly never have happened if someone had not encouraged his mentor to engage her own right brain as an advertising creative.

Some opportunities to influence lives fell a lot closer to home. As I've mentioned, my son seemed to have inherited his father's love of sports directly through the genes. By the time Brian was eight years old, it was clear that he needed his own TV to satisfy his desire to watch nearly every televised game. As he grew older, that passion and his encyclopedic knowledge of sports grew with him, and he has now spent more than a decade working for professional teams. While it might be a stretch to describe his job as a sales executive as "creative," his approach to the work is always innovative, and real imagination was required to believe that he could ever do such a thing for a living. So what if he didn't know anyone who had ever actually worked for a team? His mom, who had never known anyone in advertising, had done pretty well for herself in that field. With his knowledge of sports, why shouldn't he be the first of his circle to break through? It was lovely to see him do it, and even more gratifying to know that he was so good that he could climb out of the pit of drug addiction and find the Detroit Lions willing to give him a chance.

The loving, self-sufficient man my son has become is the product of the proverbial village, from Mama and Daddy to the Cooper family. I needed and got so much help in raising Brian that I often see other people's influences in his personality. He is traditionally religious like his grandmother, generous and nonjudgmental like Mama Cooper and her daughter Alla Mary, cautious with his money like Daddy. But in one small corner of his character, I can firmly stake a claim. His ability to dream a life and make it real—he gets that from me. Now he has shown his own son, a budding photographer, that life as an artist is not beyond his grasp if he is willing to supplement his talent with passion and irrational optimism. For a young African American man who is confronted daily with gloomy statistics about people who share his color and generation, that is no small gift to receive from a father.

They say that family traits sometimes skip a generation. In my family, they also slide sideways. So far, three of my brother's talented children, who tell me my career encouraged them to try, have moved to New York to pursue creative careers. For the most part, they are enjoying a degree of success that makes me feel I should have dreamed even bigger in my own life.

In the Jennifer Aniston movie *Picture Perfect*, her character, a copywriter, is asked by her boss what she wants out of her career. Aniston's character says, "I want a billboard in the middle of Times Square . . . That's what I want," as if those bright, gigantic messages represent ultimate success. There is no denying that UniWorld's towering Busta Rhymes billboard in Times Square, my work on President Clinton's campaign, and my appearance on the *Today* show were career highlights I will never forget. But absolutely nothing can compare to the achievement of seeing my big old African footprint on someone else's path to success.

CHAPTER 20

What a Legend Becomes Most

Wise people say that you can't receive anything while your hand is clutching what you already have. One night back in 2011, I had just watched *The Pitch*, a reality show on which ad agencies compete to win an account, and my spiritual hand was a tightly clenched fist. Inside it was my hard-won image as one of the most desirable creative specialists in the business. The agency that had just won *The Pitch*, DIGO, was the one I had thought I'd be working with by the time that show aired. Instead I was lying in bed watching their success as fifty inches of high definition magnified my absence from the team.

This agency had even been willing to wait out the contractual noncompete year until I became available, and had reiterated their offer two months before the year was up. Then, one month before I would be available, the agency reneged, citing a change in direction. I had wasted eleven months not thinking about my future beyond how I would integrate myself into a general market agency again, even one that sold itself as "the agency for a social world." Like other big opportunities in my career, their approach had appeared out of the blue. Once they made the offer, though, it seemed to be a perfect Valerie Graves comeback: large and unexpected.

Then, suddenly, they had rejected me. Now here they were, doing something big that I was not part of. I was jealous as hell and felt cheated too. I was convinced that I could have made their winning concept better, and the agency sure as hell would have looked more millennial with more melanin at the table. I sat there clutching my status as "somebody" so tightly, it would have been impossible to squeeze a winning lottery ticket into my palm.

I was so upset at not being part of the agency's success that I forgot the ambivalence their offer had inspired in me. When they withdrew it, I hadn't tried to change their minds or fight for the deal at all. For one thing, not working was an attractive option. I could walk away with awards, accolades, and Who's Who listings to salve my wounded ego. I had even experienced the vain, gratifying rush of introducing myself to someone in advertising and having their expression change as they realized they were talking to "the" Valerie Graves. Why was I turning green because this little agency was having its fifteen minutes of fame?

I hadn't experienced fear in so long, I had almost forgotten the feeling. But the pangs that rippled through my chest when I thought about that agency and its TV victory were a companion that had traveled with me too many times to go totally unrecognized. Like the day I admitted to myself that I was really pregnant and the moment I was handed a severance check from BBDO, what I was feeling now was galloping identity anxiety. If I was no longer a high-profile, highly paid executive, who was I?

I turned to meditation, which I had come to rely on to provide the answers of my life. *What's wrong?* I asked my subconscious. *Why am I worrying about where my next meal is coming from?*

You are not worried about your next meal, my subconscious eventually answered. *You are worrying about your next success.*

Instantly, I experienced "the shift," a moment of almost palpable insight. If you've ever gone on a trip with the nagging feeling you've forgotten something, endlessly run through the possibilities in your head, then breathed a sigh of relief when you realized it was only the photographs you meant to bring with you to show a friend, you've felt the shift. You suddenly know something you didn't know a moment before, and that knowing is the difference between being wracked with anxiety and filled with calm. This time, the calm lay in remembering all the times I had fallen into fulfillment and prosperity through very little conscious effort of my own. I thought about what the course of my life had taught me: if that agency job had been meant for me, nothing could have kept it from me. With that thought came one of the most important realizations of my life.

In every perceived failure the next triumph is germinating. Success is unlikely to come exactly as we envision it, and if we are too specific in defining it, we might not recognize it when it appears. The universe has a big imagination and zero inclination to limit its creativity. Sure enough, from the crucible of my perceived defeat came the freedom to create a victory. A couple of weeks after that episode of *The Pitch,* an author friend and his agent presented me with the opportunity to write this book. Because I had no job, I had the time to accept that gift.

The words that you are reading are the universe coming through for me again. Whether it ever sells more than a few copies, my book is already a success because of the joy and the lesson that writing it has brought me. When I was a little girl, I once complained to my mother that there was nothing to do.

That hardworking woman looked up from a book that she had found a few precious moments to be alone with and said, "It is not the world's job to entertain you. Find something to do." I stomped off to my room, making as much noise as my Keds would allow, scraped back the desk chair she had scrimped to buy me, and plopped myself down at my desk. I wished with all my heart that I were a little blond girl who could throw things around the room without getting a stinging rebuke from my mother's skinny but effective belt. The only thing I actually threw was myself—into the world of words, where I always seemed to land on my feet. That particular day, I finally got around to writing a speech that I was to give for Mother's Day at church. It was a sweetly hypocritical ode of appreciation to the mothers of the world, calling for us kids to show them on a daily basis the love they deserve. Afterward, my mother took note of the audience's warm reception and quietly said to me, "Nice speech. Don't forget it when you get home." As usual, writing had been my refuge from the world of what is, and my key to a better world I could consciously create.

There is no doubt that advertising copywriting has created a wonderful career for me. Still, "legends" make history, and then are often consigned to it. My Motown boss Andre Harrell used to describe the dilemma of the legends of Motown this way: "To hip-hop kids, they are icons. They are people you respect, but not the people you party with."

In the world of what is, I was near the end of a pretty hot career. For all the shortcomings of the advertising industry, it has offered me lasting friendships, singular experiences, my share of recognition, and a very rewarding livelihood. My circle of friends and neighbors is a vibrant spectrum that contradicts the struggle for racial reconciliation that still bedevils the ad industry. My life and career have produced more good than can easily be undone, no matter what changes lie ahead.

What if I could recreate myself for as long as I live? What if the end of something good is actually the commencement of something better? What if that little girl inside of me has been growing and maturing alongside the "official" me, waiting to emerge as an artist, free to work and to inspire others without the limitations of commerce?

I made the simple decision not to accept an ending, but to embrace a change. As soon as I did, I recalled the colleague who had said to me, "You don't really want another advertising job, do you?" as if to let me know I wasn't doing what it takes to get one. Another opined, "You could've gotten that job if you really wanted it." And then, a renowned theater director approached me to be the producer of the star-studded anniversary gala of a treasured African American arts institution. That offer went beyond anything I would have thought of for myself, which is the way of the universe.

These people had seen the change in me before I had opened my hand to receive it. To be a writer, an artist, was the original dream of the little girl I was. The producer in me had been around since the days of those backyard extravaganzas and the junior high school Personality Week. More importantly, being an artist had also been the improbable desire of the driven career woman I had become. So many times, I had thought the reality of my career outpaced my dreams. In fact, some dreams now seemed to have bided their time, waiting for the career to run its course. Change, the only real constant in our world, often seems to suddenly confront us, when it is actually our dreams finally taking charge.

Like the saga of my hometown, my story doesn't yet have an ending, and that's a good thing. I am still alive and well. Alvin and I remain together, still loving, laughing, and even occasionally surprising each other. The beautiful baby whose birth changed my life is now a successful man with a grown son who shares his name and feels his love. My Brian has never lost his sunny personality and positive outlook. Daddy departed this life several years ago, but Mama, still lovely in her eighties, lives an independent life and provides the occasional home-cooked meal for my divorced brother Gary and an ailing cousin. My happily married brother Isa lives, like Gary, a devoutly Muslim life, making a living as a teacher and a chaplain. Neither has ever wavered from the faith that seems to give their lives purpose. My brothers' many children and grandchildren have enlarged what might have been a dwindling family and invigorated it with beauty, creativity, and diversity.

The quest to put Mud Lake behind me has not been the driving force of my life for a very long time. The child pretending past Mud Lake has become a woman who happily basks in the warmth of once-scorned Harlem.

Now I see the uncertainty in my world as the cradle of creativity. Sometimes, the habit of fear still wafts into my consciousness, but I have learned to embrace it as a sign that I am about to do something new. My career in agency advertising may or may not be over, but life as a writer would be the achievement of a dream that has nothing to do with escape and everything to do with always moving forward.

A friend of mine once told me, as I lamented what I perceived to be a stall in my career, "Never forget how many people would kiss your ass in Macy's window to have the life you have right now." No ass-kissing required. I have learned to celebrate challenge, joy, and disappointment for the rich life they give me. Having experienced the civil rights struggle, the black consciousness revolution, the rise of feminism, the sexual revolution, the antiwar movement, and the election of the first African American president, I can never lack for material as a writer. My life story is in some ways the story of a person and a career, and in others, the story of a people. And yet, because two people can never take the same walk, there are many stories to tell. I have merely started with the one I know best.

AFTERWORD

When I accepted my ADCOLOR Legend award in front of an audience of peers and clients, I thought about what it meant, early in the new millennium, to be near the pinnacle of the minority side of the business. No matter how many articles and columns might appear in the *New York Times* or *Wall Street Journal*, regardless of an appearance on the *Today* show or inclusion of our work in a Hollywood movie, in spite of the research and sales data that showed us to be more effective than many general market agencies, no matter that I had been paid more than many people make in their lifetimes NOT to compete against former employers, it seemed our general agency counterparts might always classify those of us who create multicultural ads as wannabes in an industry that belonged to them. On that night I realized I had reached the 180th degree of my Mud Lake journey: I no longer shared their opinion.

James Baldwin wrote, *The power of the white world is threatened whenever a black man refuses to accept the white world's definitions.* I had long since come to know that my life on the underdog side of America made me an expert on how to communicate with those who shared my experience. I felt empathy, from the underpinnings of our common souls, with what touched them, as no general market creative could. General ads were like a notice posted on a public bulletin board.

Mine were an engraved invitation sent to the customer's house. And, as diminutive former NBA star Muggsy Bogues once said, "The game is for who can play." Now, vigilance is required to make sure that general market agencies are not given credit for work that was created by Vigilante. Seismic shifts in the racial makeup of America are changing the game in favor of those with the most expansive court vision. All of America was shown this by the results of the 2012 election in which the Republican Party was smacked upside the head by its willful ignorance of the demographic truth.

I am still curious to see where my industry will go. Just as the business world recognizes the importance of consumers of color, white-controlled giant agencies seem to be consolidating their power and multicultural shops often appear overwhelmed by daunting odds. Something will happen—most likely something unforeseen and in keeping with America's emerging, ambiguous racial identity; multiculturalism may have brought on the last gasps of the old black/white divide. What we see as progress is a matter of perspective. Some say that cultural marketing, like the celebration of a president's blackness, is an old-fashioned, divisive phenomenon that obscures our common humanity. Mosaicists like me trust that our differences come together to create a pattern far more interesting than some bland amalgam without distinguishing features. Something will happen. In the meantime, maybe we should all take a deep breath and look around.

Just as Mud Lake and Crystal Lake are a single body of water divided only by perspective, advertising is a single industry and America is one country, the sum of its multicolored parts. While some in power waste their time denying the existence of racial bias, Americans are busily muddying the waters of race itself. For evidence of this, I can look in places as disparate as the White House, currently inhabited by a "black" president born of a white mother, and my family's Thanksgiving table. The collection of people who make up my family today would be unrecognizable to the family I grew up in. My fruitful Islamic convert brothers and their offspring have caused the Muslims to outnumber the Christians. Their children's more relaxed racial attitudes and global worldview have brought a Dominican woman, a Frenchman, and a Russian American male to the feast. My nephew's last girlfriend is a mixture of black, white, and Native American that defies neat classification, even by her. Her kinky hair might cause some to call her black, but her white skin, white mother, and upbringing on the plains of Oklahoma argue for a less restrictive call. Now that she is gone, the woman next to him is a biracial beauty of white French and black Kenyan parents. My mother's great-grandchildren are a paint-store color chart: from the palest of yellows to deepest black. When these children look at each other, they see cousins, not color. Their experience in the Muslim community, unlike mine in the black Baptist church, has divorced religion from race. The Frenchman shrugs at the American obsession with the nuances of race, including his wife's preference to describe him as French, rather than white. The white-skinned Dominican woman has married an African American who resembles her dark Hispanic father. The Russian, in love with a black-skinned beauty who is working out childhood color trauma, projects the racial agnosticism and atheism of his formerly communist homeland. At our table, the halal turkey, porkless side dishes, and choice of a nonreligious holiday as our largest gathering of the year are reflections of our cultural indentations on each other.

Somehow, a family of transplanted Southern Baptist farmers and miners from the black side of town has morphed into this polyglot of races, religions, nationalities, and complexions that lives where it pleases. Almost miraculously, all this change in the family, particularly when it comes to race, has been met with nothing but acceptance. While it tickles me when the Frenchman calls my husband "Oncle Alveen," my great-nieces think nothing of having a white French Uncle "G" and a black Uncle Qasim. Now that my niece and her husband have started a family, the first biracial children of our clan have been greeted only with love. We are, more than ever, an American family: diverse and devoted. I believe that I will always be as culturally black as I have ever been. So will this rainbow of children be as black as they are, which is less than I am. For now, we call ourselves a black family, but in a generation, who knows? Our love of family may trump our identity as a black family because we have no choice. Indeed, our country is in a similar situation.

I give America two generations before it becomes too much trouble to have races at all. Racial classification will become optional, barely beneficial, and generally too much of a hassle. "Other" is already the fastest-growing racial group, and as one of my Pontiac friends would say, "Other ain't no damn group." Other belongs to no culture. The only thing binding Other together is what Other is not. If a young friend's black/East Indian daughter should have a child with a son of my black nephew and his black/white/Native American girlfriend, what race is the child? Other. Two biracial friends of mine married and produced a white child. But he also is Other. There will still be some, white and black, who invoke the "one drop" rule. However, should affirmative action survive another generation, only black people, accustomed to one-drop kinfolk, will be okay when that little boy gets a slot in med school that is reserved for a qualified minority. How long before whites realize there might be advantages to letting the race thing go? Not long. But who will we be when we are no longer who we were?

We are a country that likes to keep things simple. Black. White. Mud Lake. Crystal Lake. In the wake of the rapist jamboree that was slavery, the whole mulatto/quadroon/octoroon thing had threatened to get too messy. After how many dilutions would you end up with a white person? Thus, the one-drop asymptote that declared that no matter how many times you divide blackness, some blackness remains. My French nephew-in-law scratches his head that Americans can look at two pale, redheaded, freckled women and label one black and the other not, depending on whether one is known to have a black relative. And when the issue was as "simple" as black and white, we got away with it. But now, America's vaunted melting pot is on the boil. We cannot determine identity based on one or two races. Immigrants of many hues stream over the borders. During Barack Obama's Hawaiian childhood, there were not a lot of African Americans around. There was, however, no shortage of little brown children of indeterminate racial backgrounds. "I was trying to raise myself to be a black man in America, and beyond the given of my appearance, no one around me seemed to know exactly what that meant," he wrote. To suss out the sources of all these perpetually tanned little people would have been way too much trouble in paradise. *Screw it, surf's up!* seemed to be the Hawaiian answer, unsatisfying as it ultimately was to the identity-hungry future president. Once white people say, "Race is an antiquated concept," attaching a race to a person will soon sound as anachronistic as saying "color TV."

If you want your postracial America even faster, get famous. From the corner of my eye, I am watching Tony Parker, the Afro-French star of the San Antonio Spurs, on TV. I am not sure whether he is an American now, but he is if he wants to be. His English carries not only the accent of his native France, but also the Ebonics tinge of the NBA. If he and ex-wife Eva Longoria had had a child in this country, how would their Afro-Franco-Mexican-American have racially identified him or herself? No matter. A little Parker-Longorian would have enjoyed the postracial status America grants to celebrities and their offspring, natural or adopted. Tom Cruise's son Connor is obviously not white, but that fact is rarely mentioned. You don't need a race when you've got it like that. The black children of Brad and Angelina, Madonna, Sandra Bullock, and Charlize Theron need not fear racism as long as anyone knows who they are. Will Smith and Jada Pinkett's kids have a VIP pass into anywhere they want to go, and Kim and Kanye's children are unlikely to meet racial obstruction no matter the direction of their lives. Ditto Michael Jordan's children, Denzel's brood, and little LeBron Jr. Chocolate-brown actor Chris Tucker does a hilarious bit about a Hollywood restaurateur clearing a prime table for him, saying, "Mr. Tucker, sit down here. Get up, get up, white man!" Even the honest militant must concede that in this country, if you are famous, race does not much intrude on the pursuit of happiness.

Not that racial classification can't be good for a laugh. I know two white Americans, originally from Capetown, South Africa, who jokingly but accurately describe themselves as African Americans. They even briefly had a company that specialized in placing African Americans in general market ad agencies. Unfortunately for them, their clientele was of the dark-skinned, mostly unplaceable African persuasion. So far, they haven't applied for any government set-asides, but if we ever get our modern-day forty acres and a mule, we may have to kick them out of line.

Unpredictable things are bound to happen when race

doesn't determine who lives next door. Light skin is likely to remain popular, given our history, but increasingly, "exotic" girls of Latin or Middle Eastern Blood will be giving blondes a run for their money in the trophy-chick sweepstakes. Collagen-poofed lips and enhanced booties are a signal that ethnic features will be considered comely. Last year, I met my first white girl named Keisha. My white friend's son is named Deonte. A Chinese American point guard, Jeremy Lin, was the sensation of the 2011 New York Knicks. The *National Review* featured an article in which a white adoptive mother chronicled her progress in caring for her black daughter's hair, mastering natural styles like cornrows, twists, and knots. One of the country's finest young amateur hockey players is black. Someday, white men will routinely jump and black women may prefer to speak sotto voce.

Proximity and the mainstreaming of urban culture are removing the facile filters of discrimination. If there's not much information in a name, if color may not represent what it seems to, if a Harlem address doesn't tell you whose résumé you are holding, there won't be enough madmen in the world to keep ad agencies segregated. Smart, multicultural agencies, already diverse, should be in a good position to capitalize on the rise of a generation of people, increasingly not black or white, who just might opt to see themselves as red, white, and blue. For lack of a more descriptive term, they might call themselves "American." And that, absolutely, is a damn group.

These new Americans might at last bring validity to the old canard, *America's diversity is her strength.* During the opening ceremonies of every Olympic games, as the athletes march in country by country, I notice the homogeneity of most nations. Blond Swedes, gangly black Kenyans, short reddish-brown Pacific Islanders, and so on. Even without their uniforms, their common gene pool often identifies them as countrymen and -women. Then, as diverse and racially disorganized as a convention of Democrats, come the Americans: white, black, yellow, red, and every shade of brown. Tall and short, stocky and slender, bound by commonalities more ephemeral than genetic, in they stride with a swagger that is not white, black, Asian, or Hispanic. It is, rather, distinctly American. We are taught from an early age that to have a nation as magnificent as ours sometimes requires a sacrifice of blood. Perhaps our attachment to bloodlines will be the next casualty.

Procreation, adoption, and popular culture—not politics—are ushering the advent of postracial America. It can't get here soon enough for me. I say this knowing that when postracialism arrives, my corner of Madison Avenue will either have claimed its rightful place at the center of the industry or become obsolete. The Mud Lake/Crystal Lake divide disappeared with a dredging that affirmed the value of all waterfront property. My hope is that the inclusiveness of postracialism will embrace the richness of all cultures and celebrate their beautiful potential. It's hard to see how else a nation of tempest-tossed ex-refugees and nomads can work. It's also hard to see why it wouldn't be the best place on earth.

Long ago, a white colleague at UniWorld shared with me that white prospective clients and folks from general market agencies would sometimes ask him, "Haven't we gotten to the point yet where people are just people?" What my coworker heard in that question was, *Haven't we gotten to the point yet where people are just WHITE people?* My response returned me to the familiar habit of dreaming a more appealing reality: "No, but when we get to the point where white people are just people, we will be headed in the right direction." E pluribus unum like a mother.